With exp[...] [...]
to roman[...] [...], good health, or career opportunities while gaining valuable insight into yourself and others.
Offering a daily outlook for 18 full months, this fascinating
guide shows you:

- The important dates in your life
- What to expect from an astrological reading
- How the stars can help you stay healthy and fit
  And more!

Let this sound advice guide you through a year of heavenly
possibilities—for today and for every day of 2010!

SYDNEY OMARR'S® DAY-BY-DAY
ASTROLOGICAL GUIDE FOR

ARIES—March 21–April 19
TAURUS—April 20–May 20
GEMINI—May 21–June 20
CANCER—June 21–July 22
LEO—July 23–August 22
VIRGO—August 23–September 22
LIBRA—September 23–October 22
SCORPIO—October 23–November 21
SAGITTARIUS—November 22–December 21
CAPRICORN—December 22–January 19
AQUARIUS—January 20–February 18
PISCES—February 19–March 20

IN 2010

SYDNEY OMARR'S®

DAY-BY-DAY ASTROLOGICAL GUIDE FOR

PISCES

FEBRUARY 19–MARCH 20

2010

by Trish MacGregor
with Carol Tonsing

A SIGNET BOOK

SIGNET
Published by New American Library, a division of
Penguin Group (USA) Inc., 375 Hudson Street,
New York, New York 10014, USA
Penguin Group (Canada), 90 Eglinton Avenue East, Suite 700, Toronto,
Ontario M4P 2Y3, Canada (a division of Pearson Penguin Canada Inc.)
Penguin Books Ltd., 80 Strand, London WC2R 0RL, England
Penguin Ireland, 25 St. Stephen's Green, Dublin 2,
Ireland (a division of Penguin Books Ltd.)
Penguin Group (Australia), 250 Camberwell Road, Camberwell, Victoria 3124,
Australia (a division of Pearson Australia Group Pty. Ltd.)
Penguin Books India Pvt. Ltd., 11 Community Centre, Panchsheel Park,
New Delhi - 110 017, India
Penguin Group (NZ), 67 Apollo Drive, Rosedale, North Shore 0645
New Zealand (a division of Pearson New Zealand Ltd.)
Penguin Books (South Africa) (Pty.) Ltd., 24 Sturdee Avenue,
Rosebank, Johannesburg 2196, South Africa

Penguin Books Ltd., Registered Offices:
80 Strand, London WC2R 0RL, England

First Printing, June 2009
10 9 8 7 6 5 4 3 2 1

First published by Signet, an imprint of New American Library,
a division of Penguin Group (USA) Inc.

CONTENTS

INTRODUCTION

Seize the Moment

"Timing is everything" is a saying worth repeating this year. Astrology is the art of interpreting moments in time, and astrology fans from the rich and famous to the readers of daily horoscope columns realize that some moments are more favorable for certain actions than others. Knowing that they can plan their actions in tune with the rhythm of the cosmic cycles gives them confidence that they are making wise choices. This could be a challenging year for many, so let this guide help you seize the moment and turn those challenges into opportunities by using the tools astrology provides.

In our toolbox for 2010, you'll find secrets of astrological timing—how to find the most auspicious dates this year. For those who are new to astrology or would like to know more about it, we offer easy techniques to start using astrology in your daily life. You'll learn all about your sun sign and how to interpret the mysterious symbols on a horoscope chart. You can use the convenient tables in this book to look up other planets in your horoscope, each of which sheds light on a different facet of your personality.

Many people turn to astrology to help them find love or figure out what went wrong with a relationship. At your service is the world's oldest dating and mating coach, ready to help you decide whether that new passion has potential or might burn out fast. We'll go through the pros and cons of all the possible sun-sign combinations, with celebrities to illustrate the romantic chemistry.

Contemplating a career change? Our sun-sign chapters can help you build your confidence and focus your job search in the most fulfilling direction by highlighting your natural talents and abilities.

Many readers have explored astrology on the Internet, where there are a mind-boggling variety of sites. Our suggestions are well worth your surfing time. We show you where to get free horoscopes, connect with other astrology fans, find the right astrology software for your ability, and even find an accredited college that specializes in astrological studies.

Whether it's money matters, fashion tips, or ideas for vacation getaways, we'll provide ways to use astrology in your life every day. Before giving yourself or your home a makeover, be sure to consult your sun sign, for the colors and styles that will complement your personality.

To make the most of each day, there are eighteen months of on-target daily horoscopes. So here's hoping this year's guide will help you use your star power wisely to make 2010 a happy, successful year!

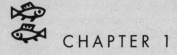

CHAPTER 1

The Top Trends of 2010: Transition Times

Astrologers judge the trends of a year by following the slow-moving planets, from Jupiter through Pluto. A change in sign indicates a new cycle, with new emphasis. The farthest planets (Uranus, Neptune, and Pluto) which stay in a sign for at least seven years, cause a very significant change in the atmosphere when they change signs. Shifts in Jupiter, which changes every year, and Saturn, every two years, are more obvious in current events and daily lives. Jupiter generally brings a fortunate, expansive emphasis to its new sign, while Saturn's two-year cycle is a reality check, bringing tests of maturity, discipline, and responsibility. This year, Jupiter in Pisces and Saturn in Libra are in auspicious signs for most of the year, which should act as a balance to more volatile elements in the comos.

Little Pluto—The Mighty Mite

Though astronomers have demoted tiny Pluto from being a full-fledged planet to a dwarf planet, astrologers have been tracking its influence since Pluto was discovered in 1930 and have witnessed that this minuscule celestial body has a powerful effect on both a personal and global level. So Pluto, which moved into the sign of Capricorn in 2008, will still be called a "planet" by astrologers and will be given just as much importance as before.

Until 2024, Pluto will exert its influence in this practical, building, healing earth sign. Capricorn relates to structures, institutions, order, mountains and mountain countries, mineral rights, issues involving the elderly and growing older—all of which will be emphasized in the coming years. It is the sign of established order, corporations, big business—all of which will be accented. Possibly, it will fall to business structures to create a new sense of order in the world.

You should now feel the rumblings of change in the Capricorn area of your horoscope and in the world at large. The last time Pluto was in Capricorn was the years up to and during the Revolutionary War; therefore this should be an important time in the U.S. political scene, as well as a reflection of the aging and maturing of American society in general. Both the rise and the fall of the Ottoman Empire happened under Pluto in Capricorn.

The Pisces Factor

This year, Jupiter moves from experimental, humanitarian Aquarius to creative, imaginative Pisces. Jupiter is the coruler of Pisces, along with Neptune, so this is a particularly auspicious place for the planet of luck and expansion to be. During the year that Jupiter remains in a sign, the fields associated with that sign are the ones that currently arouse excitement and enthusiasm, usually providing excellent opportunities.

Jupiter in Pisces expands the influence of Neptune in Aquarius; there should be many artistic and scientific breakthroughs. International politics also comes under this influence, as Neptune in Aquarius raises issues of global boundaries and political structures not being as solid as they seem. This could continue to produce rebellion and chaos in the environment. However, with the generally benevolent force of Jupiter backing up the creative side of Neptune, it is possible that highly original and effective solutions to global problems will be found, which could transcend the current social and cultural barriers.

Another place we notice the Jupiter influence is in fashion, which should veer into a Pisces fantasy mood, with more theatrical, dramatic styles and a special emphasis on footwear. Look for exciting beachwear and seaside resorts that appeal to our desire to escape reality.

Those born under Pisces should have many opportunities during the year. However, the key is to keep your feet on the ground. The flip side of Jupiter is that there are no limits. You can expand off the planet under a Jupiter transit, which is why the planet is often called the "Gateway to Heaven." If something is going to burst (such as an artery) or overextend or go over the top in some way, it could happen under a supposedly lucky Jupiter transit, so be aware.

Those born under Virgo may find their best opportunities working with partners this year, as Jupiter will be transiting their seventh house of relationships.

During the summer months, Jupiter dips into Aries, which should give us a preview of happenings next year. In this headstrong fire sign, Jupiter promotes pioneering ventures, start-ups, all that is new and exciting. It can also promote impatience with more conservative forces, especially in early summer, which looks like the most volatile time this year. Jupiter returns to Pisces in September for the rest of the year.

Saturn in Libra

Saturn, the planet of limitation, testing, and restriction, will be moving through Libra, the sign of its exaltation and one of its most auspicious signs, this year. In Libra, Saturn can steady the scales of justice and promote balanced, responsible judgment. There should be much deliberation over duty, honor, and fairness, which will be ongoing for the next two years, balancing the more impulsive energy of other planets. Far-reaching new legislation and diplomatic moves are possible, perhaps resolving difficult international standoffs. As this placement works well with the humanitarian Aquarius influence of Neptune, there should be new hope of resolving conflicts. Previously, Saturn was in Libra during the early 1920s, the early 1950s, and again in the early 1980s.

Continuing Trends

Uranus and Neptune continue to do a kind of astrological dance called a "mutual reception." This is a supportive relationship where Uranus is in Pisces, the sign ruled by Neptune, while Neptune is in Aquarius, the sign ruled by Uranus. When this dance is over in 2011, it is likely that we will be living under very different political and social circumstances.

Uranus in Pisces and Aries

Uranus, known as the Great Awakener, tends to cause both upheaval and innovation in the sign it transits. This year, it is accompanied by Jupiter, as it is preparing to leave Pisces and dip its toe into Aries from June to mid-August. However, the Pisces influence will predominate, since Jupiter will be in Pisces most of the year.

During previous episodes of Uranus in Pisces, great religions and spiritual movements have come into being, most recently Mormonism and Christian Fundamentalism. In its most positive mode, Pisces promotes imagination and creativity, the art of illusion in theater and film, and the inspiration of great artists.

A water sign, Pisces is naturally associated with all things liquid—such as oceans, oil, and alcohol—and with those creatures that live in the water—fish, the fishing industry, fish habitats, and fish farming. Currently there is a great debate going on about overfishing, contamination of fish, and fish farming. The underdogs, the enslaved, and the disenfranchised should also benefit from Uranus in Pisces. Since Uranus is a disruptive influence that aims to challenge the status quo, the forces of nature that manifest now will most likely be in the Pisces area—the oceans, seas, and rivers. We have so far seen unprecedented rainy seasons, floods, mud slides, and disastrous hurricanes. Note that 2005's devastating Hurricane Katrina hit an area known for both the oil and fishing industries.

Pisces is associated with the prenatal phase of life, which is related to regenerative medicine. The controversy over embryonic stem cell research will continue to be debated, but recent developments may make the arguments moot. Petroleum issues, both in the oil-producing countries and offshore oil drilling, will come to a head. Uranus in Pisces suggests that development of new hydroelectric sources may provide the power we need to continue our current power-thirsty lifestyle.

As in previous eras, there should continue to be a flourishing of the arts. We are seeing many new artistic forms developing now, such as computer-created actors and special effects. The sky's the limit on this influence.

Those who have problems with Uranus are those who resist change, so the key is to embrace the future.

As Uranus prepares to enter Aries, an active fire sign, we should have a preview of coming influences over the summer.

Neptune in Aquarius

Neptune is a planet of imagination and creativity, but also of deception and illusion. Neptune is associated with hospitals, which have been the subject of much controversy. On the positive side, hospitals are acquiring cutting-edge technology. The atmosphere of many hospitals is already changing from the intimidating and sterile environment of the past to that of a health-promoting spa. Alternative therapies, such as massage, diet counseling, and aromatherapy, are becoming commonplace, which expresses this Neptune trend. New procedures in plastic surgery, also a Neptune glamour field, and antiaging therapies are giving the illusion of youth.

However, issues involving the expense and quality of health care, medication, and the evolving relationship between doctors, drug companies, and HMOs reflect a darker side of this trend.

Neptune is finishing up its stay in Aquarius and will begin its transit of Pisces, which it rules, in 2011. So this should be a time of transition into a much more Neptunian era, when Pisces-related issues will be of paramount importance.

Lunar Eclipses Are Movers and Shakers

Eclipses could shake up the financial markets and rock your world in 2010. The eclipses in late June and July are the ones to watch as they coincide with a close contact of Jupiter and Uranus in Aries. This is a potentially volatile time, so it would be wise to be prepared. As several recent studies have shown the stock market to be linked to the lunar cycle, track investments more carefully during this time.

New Celestial Bodies

Our solar system is getting crowded, as astronomers continue to discover new objects circling the sun. In addition to the familiar planets, there are dwarf planets, comets, cometoids, asteroids, and strange icy bodies in the Kuiper Belt beyond Neptune. A dwarf planet christened Eris, discovered in 2005, is now being observed and analyzed by astrologers. Eris was named after a goddess of discord and strife. In mythology, she was a troublemaker who made men think their opinions were right and others wrong. What an appropriate name for a planet discovered during a time of discord in the Middle East and elsewhere! Eris has a companion moon named Dysnomia for her daughter, described as a demon spirit of lawlessness. With mythological associations like these, we wonder what the effect of this mother-daughter duo will be. Once Eris's orbit is established, astrologers will track the impact of this planet on our horoscopes. Eris takes about 560 years to orbit the sun, which means its emphasis in a given astrological sign will affect several generations.

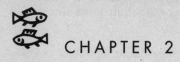

CHAPTER 2

How to Find Your Best Times This Year

It's no secret that some of the most powerful and famous people, from Julius Caesar to Queen Elizabeth I, from financier J. P. Morgan to Ronald Reagan, have consulted astrologers before they made their moves. If astrology helps the rich and famous stay on course through life's ups and downs, why not put it to work for you? Anyone can follow the planetary movements, and once you know how to interpret them, you won't need an expert to grasp the overall trends and make use of them.

For instance, when mischievous Mercury creates havoc with communications, it's time to back up your vital computer files, read between the lines of contracts, and be very patient with coworkers. When Venus passes through your sign, you're more alluring, so it's time to try out a new outfit or hairstyle, and then ask someone you'd like to know better to dinner. Venus timing can also help you charm clients with a stunning sales pitch or make an offer they won't refuse.

In this chapter you will find the tricks of astrological time management. You can find your red-letter days as well as which times to avoid. You will also learn how to make the magic of the moon work for you. Use the information in this chapter and the planet tables in this book and also the moon sign listings in your daily forecasts.

Here are the happenings to note on your agenda:

- Dates of your sun sign (high-energy period)
- The month previous to your sun sign (low-energy time)

- Dates of planets in your sign this year
- Full and new moons (Pay special attention when these fall in your sun sign!)
- Eclipses
- Moon in your sun sign every month, as well as moon in the opposite sign (listed in daily forecast)
- Mercury retrogrades
- Other retrograde periods

Your Most Proactive Time

Every birthday starts off a new cycle of solar energy for you. You should feel a new surge of vitality as the powerful sun enters your sign. This is the time when predominant energies are most favorable to you. So go for it! Start new projects, and make your big moves (especially when the new moon is in your sign, doubling your charisma). You'll get the recognition you deserve now, when everyone is attuned to your sun sign. Look in the tables in this book to see if other planets will also be passing through your sun sign at this time. Venus (love, beauty), Mars (energy, drive), and Mercury (communication, mental sharpness) reinforce the sun and give an extra boost to your life in the areas they affect. Venus will rev up your social and love life, making you seem especially attractive. Mars amplifies your energy and drive. Mercury fuels your brainpower and helps you communicate. Jupiter signals an especially lucky period of expansion.

There are two downtimes related to the sun. During the month before your birthday period, when you are winding up your annual cycle, you could be feeling especially vulnerable and depleted. So at that time get extra rest, watch your diet, and take it easy. Don't overstress yourself. Use this time to gear up for a big push when the sun enters your sign.

Another downtime is when the sun is in the sign opposite your sun sign (six months from your birthday). This is a reactive time, when the prevailing energies are very different from yours. You may feel at odds with the world. You'll have to work harder for recognition because people are not on your wavelength. However, this could be a good time to work on a team, in cooperation with others, or behind the scenes.

Be a Moon Watcher

The moon is a powerful tool to divine the mood of the moment. You can work with the moon in two ways. Plan by the sign the moon is in; plan by the phase of the moon. The sign will tell you the kind of activities that suit the moon's mood. The phase will tell you the best time to start or finish a certain activity.

Working with the phases of the moon is as easy as looking up at the night sky. During the new moon, when both the sun and moon are in the same sign, begin new ventures—especially activities that are favored by that sign. Then you'll utilize the powerful energies pulling you in the same direction. You'll be focused outward, toward action, and in a doing mode. Postpone breaking off, terminating, deliberating, or reflecting—activities that require introspection and passive work. These are better suited to a later moon phase.

Get your project under way during the first quarter. Then go public at the full moon, a time of high intensity, when feelings come out into the open. This is your time to shine—to express yourself. Be aware, however, that because pressures are being released, other people will also be letting off steam. Since confrontations are possible, take advantage of this time either to air grievances or to avoid arguments.

About three days after the full moon comes the disseminating phase, a time when the energy of the cycle begins to wind down. From the last quarter of the moon to the next new moon, it's a time to cut off unproductive relationships, do serious thinking, and focus on inward-directed activities.

You'll feel some new and full moons more strongly than others, especially when they fall in your sun sign. That full moon happens at your low-energy time of year, and is likely to be an especially stressful time in a relationship, when any hidden problems or unexpressed emotions could surface.

11

Full and New Moons in 2010

All dates are calculated for eastern standard time and eastern daylight time.

New Moon—January 15 in Capricorn (solar eclipse)
Full Moon—January 30 in Leo

New Moon—February 13 in Aquarius
Full Moon—February 28 in Virgo

New Moon—March 15 in Pisces
Full Moon—March 29 in Libra

New Moon—April 14 in Aries
Full Moon—April 28 in Scorpio

New Moon—May 13 in Taurus
Full Moon—May 27 in Sagittarius

New Moon—June 12 in Gemini
Full Moon—June 26 in Capricorn (lunar eclipse)

New Moon—July 11 in Cancer (solar eclipse)
Full Moon—July 25 in Aquarius

New Moon—August 9 in Leo
Full Moon—August 24 in Pisces

New Moon—September 8 in Virgo
Full Moon—September 23 in Aries

New Moon—October 7 in Libra
Full Moon—October 22 in Aries

New Moon—November 5 in Scorpio
Full Moon—November 21 in Taurus

New Moon—December 5 in Sagittarius
Full Moon—December 21 in Gemini (lunar eclipse)

Timing by the Moon's Sign

To forecast the daily emotional "weather," to determine your monthly high and low days, or to synchronize your activities with the cycles of the moon, take note of the moon's sign under your daily forecast at the end of the book. Here are some of the activities favored and the moods you are likely to encounter under each moon sign.

Moon in Aries: Get Moving

The new moon in Aries is an ideal time to start new projects. Everyone is pushy, raring to go, rather impatient, and short-tempered. Leave details and follow-up for later. Competitive sports or martial arts are great ways to let off steam. Quiet types could use some assertiveness, but it's a great day for dynamos. Be careful not to step on too many toes.

Moon in Taurus: Lay the Foundations for Success

Do solid, methodical tasks like follow-through or backup work. Make investments, buy real estate, do appraisals, or do some hard bargaining. Attend to your property. Get out in the country or spend some time in your garden. Enjoy creature comforts, music, a good dinner, or sensual lovemaking. Forget starting a diet—this is a day when you'll feel self-indulgent.

Moon in Gemini: Communicate

Talk means action today. Telephone, write letters, and fax! Make new contacts; stay in touch with steady customers. You can juggle lots of tasks today. It's a great time for mental activity of any kind. Don't try to pin people down—they too are feeling restless. Keep it light. Flirtations and socializing are good. Watch gossip—and don't give away secrets.

Moon in Cancer: Pay Attention to Loved Ones

This is a moody, sensitive, emotional time. People respond to personal attention and mothering. Stay at home, have a family dinner, or call your mother. Nostalgia, memories, and psychic powers are heightened. You'll want to hang on to people and things (don't clean out your closets now). You could have shrewd insights into what others really need and want. Pay attention to dreams, intuition, and gut reactions.

Moon in Leo: Be Confident

Everybody is in a much more confident, warm, generous mood. It's a good day to ask for a raise, show what you can do, or dress like a star. People will respond to flattery and enjoy a bit of drama and theater. You may be extravagant, treat yourself royally, and show off a bit—but don't break the bank! Be careful not to promise more than you can deliver.

Moon in Virgo: Be Practical

Do practical, down-to-earth chores. Review your budget, make repairs, or be an efficiency expert. Not a day to ask for a raise. Tend to personal care and maintenance. Have a health checkup, go on a diet, or buy vitamins or health food. Make your home spotless. Take care of details and piled-up chores. Reorganize your work and life so they run more smoothly and efficiently. Save money. Be prepared for others to be in critical, fault-finding moods.

Moon in Libra: Be Diplomatic

Attend to legal matters. Negotiate contracts. Arbitrate. Do things with your favorite partner. Socialize. Be romantic. Buy a special gift or a beautiful object. Decorate yourself or your surroundings. Buy new clothes. Throw a party. Have an elegant, romantic evening. Smooth over any ruffled feathers. Avoid confrontations. Stick to civilized discussions.

Moon in Scorpio: Solve Problems

This is a day to do things with passion. You'll have excellent concentration and focus. Try not to get too intense emotionally. Avoid sharp exchanges with loved ones. Others may tend to go to extremes, get jealous, or overreact. Great for troubleshooting, problem solving, research, scientific work—and making love. Pay attention to those psychic vibes.

Moon in Sagittarius: Sell and Motivate

A great time for travel, philosophical discussions, or setting long-range career goals. Work out, do sports, or buy athletic equipment. Others will be feeling upbeat, exuberant, and adventurous. Taking risks is favored. You may feel like gambling, betting on the horses, visiting a local casino, or buying a lottery ticket. Teaching, writing, and spiritual activities also get the green light. Relax outdoors. Take care of animals.

Moon in Capricorn: Get Organized

You can accomplish a lot now, so get on the ball! Attend to business. Issues concerning your basic responsibilities, duties, family, and elderly parents could crop up. You'll be expected to deliver on promises. Weed out the deadwood from your life. Get a dental checkup. Not a good day for gambling or taking risks.

Moon in Aquarius: Join the Group

A great day for doing things with groups—clubs, meetings, outings, politics, or parties. Campaign for your candidate. Work for a worthy cause. Deal with larger issues that affect humanity—the environment and metaphysical questions. Buy a computer or electronic gadget. Watch TV. Wear something outrageous. Try something you've never done before. Present an original idea. Don't stick to a rigid schedule; go with the flow. Take a class in meditation, mind control, or yoga.

Moon in Pisces: Be Creative

This can be a very creative day, so let your imagination work overtime. Film, theater, music, and ballet could inspire you. Spend some time resting and reflecting, reading, or writing poetry. Daydreams can also be profitable. Help those less fortunate. Lend a listening ear to someone who may be feeling blue. Don't overindulge in self-pity or escapism. People are especially vulnerable to substance abuse. Turn your thoughts to romance and someone special.

Eclipses Clear the Air

Eclipses can bring on milestones in your life, if they aspect a key point in your horoscope. In general, they shake up the status quo, bringing hidden areas out into the open. During this time, problems you've been avoiding or have brushed aside can surface to demand your attention. A good coping strategy is to accept whatever comes up as a challenge that could make a positive difference in your life. And don't forget the power of your sense of humor. If you can laugh at something, you'll never be afraid of it.

When the natural rhythms of the sun and moon are disturbed, it's best to postpone important activities. Be sure to mark eclipse days on your calendar, especially if the eclipse falls in your birth sign. This year, those born under Capricorn, Cancer, and Gemini should take special note of the feelings that arise. If your moon is in one of these signs, you may be especially affected. With lunar eclipses, some possibilities could be a break from attachments, or the healing of an illness or substance abuse that was triggered by the subconscious. The temporary event could be a healing time, when you gain perspective. During solar eclipses, when you might be in a highly subjective state, pay attention to the hidden subconscious patterns that surface, the emotional truth that is revealed at this time.

The effect of the eclipse can reverberate for some time, often months after the event. But it is especially important to stay cool and make no major moves during the period known as the shadow of the eclipse, which begins about a week before and lasts until at least three days after the eclipse. After three days, the daily rhythms should return to normal, and you can proceed with business as usual.

This Year's Eclipse Dates

January 15: Solar Eclipse in Capricorn
June 26: Lunar Eclipse in Capricorn
July 11: Solar Eclipse in Cancer
December 21: Lunar Eclipse in Gemini

Retrogrades: When the Planets Seem to Backstep

All the planets, except for the sun and moon, have times when they appear to move backward—or retrograde—as it seems from our point of view on Earth. At these times, planets do not work as they normally do. So it's best to "take a break" from that planet's energies in our life and to do some work on an inner level.

Mercury Retrograde: The Key Is in "Re"

Mercury goes into retrograde most often, and its effects can be especially irritating. When it reaches a short distance ahead of the sun several times a year, it seems to move backward from our point of view. Astrologers often compare retrograde motion to the optical illusion that occurs when we ride on a train that passes another train traveling at a different speed—the second train appears to be moving in reverse.

What this means to you is that the Mercury-ruled areas of your life—analytical thought processes, communications, scheduling—are subject to all kinds of confusion. Be prepared. Communications equipment can break down. Schedules may be changed on short notice. People are late for appointments or don't show up at all. Traffic is terrible. Major purchases malfunction, don't work out, or get delivered in the wrong color. Letters don't arrive or are delivered to the wrong address. Employees will make errors that have to be corrected later. Contracts don't work out or must be renegotiated.

Since most of us can't put our lives on "hold" during Mercury retrogrades, we should learn to tame the trickster and make it work for us. The key is in the prefix re-. This is the time to go back over things in your life, reflect on what you've done during the previous months. Now you can get deeper insights, and spot errors you've missed. So take time to review and reevaluate what has happened. Rest and reward yourself—it's a good time to take a vacation, especially if you revisit a favorite place. Reorganize your work and finish up projects that are backed up. Clean out your desk and closets. Throw away what you can't recycle. If you must sign contracts or agreements, do so with a contingency clause that lets you reevaluate the terms later.

Postpone major purchases or commitments for the time being. Don't get married (unless you're remarrying the same person). Try not to rely on other people keeping appointments, contracts, or agreements to the letter; have several alternatives. Double-check and read between the lines. Don't buy anything connected with communications or transportation (if you must, be sure to cover yourself).

Mercury retrograding through your sun sign will intensify its effect on your life.

If Mercury was retrograde when you were born, you may be one of the lucky people who don't suffer the frustrations of this period. If so, your mind probably works in a very intuitive, insightful way.

The sign in which Mercury is retrograding can give you an idea of what's in store—as well as the sun signs that will be especially challenged.

Mercury Retrogrades in 2010

Mercury has four retrograde periods this year, since it will be retrograde as the year begins. During the retrograde periods, it will be especially important to watch all activities which involve mental processes and communication.

December 26, 2009, to January 15 in Capricorn
April 17 to May 11 in Taurus
August 20 to September 12 in Virgo
December 10 to December 30 from Capricorn to Sagittarius

Venus Retrograde: Relationships Are Affected

Retrograding Venus can cause your relationships to take a backward step, or you may feel that a key relationship is on hold. Singles may be especially lonely, yet find it difficult to connect with someone special. If you wish to make amends in an already troubled relationship, make peaceful overtures at this time. You may feel more extravagant or overindulge in shopping or sweet treats. Shopping till you drop and buying what you cannot afford are bad at this time. It's *not* a good time to redecorate—you'll hate the color of the walls later. Postpone getting a new hairstyle. It only lasts for a relatively short time this year; however, Scorpio and Libra should take special note.

Venus Retrogrades in 2010

Venus retrogrades from October 8 to November 18, from Scorpio to Libra.

Use the Power of Mars

Mars shows how and when to get where you want to go. Timing your moves with Mars on your side can give you a big push. On the other hand, pushing Mars the wrong way can guarantee that you'll run into frustrations around every corner. Your best times to forge ahead are during the weeks when Mars is traveling through your sun sign or your Mars sign (look these up in the planet tables in this book). Also consider times when Mars is in a compatible sign (fire signs with air signs, or earth signs with water signs). You'll be sure to have planetary power on your side.

Mars began a lengthy retrograde in extravagant Leo on December 20, 2009. Your patience may have been tested more

19

than usual during last year's festivities. The Mars retrograde in Leo will last until March 10, during which time there are sure to be repercussions on the international level.

Mars Retrogrades in 2010

Mars turns retrograde in Leo on December 20, 2009, until March 10, 2010.

When Other Planets Retrograde

The slower-moving planets stay retrograde for many months at a time (Jupiter, Saturn, Neptune, Uranus, and Pluto).

When Saturn is retrograde, it's an uphill battle with self-discipline. You may not be in the mood for work. You may feel more like hanging out at the beach than getting things done.

Neptune retrograde promotes a dreamy escapism from reality, when you may feel you're in a fog (Pisces will feel this, especially).

Uranus retrograde may mean setbacks in areas where there have been sudden changes, when you may be forced to regroup or reevaluate the situation.

Pluto retrograde is a time to work on establishing proportion and balance in areas where there have been recent dramatic transformations.

When the planets move forward again, there's a shift in the atmosphere. Activities connected with each planet start moving ahead; plans that were stalled get rolling. Make a special note of those days on your calendar and proceed accordingly.

Other Retrogrades in 2010

The five slower-moving planets all go retrograde in 2010.

Jupiter retrogrades from July 23 in Aries to November 18 in Pisces.

Saturn retrogrades from January 13 in Libra to May 30 in Virgo.

Uranus retrogrades from July 5 in Aries to December 5 in Pisces.

Neptune retrogrades from May 31 to November 7 in Aquarius.

Pluto retrogrades from April 6 to September 13 in Capricorn.

CHAPTER 3

Introduction to Astrology

Astrology is a powerful tool that can help you discover and access your personal potential, understand others and interpret events in your life and the world at large. You don't have to be an expert in astrology to put it to work for you. It's easy to pick up enough basic knowledge to go beyond the realm of your sun sign into the deeper areas of this fascinating subject, which combines science, art, spirituality, and psychology. Perhaps from here you'll upgrade your knowledge with computer software that calculates charts for everyone you know in a nanosecond or join an astrology group in your city.

In this chapter, we'll introduce you to the basics of astrology. You'll be able to define a sign and figure out why astrologers say what they do about each sign. As you look at your astrological chart, you'll have a good idea of what's going on in each portion of the horoscope. Let's get started.

Know the Difference Between Signs and Constellations

Most readers know their signs, but many often confuse them with constellations. *Signs* are actually a type of celestial real estate, located on the *zodiac*, an imaginary 360-degree belt circling the earth. This belt is divided into twelve equal 30-degree portions, which are the *signs*. There's a lot of confusion about the difference between the *signs* and the *constellations* of the zodiac, patterns of stars which originally marked the twelve divisions, like signposts. Though a *sign* is named after the *constellation* that once marked the same area, the constellations are no longer in the same place relative to the earth that they were many centuries ago. Over hundreds of years, the earth's orbit has shifted, so that from our point of view here on earth, the constellations seem to have moved. However, the signs remain in place. (Most Western astrology uses the twelve-equal-part division of the zodiac, though there are some other methods of astrology that still use the constellations instead of the signs.)

Most people think of themselves in terms of their sun sign. A *sun sign* refers to the sign the sun is orbiting through at a given moment (from our point of view here on earth). For instance, if someone says, "I'm an Aries," the sun was passing through Aries when that person was born. However, there are nine other planets (plus asteroids, fixed stars, and sensitive points) that also form our total astrological personality, and some or many of these will be located in other signs. No one is completely "Aries," with all their astrological components in one sign! (Please note that, in astrology, the sun and moon are usually referred to as "planets," though of course they're not. Though there is some controversy over Pluto, it is still called a "planet" by astrologers.)

As we mentioned before, the sun signs are *places* on the zodiac. They do not *do* anything (the planets are the doers). However, they are associated with many things, depending on their location on the zodiac.

How Do We Define a Sign's Characteristics?

The definitions of the signs evolved systematically from four interrelated components: a sign's element, its quality, its polarity or sex, and its order in the progression of the zodiac. All these factors work together to tell us what the sign is like.

The system is magically mathematical: the number 12—as in the twelve signs of the zodiac—is divisible by 4, by 3, and by

2. There are four elements, three qualities, and two polarities, which follow one another in sequence around the zodiac.

The four elements (earth, air, fire, and water) are the building blocks of astrology. The use of an element to describe a sign probably dates from man's first attempts to categorize what he saw. Ancient sages believed that all things were composed of combinations of these basic elements—earth, air, fire, and water. This included the human character, which was fiery/choleric, earthy/melancholy, airy/sanguine, or watery/phlegmatic. The elements also correspond to our emotional (water), physical (earth), mental (air), and spiritual (fire) natures. The energies of each of the elements were then observed to relate to the time of year when the sun was passing through a certain segment of the zodiac.

Those born with the sun in fire signs—Aries, Leo, Sagittarius—embody the characteristics of that element. Optimism, warmth, hot tempers, enthusiasm, and "spirit" are typical of these signs. Taurus, Virgo, and Capricorn are "earthy"—more grounded, physical, materialistic, organized, and deliberate than fire sign people. Air sign people—Gemini, Libra, and Aquarius—are mentally oriented communicators. Water signs—Cancer, Scorpio, and Pisces—are emotional, sensitive, and creative.

Think of what each element does to the others: water puts out fire or evaporates under heat. Air fans the flames or blows them out. Earth smothers fire, drifts and erodes with too much wind, and becomes mud or fertile soil with water. Those are often perfect analogies for the relationships between people of different sun-sign elements. This astrochemistry was one of the first ways man described his relationships. Fortunately, no one is entirely "air" or "water." We all have a bit, or a lot, of each element in our horoscopes. It is this unique mix that defines each astrological personality.

Within each element, there are three qualities that describe types of behavior associated with the sign. Those of cardinal signs are activists, go-getters. These four signs—Aries, Cancer, Libra, and Capricorn—begin each season. Fixed signs, which happen in the middle of the season, are associated with builders and stabilizers. You'll find that Taurus, Leo, Scorpio, and Aquarius are usually gifted with concentration, stamina, and focus. Mutable signs—Gemini, Virgo, Sagittarius, and Pisces—fall at the end of each season and thus are considered catalysts for change. People born under mutable signs are flexible and adaptable.

The polarity of a sign is either its positive or negative "charge." It can be masculine, active, positive, and yang, like air or fire signs, or it can be feminine, reactive, negative, and yin, like the water and earth signs. The polarities alternate, moving energy around the zodiac like the poles of a battery.

Finally, we consider the sign's place in the order of the zodiac. This is vital to the balance of all the forces and the transmission of energy moving through the signs. You may have noticed that your sign is quite different from your neighboring sign on either side. Yet each seems to grow out of its predecessor like links in a chain and transmits a synthesis of energy gathered along the "chain" to the following sign, beginning with the fire-powered positive charge of Aries.

How the Signs Add Up

SIGN	ELEMENT	QUALITY	POLARITY	PLACE
Aries	fire	cardinal	masculine	first
Taurus	earth	fixed	feminine	second
Gemini	air	mutable	masculine	third
Cancer	water	cardinal	feminine	fourth
Leo	fire	fixed	masculine	fifth
Virgo	earth	mutable	feminine	sixth
Libra	air	cardinal	masculine	seventh
Scorpio	water	fixed	feminine	eighth
Sagittarius	fire	mutable	masculine	ninth
Capricorn	earth	cardinal	feminine	tenth
Aquarius	air	fixed	masculine	eleventh
Pisces	water	mutable	feminine	twelfth

Each Sign Has a Special Planet

Each sign has a "ruling" planet that is most compatible with
its energies. Mars adds its fiery assertive characteristics to
Aries. The sensual beauty and comfort-loving side of Venus
rules Taurus, whereas the idealistic side of Venus rules Libra.
Quick-moving Mercury rules two mutable signs, Gemini and
Virgo. Its mental agility belongs to Gemini while its analytical side is best expressed in Virgo. The changeable emotional
moon is associated with Cancer, while the outgoing Leo personality is ruled by the sun. Scorpio originally shared Mars,
but when Pluto was discovered in the last century, its powerful
magnetic energies were deemed more suitable to the intense
vibrations of the fixed water sign Scorpio. Though Pluto has,
as of this writing, been downgraded, it is still considered by astrologers to be a powerful force in the horoscope. Disciplined
Capricorn is ruled by Saturn, and expansive Sagittarius by Jupiter. Unpredictable Aquarius is ruled by Uranus and creative,
imaginative Pisces by Neptune. In a horoscope, if a planet is
placed in the sign it rules, it is sure to be especially powerful.

The Layout of a Horoscope Chart

A horoscope chart is a map of the heavens at a given moment
in time. It looks like a wheel with twelve spokes. In between
each of the "spokes" is a section called a *house*.

Each house deals with a different area of life and is influenced by a special sign and a planet. Astrologers look at the
houses to tell in what area of life an event is happening or
about to happen.

The house is governed by the sign passing over the spoke
(or cusp of the house) at that particular moment. Though
the first house is naturally associated with Aries and Mars, it
would also have an additional Capricorn influence if that sign
was passing over the house cusp at the time the chart was cast.
The sequence of the houses starts with the first house located
at the left center spoke (or the number 9 position, if you were
reading a clock). The houses are then read *counterclockwise*

around the chart, with the fourth house at the bottom of the chart, the tenth house at the top or twelve o'clock position.

Where do the planets belong? Around the horoscope, planets are placed within the houses according to their location at the time of the chart. That is why it is so important to have an accurate time; with no specific time, the planets have no specific location in the houses and one cannot determine which area of life they will apply to. Since the signs move across the houses as the earth turns, planets in a house will naturally intensify the importance of that house. The house that contains the sun is naturally one of the most prominent.

The First House: Self

The sign passing over the first house at the time of your birth is known as your ascendant, or rising sign. The first house is the house of "firsts"—the first impression you make, how you initiate matters, the image you choose to project. This is where you advertise yourself, where you project your personality. Planets that fall here will intensify the way you come across to others. It is the home of Aries and the planet Mars.

The Second House: The Material You

This house is where you experience the material world, what you value. Here are your attitudes about money, possessions, and finances, as well as your earning and spending capacity. On a deeper level, this house reveals your sense of self-worth, the inner values that draw wealth in various forms. It is the natural home of Taurus and the planet Venus.

The Third House: Your Thinking Process

This house describes how you communicate with others, how you reach out to others nearby and interact with the immediate environment. It shows how your thinking process works and the way you express your thoughts. Are you articulate or tongue-tied? Can you think on your feet? This house also shows your first relationships, your experiences with brothers and sisters, as well as how you deal with people close to you, such as your neighbors or pals. It's where you take short trips, write letters, or use the telephone. It shows how your mind works in terms of left-brain logical and analytical functions. It is the home of Gemini and the planet Mercury.

The Fourth House: Your Home Life

The fourth house shows the foundation of life, the psychological underpinnings. Located at the bottom of the chart, this house shows how you are nurtured and made to feel secure—your roots! It shows your early home environment and the circumstances at the end of your life (your final "home"), as well as the place you call home now. Astrologers look here for information about the parental nurturers in your life. It is the home of Cancer and the moon.

The Fifth House: Your Self-Expression

The Leo house is where the creative potential develops. Here you express yourself and procreate, in the sense that children are outgrowths of your creative ability. But this house most represents your inner childlike self, who delights in play. If your inner security has been established by the time you reach this house, you are now free to have fun, romance, and love affairs and to give of yourself. This is also the place astrologers look for playful love affairs, flirtations, and brief romantic encounters (rather than long-term commitments). It is the home of Leo and the sun.

The Sixth House: Care and Maintenance

The sixth house has been called the "care and maintenance" department. This house shows how you take care of your body and organize yourself to perform efficiently in the world. Here is where you get things done, where you look after others and fulfill service duties, such as taking care of pets. Here is what you do to survive on a day-to-day basis. The sixth house demands order in your life; otherwise there would be chaos. The house is your "job" (as opposed to your career, which is the domain of the tenth house), your diet, and your health and fitness regimens. It is the home of Virgo and the planet Mercury.

The Seventh House: Your Relationships

This house shows your attitude toward your partners and those with whom you enter commitments, contracts, or agreements. Here is the way you relate to others, as well as your close, intimate, one-on-one relationships (including open enemies—those you "face off" with). Open hostilities, lawsuits, divorces, and marriages happen here. If the first house represents the "I," the seventh or opposite house is the "not I"—the complementary partner you attract by the way you come across. If you are having trouble with partnerships, consider what you are attracting by the energies of your first and seventh house. It is the home of Libra and the planet Venus.

The Eighth House: Your Power House

The eighth house refers to how you merge with something or someone, and how you handle power and control. This is one of the most mysterious and powerful houses, where your energy transforms itself from "I" to "we." As you give up power and control by uniting with something or someone, two kinds of energies merge and become something greater, leading to a regeneration of the self on a higher level. Here are your attitudes toward sex, shared resources, and taxes (what you share with the government). Because this house involves what belongs to others, you face issues of control and power struggles, or undergo a deep psychological transformation as you bond with another. Here you transcend yourself through dreams, drugs, and occult or psychic experiences that reflect the collective unconscious. It is the home of Scorpio and the planet Pluto.

The Ninth House: Your Worldview

The ninth house shows your search for wisdom and higher knowledge: your belief system. As the third house represents the "lower mind," its opposite on the wheel, the ninth house, is the "higher mind," the abstract, intuitive, spiritual mind that asks "big" questions, like "Why we are here?" After the third house has explored what was close at hand, the ninth stretches out to broaden you mentally with higher education and travel. Here you stretch spiritually with religious activity. Since you are concerned with how everything is related, you tend to push boundaries and take risks. Here is where you express your ideas in a book or thesis, where you pontificate, philosophize, or preach. It is the home of Sagittarius and the planet Jupiter.

The Tenth House: Your Public Life

The tenth house is associated with your public life and high-profile activities. Located directly overhead at the "high noon" position on the horoscope wheel, this is the most "visible" house in the chart, the one where the world sees you. It deals with your career (but not your routine "job") and your reputation. Here is where you go public, take on responsibilities (as opposed to the fourth house, where you stay home). This will affect the career you choose and your "public relations." This house is also associated with your father figure or the main authority figure in your life. It is the home of Capricorn and the planet Saturn.

The Eleventh House: Your Social Concerns

The eleventh house is where you extend yourself to a group, a goal, or a belief system. This house is where you define what you really want: the kinds of friends you have, your political affiliations, and the kind of groups you identify with as an equal. Here is where you become concerned with "what other people think" or where you rebel against social conventions. It's where you become a socially conscious humanitarian or a partying social butterfly. It's where you look to others to stimulate you and discover your kinship to the rest of humanity. The sign on this house can help you understand what you gain and lose from friendships. It is the home of Aquarius and the planet Uranus.

The Twelfth House:
Where You Become Selfless

Old-fashioned astrologers used to put a rather negative spin on this house, calling it the "house of self-undoing." When we "undo ourselves," we surrender control, boundaries, limits, and rules. The twelfth house is where the boundaries between yourself and others become blurred and you become selfless. But instead of being self-undoing, the twelfth house can be a place of great creativity and talent. It is the place where you can tap into the collective unconscious, where your imagination is limitless.

In your trip around the zodiac, you've gone from the "I" of self-assertion in the first house to the final house, which symbolizes the dissolution that happens before rebirth. The twelfth house is where accumulated experiences are processed in the unconscious. Spiritually oriented astrologers look to this house for evidence of past lives and karma. Places where we go for solitude or to do spiritual or reparatory work belong here, such as retreats, religious institutions, or hospitals. Here is also where we withdraw from society voluntarily or involuntarily, and where we are put in prison because of antisocial activity. Selfless giving through charitable acts is part of this house, as is helpless receiving or dependence on charity.

In your daily life, the twelfth house reveals your deepest intimacies, your best-kept secrets, especially those you hide from yourself and repress deep in the unconscious. It is where we surrender a sense of a separate self to a deep feeling of wholeness, such as selfless service in religion or any activity that involves merging with the greater whole. Many sports stars have important planets in the twelfth house, which enable them to play in the zone, finding an inner, almost mystical, strength that transcends their limits. The twelfth house is the home of Pisces and the planet Neptune.

Which Are the Most Powerful Houses?

Houses are stronger or weaker depending on how many planets are inhabiting them. If there are many planets in a given house, it follows that the activities of that house will be especially important in your life. If the planet that rules the house is also located there, this too adds power to the house. The most powerful houses are the first, fourth, seventh, and tenth. These are the houses on "the angles" of a horoscope.

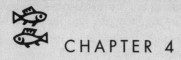

CHAPTER 4

The Moon: Your Inner Light

In some astrology-conscious lands, the moon is given as much importance in a horoscope as the sun. Astrologers often refer to these two bodies as the "lights," an appropriate description, since the sun and moon are not planets, but a star and a satellite. But it is also true that these two bodies shed the most "light" on a horoscope reading.

As the sun shines *out* in a horoscope, revealing the personality, the moon shines *in*. The sign the moon was transiting at the time of your birth reveals much about the inner you, secrets like what you really care about, what makes you feel comfortable and secure. It represents the receptive, reflective, female, nurturing self. It also reflects the one who nurtured you, the mother or mother figure in your chart. In a man's chart, the moon position describes his receptive, emotional, yin side, as well as the woman in his life who will have the deepest effect, usually his mother. (Venus reveals the kind of woman who will attract him physically.)

The moon is more at home in some signs than in others. It rules maternal Cancer and is exalted in Taurus—both comforting, home-loving signs where the natural emotional energies of the moon are easily and productively expressed. But when the moon is in the opposite signs—Capricorn and Scorpio—it leaves the comfortable nest and deals with emotional issues of power and achievement in the outside world. If you were born with the moon in one of these signs, you may find your emotional role in life more challenging.

To determine your moon sign, it is worthwhile to have an accurate horoscope cast, either by an astrologer, a computer program, or one of the online astrology sites that offer free charts. Since detailed moon tables are too extensive for this book, check through the following listing to find the moon sign that feels most familiar.

Moon in Aries

This placement makes you both independent and ardent. You are an idealist, and you tend to fall in and out of love easily. You love a challenge but could cool once your quarry is captured. Your emotional reactions are fast and fiery, quickly expressed and quickly forgotten. You may not think before expressing your feelings. It's not easy to hide how you feel. Channeling all your emotional energy could be one of your big challenges.

   Celebrity example: Angelina Jolie

Moon in Taurus

You are a sentimental soul who is very fond of the good life and gravitates toward solid, secure relationships. You like displays of affection and creature comforts—all the tangible trappings of a cozy, safe, calm atmosphere. You are sensual and steady emotionally, but very stubborn, possessive, and determined. You can't be pushed and tend to dislike changes. You should make an effort to broaden your horizons and to take a risk sometimes. You may become very attached to your home turf, your garden, and your possessions. You may also be a collector of objects that are meaningful to you.

   Celebrity example: Prince Charles

Moon in Gemini

You crave mental stimulation and variety in life, which you usually get via a varied social life, the excitement of flirtation, or multiple professional involvements. You may marry more than once and have a rather chaotic emotional life due to your difficulty with commitment and settling down, as well as your need to be constantly on the go. (Be sure to find a partner who is as outgoing as you are.) You will have to learn at some point to focus your energies because you tend to be somewhat fragmented—to do two things at once, to have two homes, or even to have two lovers. If you can find a creative way to express your many-faceted nature, you'll be ahead of the game.

Celebrity example: Jim Carrey

Moon in Cancer

This is the most powerful lunar position, which is sure to make a deep imprint on your character. Your needs are very much associated with your reaction to the needs of others. You are very sensitive, caring, and self-protective, though some of you may mask this with a hard shell, like the moon-sensitive crab. This placement also gives an excellent memory, keen intuition, and an uncanny ability to perceive the needs of others. All of the lunar phases will affect you, especially full moons and eclipses, so you would do well to mark them on your calendar. Because you're happiest at home, you may work at home or turn your office into a second home, where you can nurture and comfort people. (You may tend to mother the world.) With natural psychic, intuitive ability, you might be drawn to occult work in some way. Or you may get professionally involved with providing food and shelter to others.

Celebrity example: Tom Cruise

Moon in Leo

This warm, passionate moon takes everything to heart. You are attracted to all that is noble, generous, and aristocratic in life (and you may be a bit of a snob). You have an innate ability to take command emotionally, but you do need strong support, loyalty, and loud applause from those you love. You are possessive of your loved ones and your turf and will roar if anyone threatens to take over your territory.

Celebrity example: Paul McCartney

Moon in Virgo

You are rather cool until you decide if others measure up. But once someone or something meets your high standards, you hold up your end of the arrangement perfectly. You may, in fact, drive yourself too hard to attain some notion of perfection. Try to be a bit easier on yourself and others. Don't always act the censor! You love to be the teacher; you are drawn to situations where you can change others for the better, but sometimes you must learn to accept others for what they are—enjoy what you have!

Celebrity example: John F. Kennedy

Moon in Libra

Like other air-sign moons, you think before you feel. Therefore, you may not immediately recognize the emotional needs of others. However, you are relationship-oriented and may find it difficult to be alone or to do things alone. After you have learned emotional balance by leaning on yourself first, you can have excellent partnerships. It is best for you to avoid extremes, which set your scales swinging and can make your love life precarious. You thrive in a rather conservative, traditional, romantic relationship, where you receive attention and flattery—but not possessiveness—from your partner. You'll be your most charming in an elegant, harmonious atmosphere.

Celebrity example: Leonardo DiCaprio

Moon in Scorpio

This is a moon that enjoys and responds to intense, passionate feelings. You may go to extremes and have a very dramatic emotional life, full of ardor, suspicion, jealousy, and obsession. It would be much healthier to channel your need for power and control into meaningful work. This is a good position for anyone in the fields of medicine, police work, research, the occult, psychoanalysis, or intuitive work, because life-and-death situations don't faze you. However, you do take personal disappointments very hard.

Celebrity example: Elizabeth Taylor

Moon in Sagittarius

You take life's ups and downs with good humor and the proverbial grain of salt. You'll love 'em and leave 'em or take off on a great adventure at a moment's notice. "Born free" could be your slogan. Attracted by the exotic, you have mental and physical wanderlust. You may be too much in search of new mental and spiritual stimulation to ever settle down.

Celebrity example: Donald Trump

Moon in Capricorn

Are you ever accused of being too cool and calculating? You have an earthy side, but you take prestige and position very seriously. Your strong drive to succeed extends to your romantic life, where you will be devoted to improving your lifestyle and rising to the top. A structured situation where you can advance methodically makes you feel wonderfully secure. You may be attracted to someone older or very much younger or from a different social world. It may be difficult to look at the lighter side of emotional relationships. Though this moon is placed in the sign to your detriment, the good news is that you tend to be very dutiful and responsible to those you care for.

Celebrity example: Brad Pitt

Moon in Aquarius

You are a people collector with many friends of all backgrounds. You are happiest surrounded by people, and you may feel uneasy when left alone. Though you usually stay friends with lovers, intense emotions and demanding one-on-one relationships turn you off. You don't like anything to be too rigid or scheduled. Though tolerant and understanding, you can be emotionally unpredictable; you may opt for an unconventional love life. With plenty of space, you will be able to sustain relationships with liberal, freedom-loving types.

Celebrity example: Princess Diana

Moon in Pisces

You are very responsive and empathetic to others, especially if they have problems or are the underdog. (Be on guard against attracting too many people with sob stories.) You'll be happiest if you can express your creative imagination in the arts or in the spiritual or healing professions. Because you may tend to escape in fantasies or overreact to the moods of others, you need an emotional anchor to help you keep a firm foothold in reality. Steer clear of too much escapism (especially in alcohol) or reclusiveness. Places near water soothe your moods. Working in a field that gives you emotional variety will also help you be productive.

Celebrity example: Elvis Presley

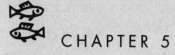

CHAPTER 5

The Planets: The Power of Ten

If you know a person's sun sign, you can learn some very useful generic information, but when you know the placement of all ten planets (eight planets plus the sun and moon), you've got a much more accurate profile of the person's character. Then the subject of the horoscope becomes a unique individual, as well as a member of a certain sun sign. You'll discover what makes him angry (Mars), pleased (Venus), or fearful (Saturn).

The planets are the doers of the horoscope, each representing a basic force in life. The sign and house where the planet is located indicate how and where its force will operate. For a moment, think of the horoscope as real estate. Prime property is close to the rising sign or at the top of the chart. If two or more planets are grouped together in one sign, they usually operate like a team, playing off each other, rather than expressing their energy singularly. But a loner, a planet that stands far away from the others, is usually outstanding and often calls the shots.

The sign of a planet also has a powerful influence. In some signs, the planet's energies are very much at home and can easily express themselves. In others, the planet has to work harder and is slightly out of sorts. The sign that most corresponds to the planet's energies is said to be ruled by that planet and obviously is the best place for that planet to be. The next best place is a sign where it is exalted, or especially harmonious. On the other hand, there are places in the horoscope where a planet has to stretch itself to play its role, such as the sign opposite a planet's rulership, which embodies the opposite area of life, and the sign opposite its exaltation. However, a planet that must work harder can also be more complete, because it must grow to meet the challenges of living in a more difficult sign. Like world leaders who've had to struggle for greatness, this planet may actually develop strength and character.

Here's a list of the best places for each planet to be. Note that, as new planets were discovered in the last century, they replaced the traditional rulers of signs which best complemented their energies.

ARIES—Mars
TAURUS—Venus, in its most sensual form
GEMINI—Mercury, in its communicative role
CANCER—the moon
LEO—the sun
VIRGO—also Mercury, this time in its more critical capacity
LIBRA—also Venus, in its more aesthetic, judgmental form
SCORPIO—Pluto, co-ruled by Mars
SAGITTARIUS—Jupiter
CAPRICORN—Saturn
AQUARIUS—Uranus, replacing Saturn, its original ruler
PISCES—Neptune, replacing Jupiter, its original ruler

Those who have many planets in exalted signs are lucky indeed, for here is where the planet can accomplish the most and be its most influential and creative.

SUN—exalted in Aries, where its energy creates action
MOON—exalted in Taurus, where instincts and reactions operate on a highly creative level
MERCURY—exalted in Aquarius, where it can reach analytical heights
VENUS—exalted in Pisces, a sign whose sensitivity encourages love and creativity
MARS—exalted in Capricorn, a sign that puts energy to work productively
JUPITER—exalted in Cancer, where it encourages nurturing and growth
SATURN—at home in Libra, where it steadies the scales of justice and promotes balanced, responsible judgment

URANUS—powerful in Scorpio, where it promotes transformation

NEPTUNE—especially favored in Cancer, where it gains the security to transcend to a higher state

PLUTO—exalted in Pisces, where it dissolves the old cycle, to make way for transition to the new

The Personal Planets:
Mercury, Venus, and Mars

These planets work in your immediate personal life.

Mercury affects how you communicate and how your mental processes work. Are you a quick study who grasps information rapidly, or do you learn more slowly and thoroughly? How is your concentration? Can you express yourself easily? Are you a good writer? All these questions can be answered by your Mercury placement.

Venus shows what you react to. What turns you on? What appeals to you aesthetically? Are you charming to others? Are you attractive to look at? Your taste, your refinement, your sense of balance and proportion are all Venus-ruled.

Mars is your outgoing energy, your drive and ambition. Do you reach out for new adventures? Are you assertive? Are you motivated? Self-confident? Hot-tempered? How you channel your energy and drive is revealed by your Mars placement.

Mercury Shows How
Your Mind Works

Since Mercury never travels far from the sun, read Mercury in your sun sign, and then the signs preceding and following it. Then decide which reflects the way you think.

Mercury in Aries

Your mind is very active and assertive. It approaches a plan aggressively. You never hesitate to say what you think, never shy away from a battle. In fact, you may relish a verbal confrontation. Tact is not your strong point, so you may have to learn not to trip over your tongue.

Mercury in Taurus

This is a much more cautious Mercury. Though you may be a slow learner, you have good concentration and mental stamina. You want to make your ideas really happen. You'll attack a problem methodically and consider every angle thoroughly, never jumping to conclusions. You'll stick with a subject until you master it.

Mercury in Gemini

You are a wonderful communicator with great facility for expressing yourself both verbally and in writing. You love gathering all kinds of information. You probably finish other people's sentences and express yourself with eloquent hand gestures. You can talk to anybody anytime and probably have phone and E-mail bills to prove it. You read anything from sci-fi to Shakespeare and might need an extra room just for your book collection. Though you learn fast, you may lack focus and discipline. Watch a tendency to jump from subject to subject.

Mercury in Cancer

You rely on intuition more than logic. Your mental processes are usually colored by your emotions, so you may seem shy or hesitant to voice your opinions. However, this placement gives you the advantage of great imagination and empathy in the way you communicate with others.

Mercury in Leo

You are enthusiastic and very dramatic in the way you express yourself. You like to hold the attention of groups and could be a great public speaker. Your mind thinks big, so you'd prefer to deal with the overall picture rather than with the details.

Mercury in Virgo

This is one of the best places for Mercury. It should give you critical ability, attention to details, and thorough analysis. Your mind focuses on the practical side of things. This type of thinking is very well suited to being a teacher or editor.

Mercury in Libra

You're either a born diplomat who smoothes over ruffled feathers or a talented debater. Many lawyers have this placement. However, since you're forever weighing the pros and cons of a situation, you may vacillate when making decisions.

Mercury in Scorpio

This is an investigative mind that stops at nothing to get the answers. You may have a sarcastic, stinging wit, a gift for the cutting remark. There's always a grain of truth to your verbal sallies, thanks to your penetrating insight.

Mercury in Sagittarius

You are a super salesman with a tendency to expound. Though you are very broad-minded, you can be dogmatic when it comes to telling others what's good for them. You won't hesitate to tell the truth as you see it, so watch a tendency toward tactlessness. On the plus side, you have a great sense of humor. This position of Mercury is often considered by astrologers to be at a disadvantage because Sagittarius opposes Gemini, the sign Mercury rules, and squares off with Virgo, another Mercury-ruled sign. What often happens is that Mercury in Sagittarius oversteps its bounds and loses sight of the facts in a situation. Do a reality check before making promises that you may not be able to deliver.

Mercury in Capricorn

This placement endows good mental discipline. You have a love of learning and a very orderly approach to your subjects. You will patiently plod through the facts and figures until you have mastered the tasks. You grasp structured situations easily, but may be short on creativity.

Mercury in Aquarius

An independent, original thinker, you'll have more cutting-edge ideas than the average person. You'll be quick to check out any unusual opportunities. Your opinions are so well-researched and grounded that once your mind is made up, it is difficult to change.

Mercury in Pisces

You have the psychic intuitive mind of a natural poet. Learn to make use of your creative imagination. You may think in terms of helping others, but check a tendency to be vague and forgetful of details.

Venus Is the Popularity Planet

Venus tells how you relate to others and to your environment. It shows where you receive pleasure and what you love to do. Find your Venus placement on the chart in this book by looking for the year of your birth in the left-hand column. Then follow the line of that year across the page until you reach the time period of your birthday. The sign heading that column will be your Venus. If you were born on a day when Venus was changing signs, check the signs preceding or following that day to determine if that feels more like your Venus nature.

Venus in Aries

You can't stand to be bored, confined, or ordered around. But a good challenge, maybe even a rousing row, turns you on. Confess—don't you pick a fight now and then just to get someone stirred up? You're attracted by the chase, not the catch, which could cause some problems in your love life, if the object of your affection becomes too attainable. You like to wear red and can spot a trend before anyone else.

Venus in Taurus

All your senses work in high gear. You love to be surrounded by glorious tastes, smells, textures, sounds, and visuals—austerity is not for you. Neither is being rushed. You like time to enjoy your pleasures. Soothing surroundings with plenty of creature comforts are your cup of tea. You like to feel secure in your nest, with no sudden jolts or surprises. You like familiar objects—in fact, you may hate to let anything or anyone go.

Venus in Gemini

You are a lively, sparkling personality who thrives in a situation that affords a constant variety and a frequent change of scenery. A varied social life is important to you, with plenty of mental stimulation and a chance to engage in some light flirtation. Commitment may be difficult, because playing the field is so much fun.

Venus in Cancer

An atmosphere where you feel protected, coddled, and mothered is best for you. You love to be surrounded by children in a cozy, homelike situation. You are attracted to those who are tender and nurturing, who make you feel secure and well provided for. You may be quite secretive about your emotional life or attracted to clandestine relationships.

Venus in Leo

First-class attention in large doses turns you on, and so does the glitter of real gold and the flash of mirrors. You like to feel like a star at all times, surrounded by your admiring audience. The side effect is that you may be attracted to flatterers and tinsel, while the real gold requires some digging.

Venus in Virgo

Everything neatly in its place? On the surface, you are attracted to an atmosphere where everything is in perfect order, but underneath are some basic, earthy urges. You are attracted to those who appeal to your need to teach, be of service, or play out a Pygmalion fantasy. You are at your best when you are busy doing something useful.

Venus in Libra

Elegance and harmony are your key words. You can't abide an atmosphere of contention. Your taste tends toward the classic, with light harmonies of color—nothing clashing, trendy, or outrageous. You love doing things with a partner and should be careful to pick one who is decisive, but patient enough to let you weigh the pros and cons. And steer clear of argumentative types.

Venus in Scorpio

Mysteries intrigue you—in fact, anything that is too open and aboveboard is a bit of a bore. You surely have a stack of whodunits by the bed, along with an erotic magazine or two. You like to solve puzzles. You may also be fascinated with the occult, crime, or scientific research. Intense, all-or-nothing situations add spice to your life, and you love to ferret out the secrets of others. But you could get burned by your flair for living dangerously. The color black, spicy food, dark wood furniture, and heady perfume put you in the right mood.

Venus in Sagittarius

If you are not actually a world traveler, your surroundings are sure to reflect your love of faraway places. You like a casual outdoor atmosphere and a dog or two to pet. There should be plenty of room for athletic equipment and suitcases. You're attracted to kindred souls who love to travel and who share your freedom-loving philosophy of life. Athletics and spiritual or New Age pursuits could be other interests.

Venus in Capricorn

No fly-by-night relationships for you! You want substance in life, and you are attracted to whatever will help you get where you are going. Status objects turn you on. And so do those who have a serious, responsible, businesslike approach, or who remind you of a beloved parent. It is characteristic of this placement to be attracted to someone of a different generation. Antiques, traditional clothing, and dignified behavior are becoming to you.

Venus in Aquarius

This Venus wants to make friends, to be "cool." You like to be in a group, particularly one pushing a worthy cause. You feel quite at home surrounded by people, and could even court fame, yet all the while, you tend to remain detached from intense commitment. Original ideas and unpredictable people fascinate you. You prefer spontaneity and delightful surprises, rather than a well-planned schedule of events.

Venus in Pisces

This Venus loves to give of yourself, and you find plenty of takers. Stray animals and people appeal to your heart and your pocketbook, but be careful to look at their motives realistically once in a while. You are extremely vulnerable to sob stories of all kinds. Fantasy, the arts (especially film, dance, and theater), and psychic or spiritual activities also speak to you.

Mars: The Action Hero

Mars is the mover and shaker in your life. It shows how you pursue your goals, whether you have energy to burn or proceed in a slow, steady pace. It will also show how you get angry. Do you explode, or do a slow burn, or hold everything inside and then get revenge later?

To find your Mars, turn to the chart on pages 82–94. Then find your birth year in the left-hand column and find the line headed by the month of your birth. There you will find an abbreviation of your Mars sign. If the description of your Mars sign doesn't ring true, read the description of the signs preceding and following it. You might have been born on a day when Mars was changing signs, in which case your Mars might fall into the adjacent sign.

Mars in Aries

In the sign it rules, Mars shows its brilliant fiery nature. You have an explosive temper and can be quite impatient. On the other hand, you have tremendous courage, energy, and drive. You'll let nothing stand in your way as you race to be first! Obstacles are met head-on and broken through by force. However, problems that require patience and persistence to solve can have you exploding in rage. You're a great starter, but not necessarily around for the finish.

Mars in Taurus

Slow, steady, concentrated energy gives you the power to last until the finish line. You've great stamina, and you never give up. Your tactic is to wear away obstacles with your persistence. Often you come out a winner because you've had the patience to hang in there. When angered, you do a slow burn.

Mars in Gemini

You can't sit still for long. This Mars craves variety. You often have two or more things going on at once—it's all an amusing game to you. Your life can get very complicated, but that only adds spice and stimulation. What drives you into a nervous, hyper state? Boredom, sameness, routine, and confinement. You can do wonderful things with your hands, and you have a way with words.

Mars in Cancer

You rarely attack head-on. Instead, you'll keep things to yourself, make plans in secret, and always cover your actions. This might be interpreted by some as manipulative, but you are only being self-protective. You get furious when anyone knows too much about you. But you do like to know all about others. Your mothering and feeding instincts can be put to good use, if you work in the food, hotel, or child-care-related businesses. You may have to overcome your fragile sense of security, which prompts you not to take risks and to get physically upset when criticized. Don't take things so personally!

Mars in Leo

You have a very dominant personality that takes center stage—modesty is not one of your traits, nor is taking a back seat. You prefer giving the orders and have been known to make a dramatic scene if they are not obeyed. Properly used, this Mars confers leadership ability, endurance, and courage.

Mars in Virgo

You are the fault-finder of the zodiac, who notices every detail. Mistakes of any kind make you very nervous. You may worry, even if everything is going smoothly. You may not express your anger directly, but you sure can nag. You have definite likes and dislikes, and you are sure you can do the job better than anyone else. You are certainly more industrious and detail-oriented than other signs. Your Mars energy is often most positively expressed in some kind of teaching role.

Mars in Libra

This Mars will have a passion for beauty, justice, and art. Generally, you will avoid confrontations at all costs. You prefer to spend your energy finding diplomatic solutions or weighing pros and cons. Your other techniques are passive aggression or exercising your well-known charm to get people to do what you want.

Mars in Scorpio

This is a powerful placement, so intense that it demands careful channeling into worthwhile activities. Otherwise, you could become obsessed with your sexuality or might use your need for power and control to manipulate others. You are strong-willed, shrewd, and very private about your affairs, and you'll usually have a secret agenda behind your actions. Your great stamina, focus, and discipline would be excellent assets for careers in the military or medical fields, especially research or surgery. When angry, you don't get mad—you get even!

Mars in Sagittarius

This expansive Mars often propels people into sales, travel, athletics or philosophy. Your energies function well when you are on the move. You have a hot temper and are inclined to say what you think before you consider the consequences. You shoot for high goals—and talk endlessly about them—but you may be weak on groundwork. This Mars needs a solid foundation. Watch a tendency to take unnecessary risks.

Mars in Capricorn

This is an ambitious Mars with an excellent sense of timing. You have an eye for those who can be of use to you, and you may dismiss people ruthlessly when you're angry. But you drive yourself hard and deliver full value. This is a good placement for an executive. You'll aim for status and a high material position in life, and keep climbing despite the odds. A great Mars to have!

Mars in Aquarius

This is the most rebellious Mars. You seem to have a drive to assert yourself against the status quo. You may enjoy provoking people, shocking them out of traditional views. Or this placement could express itself in an offbeat sex life. Somehow you often find yourself in unconventional situations. You enjoy being a leader of an active group, which pursues forward-looking studies, politics, or goals.

Mars in Pisces

This Mars is a good actor who knows just how to appeal to the sympathies of others. You create and project wonderful fantasies or use your sensitive antennae to crusade for those less fortunate. You get what you want through creating a veil of illusion and glamour. This is a good Mars for someone in the creative and imaginative fields—a dancer, a performer, a photographer, or an actor. Many famous film stars have this placement. Watch a tendency to manipulate by making others feel sorry for you.

Jupiter Is the Optimist

This big, bright, swirling mass of gases is associated with abundance, prosperity, and the kind of windfall you get without too much hard work. You're optimistic under Jupiter's influence, when anything seems possible. You'll travel, expand your mind with higher education, and publish to share your knowledge widely. On the other hand, Jupiter's influence is neither discriminating nor disciplined. It represents the principle of growth without judgment. Therefore, if not kept in check, it could result in extravagance, weight gain, laziness, and carelessness.

Be sure to look up your Jupiter in the tables in this book. When the current position of Jupiter is favorable, you may get that lucky break. This is a great time to try new things, take risks, travel, or get more education. Opportunities seem to open up easily, so take advantage of them.

Once a year, Jupiter changes signs. That means you are due for an expansive time every twelve years, when Jupiter travels through your sun sign. You'll also have periods every four years when Jupiter is in the same element as your sun sign.

Jupiter in Aries

You are the soul of enthusiasm and optimism. Your luckiest times are when you are getting started on an exciting project or selling an ideal that you really believe in. You may have to watch a tendency to be arrogant with those who do not share your enthusiasm. You follow your impulses, often ignoring budget or other commonsense limitations. To produce real, solid benefits, you'll need patience and the will to follow through wherever this Jupiter falls in your horoscope.

Jupiter in Taurus

You'll spend money on beautiful material things, especially those that come from nature—items made of rare woods, natural fabrics, or precious gems, for instance. You can't have too much comfort or too many sensual pleasures. Watch a tendency to overindulge in good food, or to overpamper yourself with nothing but the best. Spartan living is not for you! You may be especially lucky in matters of real estate.

Jupiter in Gemini

You are the great talker of the zodiac, and you may be a great writer too. But restlessness could be your weak point. You jump around and talk too much; you could be a jack-of-all-trades. Keeping a secret is especially difficult, so you'll also have to watch a tendency to spill the beans. Since you love to be at the center of a beehive of activity, you'll have a vibrant social life. Your best opportunities will come through your talent for language: speaking, writing, communicating, and selling.

Jupiter in Cancer

You are luckiest in situations where you can find emotional closeness or deal with basic security needs, such as food, nurturing, or shelter. You may be a great collector, and you may simply love to accumulate things—you are the one who stashes things away for a rainy day. You probably have a very good memory and love children—in fact, you may have many children to care for. The food, hotel, child-care, and shipping businesses hold good opportunities for you.

Jupiter in Leo

You are a natural showman who loves to live in a larger-than-life way. Yours is a personality full of color that always finds its way into the limelight. You can't have too much attention. Showbiz is a natural place for you, and so is any area where you can play to a crowd. Exercising your flair for drama, your natural playfulness, and your romantic nature brings you good fortune. But watch a tendency to be overextravagant or to monopolize center stage.

Jupiter in Virgo

You actually love those minute details others find boring. To you, they make all the difference between the perfect and the ordinary. You are the fine craftsman who spots every flaw. You expand your awareness by finding the most efficient methods and by being of service to others. Many will be drawn to medical or teaching fields. You'll also have luck in publishing, crafts, nutrition, and service professions. Watch out for a tendency to overwork.

Jupiter in Libra

This is an other-directed Jupiter that develops best with a partner, for the stimulation of others helps you grow. You are also most comfortable in harmonious, beautiful situations, and you work well with artistic people. You have a great sense of fair play and an ability to evaluate the pros and cons of a situation. You usually prefer to play the role of diplomat rather than that of adversary.

Jupiter in Scorpio

You love the feeling of power and control, of taking things to their limit. You can't resist a mystery, and your shrewd, penetrating mind sees right through to the heart of most situations and people. You have luck in work that provides for solutions to matters of life and death. You may be drawn to undercover work, behind-the-scenes intrigue, psychotherapy, the occult, and sex-related ventures. Your challenge will be to develop a sense of moderation and tolerance for other beliefs. You may have luck in handling other people's money—insurance, taxes, and inheritance can bring you a windfall.

Jupiter in Sagittarius

Independent, outgoing, and idealistic, you'll shoot for the stars. This Jupiter compels you to travel far and wide, both physically and mentally, via higher education. You may have luck while traveling in an exotic place. You also have luck with outdoor ventures, exercise, and animals, particularly horses. Since you tend to be very open about your opinions, watch a tendency to be tactless and to exaggerate. Instead, use your wonderful sense of humor to make your point.

Jupiter in Capricorn

Jupiter is much more restrained in Capricorn, the sign of rules and authority. Here, Jupiter can make you overwork and heighten any ambition or sense of duty you may have. You'll expand in areas that advance your position, putting you higher up the social or corporate ladder. You are lucky working within the establishment in a very structured situation, where you can show off your ability to organize and reap rewards for your hard work.

Jupiter in Aquarius

This is another freedom-loving Jupiter, with great tolerance and originality. You are at your best when you are working for a humanitarian cause and in the company of many supporters. This is a good Jupiter for a political career. You'll relate to all kinds of people on all social levels. You have an abundance of original ideas, but you are best off away from routine and any situation that imposes rigid rules. You need mental stimulation!

Jupiter in Pisces

You are a giver whose feelings and pocketbook are easily touched by others, so choose your companions with care. You could be the original sucker for a hard-luck story. Better find a worthy hospital or charity to appreciate your selfless support. You have a great creative imagination and may attract good fortune in fields related to oil, perfume, pharmaceuticals, petroleum, dance, footwear, and alcohol. But beware not to overindulge in alcohol—focus on a creative outlet instead.

Saturn Puts on the Brakes

Jupiter speeds you up with lucky breaks, and then along comes Saturn to slow you down with the disciplinary brakes. It is the planet that can help you achieve lasting goals. Saturn has unfairly been called a malefic planet, one of the bad guys of the zodiac. On the contrary, Saturn is one of our best friends—the kind who tells you what you need to hear, even if it's not good news. Under a Saturn transit, we grow up, take responsibility for our lives, and emerge from whatever test this planet has in store as far wiser, more capable, and mature human beings. After all, it is when we are under pressure that we grow stronger.

When Saturn hits a critical point in your horoscope, you can count on an experience that will make you slow up, pull back, and reexamine your life. It is a call to eliminate what is not working and to shape up. By the end of its twenty-eight-year trip around the zodiac, Saturn will have tested you in all areas of your life. The major tests happen in seven-year cycles, when Saturn passes over the angles of your chart—your rising sign, the top of your chart or midheaven, your descendant, and the nadir or bottom of your chart. This is when the real life-changing experiences happen. But you are also in for a testing period whenever Saturn passes a planet in your chart or stresses that planet from a distance. Therefore, it is useful to check your planetary positions with the timetable of Saturn to prepare in advance, or at least to brace yourself.

When Saturn returns to its location at the time of your birth, at approximately age twenty-eight, you'll have your first Saturn return. At this time, a person usually takes stock or settles down to find his mission in life and assumes full adult duties and responsibilities.

Another way Saturn helps us is to reveal the karmic lessons from previous lives and give us the chance to overcome them. So look at Saturn's challenges as much-needed opportunities for self-improvement. Under a Jupiter influence, you'll have more fun, but Saturn gives you solid, long-lasting results.

Look up your natal Saturn in the tables in this book for clues on where you need work.

Saturn in Aries

Saturn here puts the brakes on Aries's natural drive and enthusiasm. There is often an angry side to this placement. You don't let anyone push you around and you know what's best for yourself. Following orders is not your strong point, nor is diplomacy. You tend to be quick to go on the offensive in relationships, attacking first, before anyone attacks you. Because no one quite lives up to your standards, you often wind up doing everything yourself. You'll have to learn to cooperate and tone down any self-centeredness. Pat Buchanan has this Saturn.

Saturn in Taurus

A big issue is getting control of the cash flow. There will be lean periods that can be frightening, but you have the patience and endurance to stick them out and the methodical drive to prosper in the end. Learn to take a philosophical attitude like Ben Franklin, who also had this placement, and who said, "A penny saved is a penny earned."

Saturn in Gemini

You are a serious student of life, who may have difficulty communicating or sharing your knowledge. You may be shy, speak slowly, or have fears about communicating, like Eleanor Roosevelt. You dwell in the realms of science, theory, or abstract analysis, even when you are dealing with the emotions, like Sigmund Freud, who also had this placement.

Saturn in Cancer

Your tests come with establishing a secure emotional base. In doing so, you may have to deal with some very basic fears centering on your early home environment. Most of your Saturn tests will have emotional roots in those early-childhood experiences. You may have difficulty remaining objective in terms of what you try to achieve, so it will be especially important for you to deal with negative feelings such as guilt, paranoia, jealousy, resentment, and suspicion. Galileo and Michelangelo also navigated these murky waters.

Saturn in Leo

This is an authoritarian Saturn—a strict, demanding parent who may deny the pleasure principle in your zeal to see that rules are followed. Though you may feel guilty about taking the spotlight, you are very ambitious and loyal. You have to watch a tendency toward rigidity, also toward overwork and holding back affection. Joseph Kennedy and Billy Graham share this placement.

Saturn in Virgo

This is a cautious, exacting Saturn, intensely hard on yourself. Most of all, you give yourself the roughest time with your constant worries about every little detail, often making yourself sick. You may have difficulties setting priorities and getting the job done. Your tests will come in learning tolerance and understanding of others. Charles de Gaulle, Mae West, and Nathaniel Hawthorne had this meticulous Saturn.

Saturn in Libra

Saturn is exalted here, which makes this planet an ally. You may choose very serious, older partners in life, perhaps stemming from a fear of dependency. You need to learn to stand solidly on your own before you commit to another. Since you are extremely cautious, you deliberate every involvement—with good reason. It is best that you find an occupation that makes good use of your sense of duty and honor. Steer clear of fly-by-night situations. Both Khrushchev and Mao Tse-tung had this placement.

Saturn in Scorpio

You have great staying power. This Saturn tests you in situations involving the control of others. You may feel drawn to some kind of intrigue or undercover work, like J. Edgar Hoover. Or there may be an air of mystery surrounding your life and death, like Marilyn Monroe and Robert Kennedy, who both had this placement. There are lessons to be learned from your sexual involvements. Often sex is used for manipulation or is somehow out of the ordinary. The Roman emperor Caligula and the transsexual Christine Jorgensen are extreme cases.

Saturn in Sagittarius

Your challenges and lessons will come from tests of your spiritual and philosophical values, as happened to Martin Luther King Jr. and Gandhi. You are high-minded and sincere with this reflective, moral placement. Uncompromising in your ethical standards, you could become a benevolent despot.

Saturn in Capricorn

With the help of Saturn at maximum strength, your judgment will improve with age. And, like Spencer Tracy's screen image, you'll be the gray-haired hero with a strong sense of responsibility. You advance in life slowly but steadily, always with a strong hand at the helm and an eye for the advantageous situation. Like Pat Robertson, you're likely to stand for conservative values. Negatively, you may be a loner, prone to periods of melancholy.

Saturn in Aquarius

Your tests come from relationships with groups. Do you care too much about what others think? Do you feel like an outsider, like Greta Garbo? You may fear being different from others and therefore slight your own unique, forward-looking gifts. Or like Lord Byron and Howard Hughes, you may take the opposite tack and rebel in the extreme. You can apply discipline to accomplish great humanitarian goals, as Albert Schweitzer did.

Saturn in Pisces

Your fear of the unknown and the irrational may lead you to the safety and protection of an institution. You may go on the run like Jesse James to avoid looking too deeply inside. Or you might go in the opposite, more positive direction and develop a disciplined psychoanalytic approach, which puts you more in control of your feelings. Some of you will take refuge in work with hospitals, charities, or religious institutions. Queen Victoria, who had this placement, symbolized an era when institutions of all kinds were sustained. Discipline applied to artistic work, especially poetry and dance, or spiritual work, such as yoga or meditation, might be helpful.

How Uranus, Neptune, and Pluto Influence Your Generation

These three planets remain in signs such a long time that a whole generation bears the imprint of the sign. Mass movements, great sweeping changes, fads that characterize a generation, and even the issues of the conflicts and wars of the time are influenced by these outer three planets. When one of these distant planets changes signs, there is a definite shift in the atmosphere, the feeling of the end of an era.

Since these planets are so far away from the sun—too distant to be seen by the naked eye—they pick up signals from the universe at large. These planetary receivers literally link the sun with distant energies, and then perform a similar function in your horoscope by linking your central character with intuitive, spiritual, transformative forces from the cosmos. Each planet has a special domain and will reflect this in the area of your chart where it falls.

Uranus Is the Surprise Ingredient

Uranus is the surprise ingredient that sets you and your generation apart. There is nothing ordinary about this quirky green planet that seems to be traveling on its side, surrounded by a swarm of moons. Is it any wonder that astrologers assigned it to Aquarius, the most eccentric and gregarious sign? Uranus seems to wend its way around the sun, marching to its own tune.

Significantly, Uranus follows Saturn, the planet of limitations and structures. Often we get caught up in the structures we have created to give ourselves a sense of security. However, if we lose contact with our spiritual roots in the process, Uranus is likely to jolt us out of our comfortable rut and wake us up.

Uranus energy is electrical, happening in sudden flashes. It is not influenced by karma or past events, nor does it regard tradition, sex, or sentiment. Uranus's key words are surprise and awakening. Suddenly, there's that flash of inspiration, that bright idea, or that totally new approach that revolutionizes whatever scheme you were undertaking. A Uranus event takes you by surprise, for better or for worse. The Uranus place in your life is where you awaken and become your own person, leaving the structures of Saturn behind. And it is probably the most unconventional place in your chart.

Look up the sign of Uranus at the time of your birth and see where you follow your own tune.

Uranus in Aries

Birth Dates:
  March 31, 1927–November 4, 1927
  January 13, 1928–June 6, 1934
  October 10, 1934–March 28, 1935

Your generation is original, creative, and pioneering. It developed the computer, the airplane, and the cyclotron. You let nothing hold you back from exploring the unknown, and you have a powerful mixture of fire and electricity behind you. Women of your generation were among the first to be liberated. You were the unforgettable style setters. You have a surprise in store for everyone. As with Yoko Ono, Grace Kelly, and Jacqueline Onassis, your life may be jolted by sudden and violent changes.

Uranus in Taurus

Birth Dates:
  June 6, 1934–October 10, 1934
  March 28, 1935–August 7, 1941
  October 5, 1941–May 15, 1942

The great territorial shakeups of World War II began during your generation. You're independent; you're probably self-employed or you would like to be. You have original ideas about making money, and you brace yourself for sudden changes of fortune. This Uranus can cause shake-ups, particularly in finances, but it can also make you a born entrepreneur, like Martha Stewart.

Uranus in Gemini

Birth Dates:
  August 7, 1941–October 5, 1941
  May 15, 1942–August 30, 1948
  November 12, 1948–June 10, 1949

You were the first children to be influenced by television, and in your adult years, your generation stocks up on answering machines, cell phones, computers, and fax machines—any new way you can communicate. You have an inquiring mind, but your interests may be rather short-lived. This Uranus can be easily fragmented if there is no structure and focus.

Uranus in Cancer

Birth Dates:
  August 30–November 12, 1948
  June 10, 1949–August 24, 1955
  January 28, 1956–June 10, 1956

This generation came at a time when divorce was becoming commonplace, so your home image is unconventional. You may have an unusual relationship with your parents, or come from a broken home or an unconventional one. You'll have unorthodox ideas about parenting, intimacy, food, and shelter. You may also be interested in dreams, psychic phenomena, and memory work.

Uranus in Leo

Birth Dates:
  August 24, 1955–January 28, 1956
  June 10, 1956–November 1, 1961
  January 10, 1962–August 10, 1962

This generation understood how to use electronic media. Many of your group are now leaders in the high-tech industries, and you also understand how to use the new media to promote yourself. Like Isadora Duncan, you may have a very eccentric kind of charisma and a life that is sparked by unusual love affairs. Your children may have traits that are out of the ordinary. Where this planet falls in your chart, you'll have a love of freedom, be a bit of an egomaniac, and show the full force of your personality in a unique way, like tennis great Martina Navratilova.

Uranus in Virgo

Birth Dates:
> November 1, 1961–January 10, 1962
> August 10, 1962–September 28, 1968
> May 20, 1969–June 24, 1969

You'll have highly individual work methods, and many will be finding newer, more practical ways to use computers. Like Einstein, who had this placement, you'll break the rules brilliantly. Your generation came at a time of student rebellions, the civil rights movement, and the general acceptance of health foods. Chances are, you're concerned about pollution and cleaning up the environment. You may also be involved with nontraditional healing methods.

Uranus in Libra

Birth Dates:
> September 28, 1968–May 20, 1969
> June 24, 1969–November 21, 1974
> May 1, 1975–September 8, 1975

Your generation will be always changing partners. Born during the era of women's liberation, you may have come from a broken home and may have no clear image of what a marriage entails. There will be many sudden splits and experiments before you settle down. Your generation will be much involved in legal and political reforms and in changing artistic and fashion looks.

Uranus in Scorpio

Birth Dates:
> November 21, 1974–May 1, 1975
> September 8, 1975–February 17, 1981
> March 20, 1981–November 16, 1981

Interest in transformation, meditation, and life after death signaled the beginning of New Age consciousness. Your generation recognizes no boundaries, no limits, and no external controls. You'll have new attitudes toward death and dying, psychic phenomena, and the occult. Like Mae West and Casanova, you'll shock 'em sexually.

Uranus in Sagittarius

Birth Dates:
    February 17, 1981–March 20, 1981
    November 16, 1981–February 15, 1988
    May 27, 1988–December 2, 1988
    Could this generation be the first to travel in outer space? The new generation with this placement included Charles Lindbergh and a time when the first zeppelins and the Wright Brothers were conquering the skies. Uranus here forecasts great discoveries, mind expansion, and long-distance travel. Like Galileo and Martin Luther, those born in these years will generate new theories about the cosmos and man's relation to it.

Uranus in Capricorn

Birth Dates:
    December 20, 1904–January 30, 1912
    September 4, 1912–November 12, 1912
    February 15, 1988–May 27, 1988
    December 2, 1988–April 1, 1995
    June 9, 1995–January 12, 1996
    This generation, now reaching adulthood, will challenge traditions. In these years, we got organized with the help of technology put to practical use. The Internet was born after the great economic boom of the 1990s. Great leaders who were movers and shakers of history, like Julius Caesar and Henry VIII, were born under this placement.

Uranus in Aquarius

Birth Dates:
    January 30, 1912–September 4, 1912
    November 12, 1912–April 1, 1919

August 16, 1919–January 22, 1920
April 1, 1995–June 9, 1995
January 12, 1996–March 10, 2003
September 15, 2003–December 30, 2003

Uranus in Aquarius is the strongest placement for this planet. Recently, we've had the opportunity to witness the full force of its power of innovation, as well as its sudden wake-up calls and insistence on humanitarian values. This was a time of high-tech development, when home computers became as ubiquitous as television. It was a time of globalization, surprise attacks (9/11), and underdeveloped countries demanding attention. The last generation with this placement produced great innovative minds, such as Leonard Bernstein and Orson Welles. The next will become another radical breakthrough generation, much concerned with global issues that involve all humanity.

Uranus in Pisces

Birth Dates:
April 1, 1919–August 16, 1919
January 22, 1920–March 31, 1927
November 4, 1927–January 12, 1928
March 10, 2003–September 15, 2003
December 30, 2003–May 28, 2010

Uranus is now in Pisces, ushering in a new generation. In the past century, Uranus in Pisces focused attention on the rise of electronic entertainment—radio and the cinema—and the secretiveness of Prohibition. This produced a generation of idealists exemplified by Judy Garland's theme, "Somewhere over the Rainbow." Uranus in Pisces also hints at stealth activities, at hospital and prison reform, at high-tech drugs and medical experiments, at shake-ups in the petroleum industry and new locations for Pisces-ruled off-shore drilling. Issues regarding the water and oil supply, water-related storm damage (Hurricane Katrina), sudden hurricanes, droughts, and floods demand our attention.

Neptune Is the Magic Solvent

Neptune is often maligned as the planet of illusions that dissolves reality, enabling you to escape the material world. Under Neptune's influence, you see what you want to see. But Neptune also encourages you to create. It embodies glamour, subtlety, mystery, and mysticism, and governs anything that takes you beyond the mundane world, including out-of-body experiences.

Neptune breaks through and transcends your ordinary perceptions to take you to another level, where you experience either confusion or ecstasy. Its force can pull you off course only if you allow this to happen. Those who use Neptune wisely can translate their daydreams into poetry, theater, design, or inspired moves in the business world, avoiding the tricky con artist side of this planet.

Find your Neptune listed below:

Neptune in Cancer

Birth Dates:
   July 19, 1901–December 25, 1901
   May 21, 1902–September 23, 1914
   December 14, 1914–July 19, 1915
   March 19, 1916–May 2, 1916

Dreams of the homeland, idealistic patriotism, and glamorization of the nurturing assets of women characterized this time. You who were born here have unusual psychic ability and deep insights into basic needs of others.

Neptune in Leo

Birth Dates:
   September 23, 1914–December 14, 1914
   July 19, 1915–March 19, 1916
   May 2, 1916–September 21, 1928
   February 19, 1929–July 24, 1929

Neptune in Leo brought us the glamour and high living of the 1920s and the big spenders of that time. Neptune temptations of gambling, seduction, theater, and lavish entertaining distracted from the realities of the age. Those born in that generation also made great advances in the arts.

Neptune in Virgo

Birth Dates:
    September 21, 1928–February 19, 1929
    July 24, 1929–October 3, 1942
    April 17, 1943–August 2, 1943
    Neptune in Virgo encompassed the 1930s, the Great Depression, and the beginning of World War II, when a new order was born. This was a time of facing what didn't work. Many were unemployed and found solace at the movies, watching the great Virgo star Greta Garbo or the escapist dance films of Busby Berkeley. New public services were born. Those with Neptune in Virgo later spread the gospel of health and fitness. This generation's devotion to spending hours at the office inspired the word *workaholic*.

Neptune in Libra

Birth Dates:
    October 3, 1942–April 17, 1943
    August 2, 1943–December 24, 1955
    March 12, 1956–October 19, 1956
    June 15, 1957–August 6, 1957
    This was the time of World War II, and the immediate postwar period, when the world regained balance and returned to relative stability. Neptune in Libra was the romantic generation who would later be concerned with relating. As this generation matured, there was a new trend toward marriage and commitment. Racial and sexual equality became important issues, as they redesigned traditional roles to suit modern times.

Neptune in Scorpio

Birth Dates:
    December 24, 1955–March 12, 1956
    October 19, 1956–June 15, 1957
    August 6, 1957–January 4, 1970

May 3, 1970–November 6, 1970

Neptune in Scorpio brought in a generation that would become interested in transformative power. Born in an era that glamorized sex, drugs, rock and roll, and Eastern religion, they matured in a more sobering time of AIDS, cocaine abuse, and New Age spirituality. As they evolve, they will become active in healing the planet from the results of the abuse of power.

Neptune in Sagittarius

Birth Dates:
   January 4, 1970–May 3, 1970
   November 6, 1970–January 19, 1984
   June 23, 1984–November 21, 1984

Neptune in Sagittarius was the time when space travel became a reality. The Neptune influence glamorized new approaches to mysticism, religion, and mind expansion. This generation will take a new approach to spiritual life, with emphasis on visions, mysticism, and clairvoyance.

Neptune in Capricorn

Birth Dates:
   January 19, 1984–June 23, 1984
   November 21, 1984–January 29, 1998

Neptune in Capricorn brought a time when delusions about material power were glamorized in the mideighties and nineties. There was a boom in the stock market, and the Internet era spawned young tycoons who later lost all their wealth. It was also a time when the psychic and occult worlds spawned a new category of business enterprise, and sold services on television.

Neptune in Aquarius

Birth Dates:
   January 29, 1998–April 4, 2011

This should continue to be a time of breakthroughs. Here the creative influence of Neptune reaches a universal audience. This is a time of dissolving barriers and globalization—when we truly become one world. During this transit of high-tech Aquarius, new kinds of entertainment media reach across cultural differences. However, the transit of Neptune has also raised boundary issues between cultures, especially in Middle Eastern countries with Neptune-ruled oil fields. As Neptune raises issues of social and political structures not being as solid as they seem, this could continue to produce rebellion and chaos in the environment. However, by using imagination (Neptune) in partnership with a global view (Aquarius), we could reach creative solutions.

Those born with this placement should be true citizens of the world, with a remarkable creative ability to transcend social and cultural barriers.

Pluto Can Transform You

Though Pluto is a tiny, mysterious body in space, its influence is great. When Pluto zaps a strategic point in your horoscope, your life changes dramatically.

Little Pluto is the power behind the scenes; it affects you at deep levels of consciousness, causing events to come to the surface that will transform you and your generation. Nothing escapes, or is sacred, with this probing planet. Its purpose is to wipe out the past so something new can happen.

The Pluto place in your horoscope is where you have invisible power (Mars governs the visible power), where you can transform, heal, and affect the unconscious needs of the masses. Pluto tells lots about how your generation projects power and what makes it seem cool to others. And when Pluto changes signs, there is a whole new concept of what's cool. Pluto's strange elliptical orbit occasionally runs inside the orbit of neighboring Neptune. Because of its eccentric path, the length of time Pluto stays in any given sign can vary from thirteen to thirty-two years. It covered only seven signs in the last century.

Pluto in Gemini

Late 1800s–May 26, 1914

This was a time of mass suggestion and breakthroughs in communications, when many brilliant writers, such as Ernest Hemingway and F. Scott Fitzgerald, were born. Henry Miller, D. H. Lawrence, and James Joyce scandalized society by using explicit sexual images and language in their literature. "Muck-raking" journalists exposed corruption. Pluto-ruled Scorpio president Theodore Roosevelt said, "Speak softly, but carry a big stick." This generation had an intense need to communicate and made major breakthroughs in knowledge. A compulsive restlessness and a thirst for a variety of experiences characterize many of this generation.

Pluto in Cancer

Birth Dates:

May 26, 1914–June 14, 1939

Dictators and mass media arose to wield emotional power over the masses. Women's rights were a popular issue. Deep sentimental feelings, acquisitiveness, and possessiveness characterized these times and people. Most of the great stars of the Hollywood era who embodied the American image were born during this period: Grace Kelly, Esther Williams, Frank Sinatra, and Lana Turner, to name a few.

Pluto in Leo

Birth Dates:

June 14, 1939–August 19, 1957

The performing arts played on the emotions of the masses. Mick Jagger, John Lennon, and rock and roll were born at this time. So were baby boomers like Bill and Hillary Clinton. Those born here tend to be self-centered, powerful, and boisterous. This generation does its own thing, for better or for worse. They are quick to embrace self-transformation in the form of antiaging and plastic surgery techniques, to stay forever young and stay relevant in society.

Pluto in Virgo

Birth Dates:
  August 19, 1957–October 5, 1971
  April 17, 1972–July 30, 1972
This is the yuppie generation that sparked a mass movement toward fitness, health, and career. It is a much more sober, serious, and driven generation than the fun-loving Pluto in Leo. During this time, machines were invented to process detail work efficiently. Inventions took a practical turn with answering machines, fax machines, car phones, and home-office equipment—all making the workplace far more efficient.

Pluto in Libra

Birth Dates:
  October 5, 1971–April 17, 1972
  July 30, 1972–November 5, 1983
  May 18, 1984–August 27, 1984
A mellower generation, people born at this time are concerned with partnerships, working together, and finding diplomatic solutions to problems. Marriage is important to this generation, and they will define it by combining traditional values with equal partnership. This was a time of women's liberation, gay rights, the ERA, and legal battles over abortion—all of which transformed our ideas about relationships.

Pluto in Scorpio

Birth Dates:
  November 5, 1983–May 18, 1984
  August 27, 1984–January 17, 1995
Pluto was in its ruling sign for a comparatively short period of time. However, this was a time of record achievements, destructive sexually transmitted diseases, nuclear power controversies, and explosive political issues. Pluto destroys in order to create new understanding—the phoenix rising from the ashes—which should be some consolation for those of you who felt Pluto's force before 1995. Sexual shockers were par for the course during these intense years, when black cloth-

ing, transvestites, body piercing, tattoos, and sexually explicit advertising pushed the boundaries of good taste.

Pluto in Sagittarius

Birth Dates:
    January 17, 1995–April 20, 1995
    November 10, 1995–January 27, 2008
    June 13, 2008–November 26, 2008

During the most recent Pluto transit, we were pushed to expand our horizons and find deeper spiritual meaning in life.

Pluto's opposition with Saturn in 2001 brought an enormous conflict between traditional societies and the forces of change. It signaled a time when religious convictions exerted power in our political life as well.

Since Sagittarius is associated with travel, Pluto, the planet of extremes, made space travel a reality for wealthy adventurers, who paid for the privilege of travel on space shuttles. Globalization transformed business and traditional societies as outsourcing became the norm.

New dimensions in electronic publishing, concern with animal rights and the environment, and an increasing emphasis on extreme forms of religion were other signs of Pluto in Sagittarius. Charismatic religious leaders asserted themselves and questions of the boundaries between church and state arose. There were also sexual scandals associated with the church, which transformed the religious power structure.

Pluto in Capricorn

Birth Dates:
    January 25, 2008–June 13, 2008
    November 26, 2008–January 20, 2024

As Pluto in Jupiter-ruled Sagittarius signaled a time of expansion and globalization, Pluto's entry into Saturn-ruled Capricorn in 2008 signaled a time of adjustment, of facing reality and limitations, then finding pragmatic solutions. It will be a time when a new structure is imposed, when we become concerned with what actually works.

As Capricorn is associated with corporations and also with

responsibility and duty, look for dramatic changes in business practices, hopefully with more attention paid to ethical and social responsibility as well as the bottom line. Big business will have enormous power during this transit, perhaps handling what governments have been unable to accomplish. There will be an emphasis on trimming down, perhaps a new belt-tightening regime. And, since Capricorn is the sign of Father Time, there will be a new emphasis on the aging of the population. The generation born now is sure to be a more practical and realistic one than that of their older Pluto in Sagittarius siblings.

VENUS SIGNS 1901–2010

	Aries	Taurus	Gemini	Cancer	Leo	Virgo
1901	3/29–4/22	4/22–5/17	5/17–6/10	6/10–7/5	7/5–7/29	7/29–8/23
1902	5/7–6/3	6/3–6/30	6/30–7/25	7/25–8/19	8/19–9/13	9/13–10/7
1903	2/28–3/24	3/24–4/18	4/18–5/13	5/13–6/9	6/9–7/7	7/7–8/17
						9/6–11/8
1904	3/13–5/7	5/7–6/1	6/1–6/25	6/25–7/19	7/19–8/13	8/13–9/6
1905	2/3–3/6	3/6–4/9	7/8–8/6	8/6–9/1	9/1–9/27	9/27–10/21
	4/9–5/28	5/28–7/8				
1906	3/1–4/7	4/7–5/2	5/2–5/26	5/26–6/20	6/20–7/16	7/16–8/11
1907	4/27–5/22	5/22–6/16	6/16–7/11	7/11–8/4	8/4–8/29	8/29–9/22
1908	2/14–3/10	3/10–4/5	4/5–5/5	5/5–9/8	9/8–10/8	10/8–11/3
1909	3/29–4/22	4/22–5/16	5/16–6/10	6/10–7/4	7/4–7/29	7/29–8/23
1910	5/7–6/3	6/4–6/29	6/30–7/24	7/25–8/18	8/19–9/12	9/13–10/6
1911	2/28–3/23	3/24–4/17	4/18–5/12	5/13–6/8	6/9–7/7	7/8–11/18
1912	4/13–5/6	5/7–5/31	6/1–6/24	6/24–7/18	7/19–8/12	8/13–9/5
1913	2/3–3/6	3/7–5/1	7/8–8/5	8/6–8/31	9/1–9/26	9/27–10/20
	5/2–5/30	5/31–7/7				
1914	3/14–4/6	4/7–5/1	5/2–5/25	5/26–6/19	6/20–7/15	7/16–8/10
1915	4/27–5/21	5/22–6/15	6/16–7/10	7/11–8/3	8/4–8/28	8/29–9/21
1916	2/14–3/9	3/10–4/5	4/6–5/5	5/6–9/8	9/9–10/7	10/8–11/2
1917	3/29–4/21	4/22–5/15	5/16–6/9	6/10–7/3	7/4–7/28	7/29–8/21
1918	5/7–6/2	6/3–6/28	6/29–7/24	7/25–8/18	8/19–9/11	9/12–10/5
1919	2/27–3/22	3/23–4/16	4/17–5/12	5/13–6/7	6/8–7/7	7/8–11/8
1920	4/12–5/6	5/7–5/30	5/31–6/23	6/24–7/18	7/19–8/11	8/12–9/4
1921	2/3–3/6	3/7–4/25	7/8–8/5	8/6–8/31	9/1–9/25	9/26–10/20
	4/26–6/1	6/2–7/7				
1922	3/13–4/6	4/7–4/30	5/1–5/25	5/26–6/19	6/20–7/14	7/15–8/9
1923	4/27–5/21	5/22–6/14	6/15–7/9	7/10–8/3	8/4–8/27	8/28–9/20
1924	2/13–3/8	3/9–4/4	4/5–5/5	5/6–9/8	9/9–10/7	10/8–11/12
1925	3/28–4/20	4/21–5/15	5/16–6/8	6/9–7/3	7/4–7/27	7/28–8/21
1926	5/7–6/2	6/3–6/28	6/29–7/23	7/24–8/17	8/18–9/11	9/12–10/5
1927	2/27–3/22	3/23–4/16	4/17–5/11	5/12–6/7	6/8–7/7	7/8–11/9

Libra	Scorpio	Sagittarius	Capricorn	Aquarius	Pisces
8/23–9/17	9/17–10/12	10/12–1/16	1/16–2/9	2/9–3/5	3/5–3/29
			11/7–12/5	12/5–1/11	
10/7–10/31	10/31–11/24	11/24–12/18	12/18–1/11	2/6–4/4	1/11–2/6
					4/4–5/7
8/17–9/6	12/9–1/5			1/11–2/4	2/4–2/28
11/8–12/9					
9/6–9/30	9/30–10/25	1/5–1/30	1/30–2/24	2/24–3/19	3/19–4/13
		10/25–11/18	11/18–12/13	12/13–1/7	
10/21–11/14	11/14–12/8	12/8–1/1/06			1/7–2/3
8/11–9/7	9/7–10/9	10/9–12/15	1/1–1/25	1/25–2/18	2/18–3/14
	12/15–12/25	12/25–2/6			
9/22–10/16	10/16–11/9	11/9–12/3	2/6–3/6	3/6–4/2	4/2–4/27
			12/3–12/27	12/27–1/20	
11/3–11/28	11/28–12/22	12/22–1/15			1/20–2/4
8/23–9/17	9/17–10/12	10/12–11/17	1/15–2/9	2/9–3/5	3/5–3/29
			11/17–12/5	12/5–1/15	
10/7–10/30	10/31–11/23	11/24–12/17	12/18–12/31	1/1–1/15	1/16–1/28
				1/29–4/4	4/5–5/6
11/19–12/8	12/9–12/31		1/1–1/10	1/11–2/2	2/3–2/27
9/6–9/30	1/1–1/4	1/5–1/29	1/30–2/23	2/24–3/18	3/19–4/12
	10/1–10/24	10/25–11/17	11/18–12/12	12/13–12/31	
10/21–11/13	11/14–12/7	12/8–12/31		1/1–1/6	1/7–2/2
8/11–9/6	9/7–10/9	10/10–12/5	1/1–1/24	1/25–2/17	2/18–3/13
	12/6–12/30	12/31			
9/22–10/15	10/16–11/8	1/1–2/6	2/7–3/6	3/7–4/1	4/2–4/26
		11/9–12/2	12/3–12/26	12/27–12/31	
11/3–11/27	11/28–12/21	12/22–12/31		1/1–1/19	1/20–2/13
8/22–9/16	9/17–10/11	1/1–1/14	1/15–2/7	2/8–3/4	3/5–3/28
		10/12–11/6	11/7–12/5	12/6–12/31	
10/6–10/29	10/30–11/22	11/23–12/16	12/17–12/31	1/1–4/5	4/6–5/6
11/9–12/8	12/9–12/31		1/1–1/9	1/10–2/2	2/3–2/26
9/5–9/30	1/1–1/3	1/4–1/28	1/29–2/22	2/23–3/18	3/19–4/11
	9/31–10/23	10/24–11/17	11/18–12/11	12/12–12/31	
10/21–11/13	11/14–12/7	12/8–12/31		1/1–1/6	1/7–2/2
8/10–9/6	9/7–10/10	10/11–11/28	1/1–1/24	1/25–2/16	2/17–3/12
	11/29–12/31				
9/21–10/14	1/1	1/2–2/6	2/7–3/5	3/6–3/31	4/1–4/26
	10/15–11/7	11/8–12/1	12/2–12/25	12/26–12/31	
11/13–11/26	11/27–12/21	12/22–12/31		1/1–1/19	1/20–2/12
8/22–9/15	9/16–10/11	1/1–1/14	1/15–2/7	2/8–3/3	3/4–3/27
		10/12–11/6	11/7–12/5	12/6–12/31	
10/6–10/29	10/30–11/22	11/23–12/16	12/17–12/31	1/1–4/5	4/6–5/6
11/10–12/8	12/9–12/31	1/1–1/7	1/8	1/9–2/1	2/2–2/26

VENUS SIGNS 1901–2010

	Aries	Taurus	Gemini	Cancer	Leo	Virgo
1928	4/12–5/5	5/6–5/29	5/30–6/23	6/24–7/17	7/18–8/11	8/12–9/4
1929	2/3–3/7	3/8–4/19	7/8–8/4	8/5–8/30	8/31–9/25	9/26–10/19
	4/20–6/2	6/3–7/7				
1930	3/13–4/5	4/6–4/30	5/1–5/24	5/25–6/18	6/19–7/14	7/15–8/9
1931	4/26–5/20	5/21–6/13	6/14–7/8	7/9–8/2	8/3–8/26	8/27–9/19
1932	2/12–3/8	3/9–4/3	4/4–5/5	5/6–7/12	9/9–10/6	10/7–11/1
			7/13–7/27	7/28–9/8		
1933	3/27–4/19	4/20–5/28	5/29–6/8	6/9–7/2	7/3–7/26	7/27–8/20
1934	5/6–6/1	6/2–6/27	6/28–7/22	7/23–8/16	8/17–9/10	9/11–10/4
1935	2/26–3/21	3/22–4/15	4/16–5/10	5/11–6/6	6/7–7/6	7/7–11/8
1936	4/11–5/4	5/5–5/28	5/29–6/22	6/23–7/16	7/17–8/10	8/11–9/4
1937	2/2–3/8	3/9–4/13	7/7–8/3	8/4–8/29	8/30–9/24	9/25–10/18
	4/14–6/3	6/4–7/6				
1938	3/12–4/4	4/5–4/28	4/29–5/23	5/24–6/18	6/19–7/13	7/14–8/8
1939	4/25–5/19	5/20–6/13	6/14–7/8	7/9–8/1	8/2–8/25	8/26–9/19
1940	2/12–3/7	3/8–4/3	4/4–5/5	5/6–7/4	9/9–10/5	10/6–10/31
			7/5–7/31	8/1–9/8		
1941	3/27–4/19	4/20–5/13	5/14–6/6	6/7–7/1	7/2–7/26	7/27–8/20
1942	5/6–6/1	6/2–6/26	6/27–7/22	7/23–8/16	8/17–9/9	9/10–10/3
1943	2/25–3/20	3/21–4/14	4/15–5/10	5/11–6/6	6/7–7/6	7/7–11/8
1944	4/10–5/3	5/4–5/28	5/29–6/21	6/22–7/16	7/17–8/9	8/10–9/2
1945	2/2–3/10	3/11–4/6	7/7–8/3	8/4–8/29	8/30–9/23	9/24–10/18
	4/7–6/3	6/4–7/6				
1946	3/11–4/4	4/5–4/28	4/29–5/23	5/24–6/17	6/18–7/12	7/13–8/8
1947	4/25–5/19	5/20–6/12	6/13–7/7	7/8–8/1	8/2–8/25	8/26–9/18
1948	2/11–3/7	3/8–4/3	4/4–5/6	5/7–6/28	9/8–10/5	10/6–10/31
			6/29–8/2	8/3–9/7		
1949	3/26–4/19	4/20–5/13	5/14–6/6	6/7–6/30	7/1–7/25	7/26–8/19
1950	5/5–5/31	6/1–6/26	6/27–7/21	7/22–8/15	8/16–9/9	9/10–10/3
1951	2/25–3/21	3/22–4/15	4/16–5/10	5/11–6/6	6/7–7/7	7/8–11/9
1952	4/10–5/4	5/5–5/28	5/29–6/21	6/22–7/16	7/17–8/9	8/10–9/3
1953	2/2–3/3	3/4–3/31	7/8–8/3	8/4–8/29	8/30–9/24	9/25–10/18
	4/1–6/5	6/6–7/7				

Libra	Scorpio	Sagittarius	Capricorn	Aquarius	Pisces
9/5–9/28	1/1–1/3	1/4–1/28	1/29–2/22	2/23–3/17	3/18–4/11
	9/29–10/23	10/24–11/16	11/17–12/11	12/12–12/31	
10/20–11/12	11/13–12/6	12/7–12/30	12/31	1/1–1/5	1/6–2/2
8/10–9/6	9/7–10/11	10/12–11/21	1/1–1/23	1/24–2/16	2/17–3/12
	11/22–12/31				
9/20–10/13	1/1–1/3	1/4–2/6	2/7–3/4	3/5–3/31	4/1–4/25
	10/14–11/6	11/7–11/30	12/1–12/24	12/25–12/31	
11/2–11/25	11/26–12/20	12/21–12/31		1/1–1/18	1/19–2/11
8/21–9/14	9/15–10/10	1/1–1/13	1/14–2/6	2/7–3/2	3/3–3/26
		10/11–11/5	11/6–12/4	12/5–12/31	
10/5–10/28	10/29–11/21	11/22–12/15	12/16–12/31	1/1–4/5	4/6–5/5
11/9–12/7	12/8–12/31		1/1–1/7	1/8–1/31	2/1–2/25
9/5–9/27	1/1–1/2	1/3–1/27	1/28–2/21	2/22–3/16	3/17–4/10
	9/28–10/22	10/23–11/15	11/16–12/10	12/11–12/31	
10/19–11/11	11/12–12/5	12/6–12/29	12/30–12/31	1/1–1/5	1/6–2/1
8/9–9/6	9/7–10/13	10/14–11/14	1/1–1/22	1/23–2/15	2/16–3/11
	11/15–12/31				
9/20–10/13	1/1–1/3	1/4–2/5	2/6–3/4	3/5–3/30	3/31–4/24
	10/14–11/6	11/7–11/30	12/1–12/24	12/25–12/31	
11/1–11/25	11/26–12/19	12/20–12/31		1/1–1/18	1/19–2/11
8/21–9/14	9/15–10/9	1/1–1/12	1/13–2/5	2/6–3/1	3/2–3/26
		10/10–11/5	11/6–12/4	12/5–12/31	
10/4–10/27	10/28–11/20	11/21–12/14	12/15–12/31	1/1–4/5	4/6–5/5
11/9–12/7	12/8–12/31		1/1–1/7	1/8–1/31	2/1–2/24
9/3–9/27	1/1–1/2	1/3–1/27	1/28–2/20	2/21–3/16	3/17–4/9
	9/28–10/21	10/22–11/15	11/16–12/10	12/11–12/31	
10/19–11/11	11/12–12/5	12/6–12/29	12/30–12/31	1/1–1/4	1/5–2/1
8/9–9/6	9/7–10/15	10/16–11/7	1/1–1/21	1/22–2/14	2/15–3/10
	11/8–12/31				
9/19–10/12	1/1–1/4	1/5–2/5	2/6–3/4	3/5–3/29	3/30–4/24
	10/13–11/5	11/6–11/29	11/30–12/23	12/24–12/31	
11/1–11/25	11/26–12/19	12/20–12/31		1/1–1/17	1/18–2/10
8/20–9/14	9/15–10/9	1/1–1/12	1/13–2/5	2/6–3/1	3/2–3/25
		10/10–11/5	11/6–12/5	12/6–12/31	
10/4–10/27	10/28–11/20	11/21–12/13	12/14–12/31	1/1–4/5	4/6–5/4
11/10–12/7	12/8–12/31		1/1–1/7	1/8–1/31	2/1–2/24
9/4–9/27	1/1–1/2	1/3–1/27	1/28–2/20	2/21–3/16	3/17–4/9
	9/28–10/21	10/22–11/15	11/16–12/10	12/11–12/31	
10/19–11/11	11/12–12/5	12/6–12/29	12/30–12/31	1/1–1/5	1/6–2/1

VENUS SIGNS 1901–2010

	Aries	Taurus	Gemini	Cancer	Leo	Virgo
1954	3/12–4/4	4/5–4/28	4/29–5/23	5/24–6/17	6/18–7/13	7/14–8/8
1955	4/25–5/19	5/20–6/13	6/14–7/7	7/8–8/1	8/2–8/25	8/26–9/18
1956	2/12–3/7	3/8–4/4	4/5–5/7 6/24–8/4	5/8–6/23 8/5–9/8	9/9–10/5	10/6–10/31
1957	3/26–4/19	4/20–5/13	5/14–6/6	6/7–7/1	7/2–7/26	7/27–8/19
1958	5/6–5/31	6/1–6/26	6/27–7/22	7/23–8/15	8/16–9/9	9/10–10/3
1959	2/25–3/20	3/21–4/14	4/15–5/10	5/11–6/6	6/7–7/8 9/21–9/24	7/9–9/20 9/25–11/9
1960	4/10–5/3	5/4–5/28	5/29–6/21	6/22–7/15	7/16–8/9	8/10–9/2
1961	2/3–6/5	6/6–7/7	7/8–8/3	8/4–8/29	8/30–9/23	9/24–10/17
1962	3/11–4/3	4/4–4/28	4/29–5/22	5/23–6/17	6/18–7/12	7/13–8/8
1963	4/24–5/18	5/19–6/12	6/13–7/7	7/8–7/31	8/1–8/25	8/26–9/18
1964	2/11–3/7	3/8–4/4	4/5–5/9 6/18–8/5	5/10–6/17 8/6–9/8	9/9–10/5	10/6–10/31
1965	3/26–4/18	4/19–5/12	5/13–6/6	6/7–6/30	7/1–7/25	7/26–8/19
1966	5/6–5/31	6/1–6/26	6/27–7/21	7/22–8/15	8/16–9/8	9/9–10/2
1967	2/24–3/20	3/21–4/14	4/15–5/10	5/11–6/6	6/7–7/8 9/10–10/1	7/9–9/9 10/2–11/9
1968	4/9–5/3	5/4–5/27	5/28–6/20	6/21–7/15	7/16–8/8	8/9–9/2
1969	2/3–6/6	6/7–7/6	7/7–8/3	8/4–8/28	8/29–9/22	9/23–10/17
1970	3/11–4/3	4/4–4/27	4/28–5/22	5/23–6/16	6/17–7/12	7/13–8/8
1971	4/24–5/18	5/19–6/12	6/13–7/6	7/7–7/31	8/1–8/24	8/25–9/17
1972	2/11–3/7	3/8–4/3	4/4–5/10 6/12–8/6	5/11–6/11 8/7–9/8	9/9–10/5	10/6–10/30
1973	3/25–4/18	4/18–5/12	5/13–6/5	6/6–6/29	7/1–7/25	7/26–8/19
1974	5/5–5/31	6/1–6/25	6/26–7/21	7/22–8/14	8/15–9/8	9/10–10/2
1975	2/24–3/20	3/21–4/13	4/14–5/9	5/10–6/6	6/7–7/9 9/3–10/4	7/10–9/2 10/5–11/9
1976	4/8–5/2	5/2–5/27	5/27–6/20	6/20–7/14	7/14–8/8	8/8–9/1
1977	2/2–6/6	6/6–7/6	7/6–8/2	8/2–8/28	8/28–9/22	9/22–10/17
1978	3/9–4/2	4/2–4/27	4/27–5/22	5/22–6/16	6/16–7/12	7/12–8/6
1979	4/23–5/18	5/18–6/11	6/11–7/6	7/6–7/30	7/30–8/24	8/24–9/17
1980	2/9–3/6	3/6–4/3	4/3–5/12 6/5–8/6	5/12–6/5 8/6–9/7	9/7–10/4	10/4–10/30
1981	3/24–4/17	4/17–5/11	5/11–6/5	6/5–6/29	6/29–7/24	7/24–8/18

Libra	Scorpio	Sagittarius	Capricorn	Aquarius	Pisces
8/9–9/6	9/7–10/22	10/23–10/27	1/1–1/22	1/23–2/15	2/16–3/11
	10/28–12/31				
9/19–10/13		1/7–2/5	2/6–3/4	3/5–3/30	3/31–4/24
	10/14–11/5	11/6–11/30	12/1–12/24	12/25–12/31	
11/1–11/25	11/26–12/19	12/20–12/31		1/1–1/17	1/18–2/11
8/20–9/14	9/15–10/9	1/1–1/12	1/13–2/5	2/6–3/1	3/2–3/25
		10/10–11/5	11/6–12/6	12/7–12/31	
10/4–10/27	10/28–11/20	11/21–12/14	12/15–12/31	1/1–4/6	4/7–5/5
11/10–12/7	12/8–12/31		1/1–1/7	1/8–1/31	2/1–2/24
9/3–9/26	1/1–1/2	1/3–1/27	1/28–2/20	2/21–3/15	3/16–4/9
	9/27–10/21	10/22–11/15	11/16–12/10	12/11–12/31	
10/18–11/11	11/12–12/4	12/5–12/28	12/29–12/31	1/1–1/5	1/6–2/2
8/9–9/6	9/7–12/31		1/1–1/21	1/22–2/14	2/15–3/10
9/19–10/12	1/1–1/6	1/7–2/5	2/6–3/4	3/5–3/29	3/30–4/23
	10/13–11/5	11/6–11/29	11/30–12/23	12/24–12/31	
11/1–11/24	11/25–12/19	12/20–12/31		1/1–1/16	1/17–2/10
8/20–9/13	9/14–10/9	1/1–1/12	1/13–2/5	2/6–3/1	3/2–3/25
		10/10–11/5	11/6–12/7	12/8–12/31	
10/3–10/26	10/27–11/19	11/20–12/13	2/7–2/25	1/1–2/6	4/7–5/5
			12/14–12/31	2/26–4/6	
11/10–12/7	12/8–12/31		1/1–1/6	1/7–1/30	1/31–2/23
9/3–9/26	1/1	1/2–1/26	1/27–2/20	2/21–3/15	3/16–4/8
	9/27–10/21	10/22–11/14	11/15–12/9	12/10–12/31	
10/18–11/10	11/11–12/4	12/5–12/28	12/29–12/31	1/1–1/4	1/5–2/2
8/9–9/7	9/8–12/31		1/1–1/21	1/22–2/14	2/15–3/10
9/18–10/11	1/1–1/7	1/8–2/5	2/6–3/4	3/5–3/29	3/30–4/23
	10/12–11/5	11/6–11/29	11/30–12/23	12/24–12/31	
10/31–11/24	11/25–12/18	12/19–12/31		1/1–1/16	1/17–2/10
8/20–9/13	9/14–10/8	1/1–1/12	1/13–2/4	2/5–2/28	3/1–3/24
		10/9–11/5	11/6–12/7	12/8–12/31	
10/3–10/26	10/27–11/19	11/20–12/13	12/14–12/31	3/1–4/6	4/7–5/4
			1/30–2/28	1/1–1/29	
11/10–12/7	12/8–12/31		1/1–1/6	1/7–1/30	1/31–2/23
9/1–9/26	9/26–10/20	1/1–1/26	1/26–2/19	2/19–3/15	3/15–4/8
10/17–11/10	11/10–12/4	12/4–12/27	12/27–1/20/78		1/4–2/2
8/6–9/7	9/7–1/7			1/20–2/13	2/13–3/9
9/17–10/11	10/11–11/4	1/7–2/5	2/5–3/3	3/3–3/29	3/29–4/23
		11/4–11/28	11/28–12/22	12/22–1/16/80	
10/30–11/24	11/24–12/18	12/18–1/11/81			1/16–2/9
8/18–9/12	9/12–10/9	10/9–11/5	1/11–2/4	2/4–2/28	2/28–3/24
			11/5–12/8	12/8–1/23/82	

VENUS SIGNS 1901–2010

	Aries	Taurus	Gemini	Cancer	Leo	Virgo
1982	5/4–5/30	5/30–6/25	6/25–7/20	7/20–8/14	8/14–9/7	9/7–10/2
1983	2/22–3/19	3/19–4/13	4/13–5/9	5/9–6/6	6/6–7/10	7/10–8/27
					8/27–10/5	10/5–11/9
1984	4/7–5/2	5/2–5/26	5/26–6/20	6/20–7/14	7/14–8/7	8/7–9/1
1985	2/2–6/6	6/7–7/6	7/6–8/2	8/2–8/28	8/28–9/22	9/22–10/16
1986	3/9–4/2	4/2–4/26	4/26–5/21	5/21–6/15	6/15–7/11	7/11–8/7
1987	4/22–5/17	5/17–6/11	6/11–7/5	7/5–7/30	7/30–8/23	8/23–9/16
1988	2/9–3/6	3/6–4/3	4/3–5/17	5/17–5/27	9/7–10/4	10/4–10/29
			5/27–8/6	8/28–9/22	9/22–10/16	
1989	3/23–4/16	4/16–5/11	5/11–6/4	6/4–6/29	6/29–7/24	7/24–8/18
1990	5/4–5/30	5/30–6/25	6/25–7/20	7/20–8/13	8/13–9/7	9/7–10/1
1991	2/22–3/18	3/18–4/13	4/13–5/9	5/9–6/6	6/6–7/11	7/11–8/21
					8/21–10/6	10/6–11/9
1992	4/7–5/1	5/1–5/26	5/26–6/19	6/19–7/13	7/13–8/7	8/7–8/31
1993	2/2–6/6	6/6–7/6	7/6–8/1	8/1–8/27	8/27–9/21	9/21–10/16
1994	3/8–4/1	4/1–4/26	4/26–5/21	5/21–6/15	6/15–7/11	7/11–8/7
1995	4/22–5/16	5/16–6/10	6/10–7/5	7/5–7/29	7/29–8/23	8/23–9/16
1996	2/9–3/6	3/6–4/3	4/3–8/7	8/7–9/7	9/7–10/4	10/4–10/29
1997	3/23–4/16	4/16–5/10	5/10–6/4	6/4–6/28	6/28–7/23	7/23–8/17
1998	5/3–5/29	5/29–6/24	6/24–7/19	7/19–8/13	8/13–9/6	9/6–9/30
1999	2/21–3/18	3/18–4/12	4/12–5/8	5/8–6/5	6/5–7/12	7/12–8/15
					8/15–10/7	10/7–11/9
2000	4/6–5/1	5/1–5/25	5/25–6/13	6/13–7/13	7/13–8/6	8/6–8/31
2001	2/2–6/6	6/6–7/5	7/5–8/1	8/1–8/26	8/26–9/20	9/20–10/15
2002	3/7–4/1	4/1–4/25	4/25–5/20	5/20–6/14	6/14–7/10	7/10–8/7
2003	4/21–5/16	5/16–6/9	6/9–7/4	7/4–7/29	7/29–8/22	8/22–9/15
2004	2/8–3/5	3/5–4/3	4/3–8/7	8/7–9/6	9/6–10/3	10/3–10/28
2005	3/22–4/15	4/15–5/10	5/10–6/3	6/3–6/28	6/28–7/23	7/23–8/17
2006	5/3–5/29	5/29–6/24	6/24–7/19	7/19–8/12	8/12–9/6	9/6–9/30
2007	2/21–3/16	3/17–4/10	4/11–5/7	5/8–6/4	6/5–7/13	7/14–8/7
					8/8–10/6	10/7–11/7
2008	4/6–4/30	5/1–5/24	5/25–6/17	6/18–7/11	7/12–8/4	8/5–8/29
2009	2/2–4/11	6/6–7/5	7/5–7/31	731/–8/26	8/26–9/20	9/20–10/14
	4/24–6/6					
2010	3/7–3/31	3/31–4/25	4/25–5/20	5/20–6/14	6/14–7/10	7/10–8/7

Libra	Scorpio	Sagittarius	Capricorn	Aquarius	Pisces
10/2–10/26	10/26–11/18	11/18–12/12	1/23–3/2 12/12–1/5/83	3/2–4/6	4/6–5/4
11/9–12/6	12/6–1/1/84			1/5–1/29	1/29–2/22
9/1–9/25	9/25–10/20	1/1–1/25 10/20–11/13	1/25–2/19 11/13–12/9	2/19–3/14 12/10–1/4	3/14–4/7
10/16–11/9	11/9–12/3	12/3–12/27	12/28–1/19		1/4–2/2
8/7–9/7	9/7–1/7			1/20–2/13	2/13–3/9
9/16–10/10	10/10–11/3	1/7–2/5 11/3–11/28	2/5–3/3 11/28–12/22	3/3–3/28 12/22–1/15	3/28–4/22
10/29–11/23	11/23–12/17	12/17–1/10			1/15–2/9
8/18–9/12	9/12–10/8	10/8–11/5	1/10–2/3 11/5–12/10	2/3–2/27 12/10–1/16/90	2/27–3/23
10/1–10/25	10/25–11/18	11/18–12/12	1/16–3/3 12/12–1/5	3/3–4/6	4/6–5/4
11/9–12/6	12/6–12/31	12/31–1/25/92		1/5–1/29	1/29–2/22
8/31–9/25	9/25–10/19	10/19–11/13	1/25–2/18 11/13–12/8	2/18–3/13 12/8–1/3/93	3/13–4/7
10/16–11/9	11/9–12/2	12/2–12/26	12/26–1/19		1/3–2/2
8/7–9/7	9/7–1/7			1/19–2/12	2/12–3/8
9/16–10/10	10/10–11/13	1/7–2/4 11/3–11/27	2/4–3/2 11/27–12/21	3/2–3/28 12/21–1/15	3/28–4/22
10/29–11/23	11/23–12/17	12/17–1/10/97			1/15–2/9
8/17–9/12	9/12–10/8	10/8–11/5	1/10–2/3 11/5–12/12	2/3–2/27 12/12–1/9	2/27–3/23
9/30–10/24	10/24–11/17	11/17–12/11	1/9–3/4	3/4–4/6	4/6–5/3
11/9–12/5	12/5–12/31	12/31–1/24		1/4–1/28	1/28–2/21
8/31–9/24	9/24–10/19	10/19–11/13	1/24–2/18 11/13–12/8	2/18–3/12 12/8	3/13–4/6
10/15–11/8	11/8–12/2	12/2–12/26	12/26/01–1/18/02	12/8/00–1/3/01	1/3–2/2
8/7–9/7	9/7–1/7/03		12/26/01–1/18	1/18–2/11	2/11–3/7
9/15–10/9	10/9–11/2	1/7–2/4 11/2–11/26	2/4–3/2 11/26–12/21	3/2–3/27 12/21–1/14/04	3/27–4/21
10/28–11/22	11/22–12/16	12/16–1/9/05		1/1–1/14	1/14–2/8
8/17–9/11	9/11–10/8	10/8–11/15	1/9–2/2 11/5–12/15	2/2–2/26 12/15–1/1/06	2/26–3/22
9/30–10/24	10/24–11/17	11/17–12/11	1/1–3/5	3/5–4/6	4/6–5/3
11/8–12/4	12/5–12/29	12/30–1/24/08		1/3–1/26	1/27–2/20
8/6–9/7	9/7–1/7			1/20–2/13	2/13–3/9
8/30–9/22	9/23–10/17	10/18–11/11	1/24–2/16 11/12–12/6	2/17–3/11 12/7–1/2/09	3/12–4/5
10/14–11/7	11/7–12/1	12/1–12/25	12/25–1/18/10	12/7/08–1/31/09	1/3–2/2 4/11–4/24
8/7–9/8	9/8–11/8			1/18/10–2/11/10	2/11–3/7
11/8–11/30	11/30–1/7/11				

How to Use the Mars, Jupiter, and Saturn Tables

Find the year of your birth on the left side of each column. The dates when the planet entered each sign are listed on the right side of each column. (Signs are abbreviated to three letters.) Your birthday should fall on or between each date listed, and your planetary placement should correspond to the earlier sign of that period.

All planet changes are calculated for the Greenwich Mean Time zone.

MARS SIGNS 1901–2010

Year	Date	Sign		Year	Date	Sign
1901	MAR 1	Leo			OCT 1	Vir
	MAY 11	Vir			NOV 20	Lib
	JUL 13	Lib		1905	JAN 13	Scp
	AUG 31	Scp			AUG 21	Sag
	OCT 14	Sag			OCT 8	Cap
	NOV 24	Cap			NOV 18	Aqu
1902	JAN 1	Aqu			DEC 27	Pic
	FEB 8	Pic		1906	FEB 4	Ari
	MAR 19	Ari			MAR 17	Tau
	APR 27	Tau			APR 28	Gem
	JUN 7	Gem			JUN 11	Can
	JUL 20	Can			JUL 27	Leo
	SEP 4	Leo			SEP 12	Vir
	OCT 23	Vir			OCT 30	Lib
	DEC 20	Lib			DEC 17	Scp
1903	APR 19	Vir		1907	FEB 5	Sag
	MAY 30	Lib			APR 1	Cap
	AUG 6	Scp			OCT 13	Aqu
	SEP 22	Sag			NOV 29	Pic
	NOV 3	Cap		1908	JAN 11	Ari
	DEC 12	Aqu			FEB 23	Tau
1904	JAN 19	Pic			APR 7	Gem
	FEB 27	Ari			MAY 22	Can
	APR 6	Tau			JUL 8	Leo
	MAY 18	Gem			AUG 24	Vir
	JUN 30	Can			OCT 10	Lib
	AUG 15	Leo			NOV 25	Scp

1909	JAN	10	Sag		MAR	9	Pic
	FEB	24	Cap		APR	16	Ari
	APR	9	Aqu		MAY	26	Tau
	MAY	25	Pic		JUL	6	Gem
	JUL	21	Ari		AUG	19	Can
	SEP	26	Pic		OCT	7	Leo
	NOV	20	Ari	1916	MAY	28	Vir
1910	JAN	23	Tau		JUL	23	Lib
	MAR	14	Gem		SEP	8	Scp
	MAY	1	Can		OCT	22	Sag
	JUN	19	Leo		DEC	1	Cap
	AUG	6	Vir	1917	JAN	9	Aqu
	SEP	22	Lib		FEB	16	Pic
	NOV	6	Scp		MAR	26	Ari
	DEC	20	Sag		MAY	4	Tau
1911	JAN	31	Cap		JUN	14	Gem
	MAR	14	Aqu		JUL	28	Can
	APR	23	Pic		SEP	12	Leo
	JUN	2	Ari		NOV	2	Vir
	JUL	15	Tau	1918	JAN	11	Lib
	SEP	5	Gem		FEB	25	Vir
	NOV	30	Tau		JUN	23	Lib
1912	JAN	30	Gem		AUG	17	Scp
	APR	5	Can		OCT	1	Sag
	MAY	28	Leo		NOV	11	Cap
	JUL	17	Vir		DEC	20	Aqu
	SEP	2	Lib	1919	JAN	27	Pic
	OCT	18	Scp		MAR	6	Ari
	NOV	30	Sag		APR	15	Tau
1913	JAN	10	Cap		MAY	26	Gem
	FEB	19	Aqu		JUL	8	Can
	MAR	30	Pic		AUG	23	Leo
	MAY	8	Ari		OCT	10	Vir
	JUN	17	Tau		NOV	30	Lib
	JUL	29	Gem	1920	JAN	31	Scp
	SEP	15	Can		APR	23	Lib
1914	MAY	1	Leo		JUL	10	Scp
	JUN	26	Vir		SEP	4	Sag
	AUG	14	Lib		OCT	18	Cap
	SEP	29	Scp		NOV	27	Aqu
	NOV	11	Sag	1921	JAN	5	Pic
	DEC	22	Cap		FEB	13	Ari
1915	JAN	30	Aqu		MAR	25	Tau

	MAY 6	Gem
	JUN 18	Can
	AUG 3	Leo
	SEP 19	Vir
	NOV 6	Lib
	DEC 26	Scp
1922	FEB 18	Sag
	SEP 13	Cap
	OCT 30	Aqu
	DEC 11	Pic
1923	JAN 21	Ari
	MAR 4	Tau
	APR 16	Gem
	MAY 30	Can
	JUL 16	Leo
	SEP 1	Vir
	OCT 18	Lib
	DEC 4	Scp
1924	JAN 19	Sag
	MAR 6	Cap
	APR 24	Aqu
	JUN 24	Pic
	AUG 24	Aqu
	OCT 19	Pic
	DEC 19	Ari
1925	FEB 5	Tau
	MAR 24	Gem
	MAY 9	Can
	JUN 26	Leo
	AUG 12	Vir
	SEP 28	Lib
	NOV 13	Scp
	DEC 28	Sag
1926	FEB 9	Cap
	MAR 23	Aqu
	MAY 3	Pic
	JUN 15	Ari
	AUG 1	Tau
1927	FEB 22	Gem
	APR 17	Can
	JUN 6	Leo
	JUL 25	Vir
	SEP 10	Lib
	OCT 26	Scp
	DEC 8	Sag
1928	JAN 19	Cap
	FEB 28	Aqu
	APR 7	Pic
	MAY 16	Ari
	JUN 26	Tau
	AUG 9	Gem
	OCT 3	Can
	DEC 20	Gem
1929	MAR 10	Can
	MAY 13	Leo
	JUL 4	Vir
	AUG 21	Lib
	OCT 6	Scp
	NOV 18	Sag
	DEC 29	Cap
1930	FEB 6	Aqu
	MAR 17	Pic
	APR 24	Ari
	JUN 3	Tau
	JUL 14	Gem
	AUG 28	Can
	OCT 20	Leo
1931	FEB 16	Can
	MAR 30	Leo
	JUN 10	Vir
	AUG 1	Lib
	SEP 17	Scp
	OCT 30	Sag
	DEC 10	Cap
1932	JAN 18	Aqu
	FEB 25	Pic
	APR 3	Ari
	MAY 12	Tau
	JUN 22	Gem
	AUG 4	Can
	SEP 20	Leo
	NOV 13	Vir
1933	JUL 6	Lib
	AUG 26	Scp
	OCT 9	Sag
	NOV 19	Cap

	DEC	28	Aqu		FEB	17	Tau
1934	FEB	4	Pic		APR	1	Gem
	MAR	14	Ari		MAY	17	Can
	APR	22	Tau		JUL	3	Leo
	JUN	2	Gem		AUG	19	Vir
	JUL	15	Can		OCT	5	Lib
	AUG	30	Leo		NOV	20	Scp
	OCT	18	Vir	1941	JAN	4	Sag
	DEC	11	Lib		FEB	17	Cap
1935	JUL	29	Scp		APR	2	Aqu
	SEP	16	Sag		MAY	16	Pic
	OCT	28	Cap		JUL	2	Ari
	DEC	7	Aqu	1942	JAN	11	Tau
1936	JAN	14	Pic		MAR	7	Gem
	FEB	22	Ari		APR	26	Can
	APR	1	Tau		JUN	14	Leo
	MAY	13	Gem		AUG	1	Vir
	JUN	25	Can		SEP	17	Lib
	AUG	10	Leo		NOV	1	Scp
	SEP	26	Vir		DEC	15	Sag
	NOV	14	Lib	1943	JAN	26	Cap
1937	JAN	5	Scp		MAR	8	Aqu
	MAR	13	Sag		APR	17	Pic
	MAY	14	Scp		MAY	27	Ari
	AUG	8	Sag		JUL	7	Tau
	SEP	30	Cap		AUG	23	Gem
	NOV	11	Aqu	1944	MAR	28	Can
	DEC	21	Pic		MAY	22	Leo
1938	JAN	30	Ari		JUL	12	Vir
	MAR	12	Tau		AUG	29	Lib
	APR	23	Gem		OCT	13	Scp
	JUN	7	Can		NOV	25	Sag
	JUL	22	Leo	1945	JAN	5	Cap
	SEP	7	Vir		FEB	14	Aqu
	OCT	25	Lib		MAR	25	Pic
	DEC	11	Scp		MAY	2	Ari
1939	JAN	29	Sag		JUN	11	Tau
	MAR	21	Cap		JUL	23	Gem
	MAY	25	Aqu		SEP	7	Can
	JUL	21	Cap		NOV	11	Leo
	SEP	24	Aqu		DEC	26	Can
	NOV	19	Pic	1946	APR	22	Leo
1940	JAN	4	Ari		JUN	20	Vir

	AUG	9	Lib		OCT	12	Cap
	SEP	24	Scp		NOV	21	Aqu
	NOV	6	Sag		DEC	30	Pic
	DEC	17	Cap	1953	FEB	8	Ari
1947	JAN	25	Aqu		MAR	20	Tau
	MAR	4	Pic		MAY	1	Gem
	APR	11	Ari		JUN	14	Can
	MAY	21	Tau		JUL	29	Leo
	JUL	1	Gem		SEP	14	Vir
	AUG	13	Can		NOV	1	Lib
	OCT	1	Leo		DEC	20	Scp
	DEC	1	Vir	1954	FEB	9	Sag
1948	FEB	12	Leo		APR	12	Cap
	MAY	18	Vir		JUL	3	Sag
	JUL	17	Lib		AUG	24	Cap
	SEP	3	Scp		OCT	21	Aqu
	OCT	17	Sag		DEC	4	Pic
	NOV	26	Cap	1955	JAN	15	Ari
1949	JAN	4	Aqu		FEB	26	Tau
	FEB	11	Pic		APR	10	Gem
	MAR	21	Ari		MAY	26	Can
	APR	30	Tau		JUL	11	Leo
	JUN	10	Gem		AUG	27	Vir
	JUL	23	Can		OCT	13	Lib
	SEP	7	Leo		NOV	29	Scp
	OCT	27	Vir	1956	JAN	14	Sag
	DEC	26	Lib		FEB	28	Cap
1950	MAR	28	Vir		APR	14	Aqu
	JUN	11	Lib		JUN	3	Pic
	AUG	10	Scp		DEC	6	Ari
	SEP	25	Sag	1957	JAN	28	Tau
	NOV	6	Cap		MAR	17	Gem
	DEC	15	Aqu		MAY	4	Can
1951	JAN	22	Pic		JUN	21	Leo
	MAR	1	Ari		AUG	8	Vir
	APR	10	Tau		SEP	24	Lib
	MAY	21	Gem		NOV	8	Scp
	JUL	3	Can		DEC	23	Sag
	AUG	18	Leo	1958	FEB	3	Cap
	OCT	5	Vir		MAR	17	Aqu
	NOV	24	Lib		APR	27	Pic
1952	JAN	20	Scp		JUN	7	Ari
	AUG	27	Sag		JUL	21	Tau

	SEP	21	Gem		NOV	6	Vir
	OCT	29	Tau	1965	JUN	29	Lib
1959	FEB	10	Gem		AUG	20	Scp
	APR	10	Can		OCT	4	Sag
	JUN	1	Leo		NOV	14	Cap
	JUL	20	Vir		DEC	23	Aqu
	SEP	5	Lib	1966	JAN	30	Pic
	OCT	21	Scp		MAR	9	Ari
	DEC	3	Sag		APR	17	Tau
1960	JAN	14	Cap		MAY	28	Gem
	FEB	23	Aqu		JUL	11	Can
	APR	2	Pic		AUG	25	Leo
	MAY	11	Ari		OCT	12	Vir
	JUN	20	Tau		DEC	4	Lib
	AUG	2	Gem	1967	FEB	12	Scp
	SEP	21	Can		MAR	31	Lib
1961	FEB	5	Gem		JUL	19	Scp
	FEB	7	Can		SEP	10	Sag
	MAY	6	Leo		OCT	23	Cap
	JUN	28	Vir		DEC	1	Aqu
	AUG	17	Lib	1968	JAN	9	Pic
	OCT	1	Scp		FEB	17	Ari
	NOV	13	Sag		MAR	27	Tau
	DEC	24	Cap		MAY	8	Gem
1962	FEB	1	Aqu		JUN	21	Can
	MAR	12	Pic		AUG	5	Leo
	APR	19	Ari		SEP	21	Vir
	MAY	28	Tau		NOV	9	Lib
	JUL	9	Gem		DEC	29	Scp
	AUG	22	Can	1969	FEB	25	Sag
	OCT	11	Leo		SEP	21	Cap
1963	JUN	3	Vir		NOV	4	Aqu
	JUL	27	Lib		DEC	15	Pic
	SEP	12	Scp	1970	JAN	24	Ari
	OCT	25	Sag		MAR	7	Tau
	DEC	5	Cap		APR	18	Gem
1964	JAN	13	Aqu		JUN	2	Can
	FEB	20	Pic		JUL	18	Leo
	MAR	29	Ari		SEP	3	Vir
	MAY	7	Tau		OCT	20	Lib
	JUN	17	Gem		DEC	6	Scp
	JUL	30	Can	1971	JAN	23	Sag
	SEP	15	Leo		MAR	12	Cap

	MAY	3	Aqu		JUN	6	Tau
	NOV	6	Pic		JUL	17	Gem
	DEC	26	Ari		SEP	1	Can
1972	FEB	10	Tau		OCT	26	Leo
	MAR	27	Gem	1978	JAN	26	Can
	MAY	12	Can		APR	10	Leo
	JUN	28	Leo		JUN	14	Vir
	AUG	15	Vir		AUG	4	Lib
	SEP	30	Lib		SEP	19	Scp
	NOV	15	Scp		NOV	2	Sag
	DEC	30	Sag		DEC	12	Cap
1973	FEB	12	Cap	1979	JAN	20	Aqu
	MAR	26	Aqu		FEB	27	Pic
	MAY	8	Pic		APR	7	Ari
	JUN	20	Ari		MAY	16	Tau
	AUG	12	Tau		JUN	26	Gem
	OCT	29	Ari		AUG	8	Can
	DEC	24	Tau		SEP	24	Leo
1974	FEB	27	Gem		NOV	19	Vir
	APR	20	Can	1980	MAR	11	Leo
	JUN	9	Leo		MAY	4	Vir
	JUL	27	Vir		JUL	10	Lib
	SEP	12	Lib		AUG	29	Scp
	OCT	28	Scp		OCT	12	Sag
	DEC	10	Sag		NOV	22	Cap
1975	JAN	21	Cap		DEC	30	Aqu
	MAR	3	Aqu	1981	FEB	6	Pic
	APR	11	Pic		MAR	17	Ari
	MAY	21	Ari		APR	25	Tau
	JUL	1	Tau		JUN	5	Gem
	AUG	14	Gem		JUL	18	Can
	OCT	17	Can		SEP	2	Leo
	NOV	25	Gem		OCT	21	Vir
1976	MAR	18	Can		DEC	16	Lib
	MAY	16	Leo	1982	AUG	3	Scp
	JUL	6	Vir		SEP	20	Sag
	AUG	24	Lib		OCT	31	Cap
	OCT	8	Scp		DEC	10	Aqu
	NOV	20	Sag	1983	JAN	17	Pic
1977	JAN	1	Cap		FEB	25	Ari
	FEB	9	Aqu		APR	5	Tau
	MAR	20	Pic		MAY	16	Gem
	APR	27	Ari		JUN	29	Can

	AUG	13	Leo	1990	JAN	29	Cap
	SEP	30	Vir		MAR	11	Aqu
	NOV	18	Lib		APR	20	Pic
1984	JAN	11	Scp		MAY	31	Ari
	AUG	17	Sag		JUL	12	Tau
	OCT	5	Cap		AUG	31	Gem
	NOV	15	Aqu		DEC	14	Tau
	DEC	25	Pic	1991	JAN	21	Gem
1985	FEB	2	Ari		APR	3	Can
	MAR	15	Tau		MAY	26	Leo
	APR	26	Gem		JUL	15	Vir
	JUN	9	Can		SEP	1	Lib
	JUL	25	Leo		OCT	16	Scp
	SEP	10	Vir		NOV	29	Sag
	OCT	27	Lib	1992	JAN	9	Cap
	DEC	14	Scp		FEB	18	Aqu
1986	FEB	2	Sag		MAR	28	Pic
	MAR	28	Cap		MAY	5	Ari
	OCT	9	Aqu		JUN	14	Tau
	NOV	26	Pic		JUL	26	Gem
1987	JAN	8	Ari		SEP	12	Can
	FEB	20	Tau	1993	APR	27	Leo
	APR	5	Gem		JUN	23	Vir
	MAY	21	Can		AUG	12	Lib
	JUL	6	Leo		SEP	27	Scp
	AUG	22	Vir		NOV	9	Sag
	OCT	8	Lib		DEC	20	Cap
	NOV	24	Scp	1994	JAN	28	Aqu
1988	JAN	8	Sag		MAR	7	Pic
	FEB	22	Cap		APR	14	Ari
	APR	6	Aqu		MAY	23	Tau
	MAY	22	Pic		JUL	3	Gem
	JUL	13	Ari		AUG	16	Can
	OCT	23	Pic		OCT	4	Leo
	NOV	1	Ari		DEC	12	Vir
1989	JAN	19	Tau	1995	JAN	22	Leo
	MAR	11	Gem		MAY	25	Vir
	APR	29	Can		JUL	21	Lib
	JUN	16	Leo		SEP	7	Scp
	AUG	3	Vir		OCT	20	Sag
	SEP	19	Lib		NOV	30	Cap
	NOV	4	Scp	1996	JAN	8	Aqu
	DEC	18	Sag		FEB	15	Pic

	MAR 24	Ari		MAY 28	Can
	MAY 2	Tau		JUL 13	Leo
	JUN 12	Gem		AUG 29	Vir
	JUL 25	Can		OCT 15	Lib
	SEP 9	Leo		DEC 1	Scp
	OCT 30	Vir	2003	JAN 17	Sag
1997	JAN 3	Lib		MAR 4	Cap
	MAR 8	Vir		APR 21	Aqu
	JUN 19	Lib		JUN 17	Pic
	AUG 14	Scp		DEC 16	Ari
	SEP 28	Sag	2004	FEB 3	Tau
	NOV 9	Cap		MAR 21	Gem
	DEC 18	Aqu		MAY 7	Can
1998	JAN 25	Pic		JUN 23	Leo
	MAR 4	Ari		AUG 10	Vir
	APR 13	Tau		SEP 26	Lib
	MAY 24	Gem		NOV 11	Sep
	JUL 6	Can		DEC 25	Sag
	AUG 20	Leo	2005	FEB 6	Cap
	OCT 7	Vir		MAR 20	Aqu
	NOV 27	Lib		MAY 1	Pic
1999	JAN 26	Scp		JUN 12	Ari
	MAY 5	Lib		JUL 28	Tau
	JUL 5	Scp	2006	FEB 17	Gem
	SEP 2	Sag		APR 14	Can
	OCT 17	Cap		JUN 3	Leo
	NOV 26	Aqu		JUL 22	Vir
2000	JAN 4	Pic		SEP 8	Lib
	FEB 12	Ari		OCT 23	Scp
	MAR 23	Tau		DEC 6	Sag
	MAY 3	Gem	2007	JAN 16	Cap
	JUN 16	Can		FEB 25	Aqu
	AUG 1	Leo		APR 6	Pic
	SEP 17	Vir		MAY 15	Ari
	NOV 4	Lib		JUNE24	Tau
	DEC 23	Scp		AUG 7	Gem
2001	FEB 14	Sag		SEP 28	Can
	SEP 8	Cap		DEC 31	Gem*
	OCT 27	Aqu	2008	MAR 4	Can
	DEC 8	Pic		MAY 9	Leo
2002	JAN 18	Ari		JUL 1	Vir
	MAR 1	Tau		AUG 19	Lib
	APR 13	Gem		OCT 3	Scp

	NOV	16	Sag		AUG	25	Can
	DEC	27	Cap		OCT	16	Leo
2009	FEB	4	Aqu	2010	JUN	7	Vir
	MAR	14	Pic		JUL	29	Lib
	APR	22	Ari		SEP	14	Scp
	MAY	31	Tau		OCT	28	Sag
	JUL	11	Gem		DEC	7	Cap

JUPITER SIGNS 1901–2010

1901	JAN	19	Cap	1927	JAN	18	Pic
1902	FEB	6	Aqu		JUN	6	Ari
1903	FEB	20	Pic		SEP	11	Pic
1904	MAR	1	Ari	1928	JAN	23	Ari
	AUG	8	Tau		JUN	4	Tau
	AUG	31	Ari	1929	JUN	12	Gem
1905	MAR	7	Tau	1930	JUN	26	Can
	JUL	21	Gem	1931	JUL	17	Leo
	DEC	4	Tau	1932	AUG	11	Vir
1906	MAR	9	Gem	1933	SEP	10	Lib
	JUL	30	Can	1934	OCT	11	Scp
1907	AUG	18	Leo	1935	NOV	9	Sag
1908	SEP	12	Vir	1936	DEC	2	Cap
1909	OCT	11	Lib	1937	DEC	20	Aqu
1910	NOV	11	Scp	1938	MAY	14	Pic
1911	DEC	10	Sag		JUL	30	Aqu
1913	JAN	2	Cap		DEC	29	Pic
1914	JAN	21	Aqu	1939	MAY	11	Ari
1915	FEB	4	Pic		OCT	30	Pic
1916	FEB	12	Ari		DEC	20	Ari
	JUN	26	Tau	1940	MAY	16	Tau
	OCT	26	Ari	1941	MAY	26	Gem
1917	FEB	12	Tau	1942	JUN	10	Can
	JUN	29	Gem	1943	JUN	30	Leo
1918	JUL	13	Can	1944	JUL	26	Vir
1919	AUG	2	Leo	1945	AUG	25	Lib
1920	AUG	27	Vir	1946	SEP	25	Scp
1921	SEP	25	Lib	1947	OCT	24	Sag
1922	OCT	26	Scp	1948	NOV	15	Cap
1923	NOV	24	Sag	1949	APR	12	Aqu
1924	DEC	18	Cap		JUN	27	Cap
1926	JAN	6	Aqu		NOV	30	Aqu

1950	APR	15	Pic	1970	APR 30	Lib
	SEP	15	Aqu		AUG 15	Scp
	DEC	1	Pic	1971	JAN 14	Sag
1951	APR	21	Ari		JUN 5	Scp
1952	APR	28	Tau		SEP 11	Sag
1953	MAY	9	Gem	1972	FEB 6	Cap
1954	MAY	24	Can		JUL 24	Sag
1955	JUN	13	Leo		SEP 25	Cap
	NOV	17	Vir	1973	FEB 23	Aqu
1956	JAN	18	Leo	1974	MAR 8	Pic
	JUL	7	Vir	1975	MAR 18	Ari
	DEC	13	Lib	1976	MAR 26	Tau
1957	FEB	19	Vir		AUG 23	Gem
	AUG	7	Lib		OCT 16	Tau
1958	JAN	13	Scp	1977	APR 3	Gem
	MAR	20	Lib		AUG 20	Can
	SEP	7	Scp		DEC 30	Gem
1959	FEB	10	Sag	1978	APR 12	Can
	APR	24	Scp		SEP 5	Leo
	OCT	5	Sag	1979	FEB 28	Can
1960	MAR	1	Cap		APR 20	Leo
	JUN	10	Sag		SEP 29	Vir
	OCT	26	Cap	1980	OCT 27	Lib
1961	MAR	15	Aqu	1981	NOV 27	Scp
	AUG	12	Cap	1982	DEC 26	Sag
	NOV	4	Aqu	1984	JAN 19	Cap
1962	MAR	25	Pic	1985	FEB 6	Aqu
1963	APR	4	Ari	1986	FEB 20	Pic
1964	APR	12	Tau	1987	MAR 2	Ari
1965	APR	22	Gem	1988	MAR 8	Tau
	SEP	21	Can		JUL 22	Gem
	NOV	17	Gem		NOV 30	Tau
1966	MAY	5	Can	1989	MAR 11	Gem
	SEP	27	Leo		JUL 30	Can
1967	JAN	16	Can	1990	AUG 18	Leo
	MAY	23	Leo	1991	SEP 12	Vir
	OCT	19	Vir	1992	OCT 10	Lib
1968	FEB	27	Leo	1993	NOV 10	Scp
	JUN	15	Vir	1994	DEC 9	Sag
	NOV	15	Lib	1996	JAN 3	Cap
1969	MAR	30	Vir	1997	JAN 21	Aqu
	JUL	15	Lib	1998	FEB 4	Pic
	DEC	16	Scp	1999	FEB 13	Ari

	JUN	28	Tau	2005	OCT	26	Scp
	OCT	23	Ari	2006	NOV	24	Sag
2000	FEB	14	Tau	2007	DEC	17	Cap
	JUN	30	Gem	2009	JAN	5	Aqu
2001	JUL	14	Can	2010	JAN	18	Pis
2002	AUG	1	Leo		JUN	6	Ari
2003	AUG	27	Vir		SEP	9	Pis
2004	SEP	24	Lib				

SATURN SIGNS 1903–2010

1903	JAN	19	Aqu		OCT	18	Pic
1905	APR	13	Pic	1938	JAN	14	Ari
	AUG	17	Aqu	1939	JUL	6	Tau
1906	JAN	8	Pic		SEP	22	Ari
1908	MAR	19	Ari	1940	MAR	20	Tau
1910	MAY	17	Tau	1942	MAY	8	Gem
	DEC	14	Ari	1944	JUN	20	Can
1911	JAN	20	Tau	1946	AUG	2	Leo
1912	JUL	7	Gem	1948	SEP	19	Vir
	NOV	30	Tau	1949	APR	3	Leo
1913	MAR	26	Gem		MAY	29	Vir
1914	AUG	24	Can	1950	NOV	20	Lib
	DEC	7	Gem	1951	MAR	7	Vir
1915	MAY	11	Can		AUG	13	Lib
1916	OCT	17	Leo	1953	OCT	22	Scp
	DEC	7	Can	1956	JAN	12	Sag
1917	JUN	24	Leo		MAY	14	Scp
1919	AUG	12	Vir		OCT	10	Sag
1921	OCT	7	Lib	1959	JAN	5	Cap
1923	DEC	20	Scp	1962	JAN	3	Aqu
1924	APR	6	Lib	1964	MAR	24	Pic
	SEP	13	Scp		SEP	16	Aqu
1926	DEC	2	Sag		DEC	16	Pic
1929	MAR	15	Cap	1967	MAR	3	Ari
	MAY	5	Sag	1969	APR	29	Tau
	NOV	30	Cap	1971	JUN	18	Gem
1932	FEB	24	Aqu	1972	JAN	10	Tau
	AUG	13	Cap		FEB	21	Gem
	NOV	20	Aqu	1973	AUG	1	Can
1935	FEB	14	Pic	1974	JAN	7	Gem
1937	APR	25	Ari		APR	18	Can

1975	SEP	17	Leo
1976	JAN	14	Can
	JUN	5	Leo
1977	NOV	17	Vir
1978	JAN	5	Leo
	JUL	26	Vir
1980	SEP	21	Lib
1982	NOV	29	Scp
1983	MAY	6	Lib
	AUG	24	Scp
1985	NOV	17	Sag
1988	FEB	13	Cap
	JUN	10	Sag
	NOV	12	Cap
1991	FEB	6	Aqu
1993	MAY	21	Pic

	JUN	30	Aqu
1994	JAN	28	Pic
1996	APR	7	Ari
1998	JUN	9	Tau
	OCT	25	Ari
1999	MAR	1	Tau
2000	AUG	10	Gem
	OCT	16	Tau
2001	APR	21	Gem
2003	JUN	3	Can
2005	JUL	16	Leo
2007	SEP	2	Vir
2009	OCT	29	Lib
2010	APR	7	Vir
	JUL	21	Lib

CHAPTER 6

Where It All Happens: Your Rising Sign

To find out what's happening in a horoscope, you first have to look east. The degree of the zodiac ascending over the eastern horizon at the time you were born, which is called the rising sign or ascendant, marks the beginning of the first house, one of twelve divisions of the horoscope, each of which represents a different area of life. These "houses" contain the planets, the doers in a chart. After the rising sign, the other houses parade around the chart in sequence, with the following sign on the next house cusp. Therefore, the setup of the chart—*what* happens *where*—depends on the rising sign.

Though you can learn much about a person by the signs and interactions of the sun, moon, and planets in the horoscope, without a valid rising sign, the collection of planets has no "homes." One would have no idea which area of life could be influenced by a particular planet. For example, you might know that a person has Mars in Aries, which will describe that person's dynamic fiery energy. But if you also know that the person has a Capricorn rising sign, this Mars will fall in the fourth house of home and family, so you know where that energy will operate.

Due to the earth's rotation, the rising sign changes every two hours, which means that babies born later or earlier on the same day in the same hospital will have most planets in the same signs, but may not have the same rising sign. Therefore, their planets may fall in different houses in the chart. For instance, if Mars is in Gemini and your rising sign is Taurus,

Mars will most likely be active in the second or financial house of your chart. Someone born later in the same day when the rising sign is Virgo would have Mars positioned at the top of the chart, energizing the tenth house of career.

Most astrologers insist on knowing the exact time of a client's birth before they analyze a chart. The more accurate your birth time, the more accurately an astrologer can position the planets in your chart by determining the correct rising sign.

How Your Rising Sign Can Influence Your Sun Sign

Your rising sign has an important relationship with your sun sign. Some will complement the sun sign; others hide it under a totally different mask, as if playing an entirely different role, making it difficult to guess the person's sun sign from outer appearances. This may be the reason why you might not look or act like your sun sign's archetype. For example, a Leo with a conservative Capricorn ascendant would come across as much more serious than a Leo with a fiery Aries or Sagittarius ascendant.

Though the rising sign usually creates the first impression you make, there are exceptions. When the sun sign is reinforced by other planets in the same sign, this might overpower the impression of the rising sign. For instance, a Leo sun plus a Leo Venus and Leo Jupiter would counteract the more conservative image that would otherwise be conveyed by the person's Capricorn ascendant.

Those born early in the morning when the sun was on the horizon will be most likely to project the image of their sun sign. These people are often called a "double Aries" or a "double Virgo" because the same sun sign and ascendant reinforce each other.

Find Your Rising Sign

Look up your rising sign on the chart at the end of this chapter. Since rising signs change every two hours, it is important to know your birth time as close to the minute as possible. Even a few minutes' difference could change the rising sign and therefore the setup of your chart. If you are unsure about the exact time, but know within a few hours, check the following descriptions to see which is most like the personality you project.

Aries Rising: Alpha Energy

You are the most aggressive version of your sun sign, with boundless energy that can be used productively if it's channeled in the right direction. Watch a tendency to overreact emotionally and blow your top. You come across as openly competitive, a positive asset in business or sports. Be on guard against impatience, which could lead to head injuries. Your walk and bearing could have the telltale head-forward Aries posture. You may wear more bright colors, especially red, than others of your sign, or be a redhead. You may also have a tendency to drive your car faster.

Can you see the alpha Aries tendency in Barbra Streisand (a sun sign Taurus) and Bette Midler (a sun sign Sagittarius)?

Taurus Rising: Down-to-Earth

You're slow-moving, with a beautiful (or distinctive) speaking or singing voice. You probably surround yourself with comfort, good food, luxurious surroundings, and other sensual pleasures. You prefer welcoming others into your home to gadding about. You may have a talent for business, especially in trading, appraising, and real estate. A Taurus ascendant gives a well-padded physique that gains weight easily, like Liza Minnelli. This ascendant can also endow females with a curvaceous beauty.

Gemini Rising: A Way with Words

You're naturally sociable, with lighter, more ethereal mannerisms than others of your sign, especially if you're female. You love to communicate with people, and express your ideas easily, like former British prime minister Tony Blair. You may have a talent for writing or public speaking. You thrive on variety, a constantly changing scene, and a lively social life. However, you may relate to others at a deeper level than might be suspected. And you will be far more sympathetic and caring than you project. You will probably travel widely, changing partners and jobs several times (or juggle two at once). Physically, your nerves are quite sensitive. Occasionally, you would benefit from a calm, tranquil atmosphere away from your usual social scene.

Cancer Rising: Nurturing Instincts

You are naturally acquisitive, possessive, private, a money-maker like Bill Gates or Michael Bloomberg. You easily pick up others' needs and feelings—a great gift in business, the arts, and personal relationships. But you must guard against overreacting or taking things too personally, especially during full-moon periods. Find creative outlets for your natural nurturing gifts, such as helping the less fortunate, particularly children. Your insights would be helpful in psychology. Your desire to feed and care for others would be useful in the restaurant, hotel, or child-care industries. You may be especially fond of wearing romantic old clothes, collecting antiques, and dining on exquisite food. Since your body may retain fluids, pay attention to your diet. To relax, escape to places near water.

Leo Rising: Diva Dazzle

You may come across as more poised than you really feel. However, you play it to the hilt, projecting a proud royal presence. A Leo ascendant gives you a natural flair for drama, like Marilyn Monroe, and you might be accused of stealing the spotlight. You'll also project a much more outgoing, optimistic, and sunny personality than others of your sign. You take care to please your public by always projecting star quality, probably tossing a luxuriant mane of hair, sporting a striking hairstyle, or dressing to impress. Females often dazzle with colorful clothing or spectacular jewelry. Since you may have a strong parental nature, you could well become a family matriarch or patriarch, like George H. W. Bush.

Virgo Rising: High Standards

Virgo rising endows you with a practical, analytical outer image. You seem neat, orderly, and more particular than others of your sign. Others in your life may feel they must live up to your high standards. Though at times you may be openly critical, this masks a well-meaning desire to have only the best for loved ones. Your sharp eye for details could be used in the financial world, or your literary skills could draw you to teaching or publishing. The healing arts, health care, and service-oriented professions attract many with a Virgo ascendant. You're likely to take good care of yourself, with great attention to health, diet, and exercise, like Madonna. You might even show some hypochondriac tendencies, like Woody Allen. Physically, you may have a very sensitive digestive system.

Libra Rising: The Charmer

Libra rising gives you a charming, social, and public persona, like John F. Kennedy and Bill Clinton. You tend to avoid confrontations in relationships, preferring to smooth the way or negotiate diplomatically rather than give in to an emotional reaction. Because you are interested in all aspects of a situation, you may be slow to reach decisions. Physically, you'll have good proportions and physical symmetry. You will move with natural grace and balance. You're likely to have pleasing, if not beautiful, facial features, with a winning smile, like Cary Grant. You'll show natural good taste and harmony in your clothes and home decor. Legal, diplomatic, or public relations professions could draw your interest.

Scorpio Rising: Air of Mystery

You project an intriguing air of mystery with this ascendant, as the Scorpio secretiveness and sense of underlying power combine with your sun sign. Like Jacqueline Kennedy Onassis, you convey that there's more to you than meets the eye. You seem like someone who is always in control and who can move comfortably in the world of power. Your physical look comes across as intense. Many of you have remarkable eyes, with a direct, penetrating gaze. But you'll never reveal your private agenda, and you tend to keep your true feelings under wraps (watch a tendency toward paranoia). You may have an interesting romantic history with secret love affairs, like Grace Kelly. Many of you heighten your air of mystery by wearing black. You're happiest near water; you should provide yourself with a seaside retreat.

Sagittarius Rising: The Explorer

You travel with this ascendant. You may also be a more outdoor, sportive type, with an athletic, casual, and outgoing air. Your moods are camouflaged with cheerful optimism or a philosophical attitude. Though you don't hesitate to speak your mind—like Ted Turner, who was called the Mouth of the South—you can also laugh at your troubles or crack a joke more easily than others of your sign. A Sagittarius ascendant can also draw you to the field of higher education or to spiritual life. You'll seem to have less attachment to things and people, and you may explore the globe. Your strong, fast legs are a physical bonus.

Capricorn Rising: Serious Business

This rising sign makes you come across as serious, goal-oriented, disciplined, and careful with cash. You are not one of the zodiac's big spenders, though you might splurge occasionally on items with good investment value. You're the conservative type in dress and environment, and you might come across as quite formal and businesslike, like Rupert Murdoch. You'll function well in a structured or corporate environment where you can climb to the top. (You are always aware of who's the boss.) In your personal life, you could be a loner or a single parent who is father and mother to your children.

Aquarius Rising: One of a Kind

You come across as less concerned about what others think and could even be a bit eccentric. Your appearance is sure to be unique and memorable. You're more at ease with groups of people than others in your sign, and you may be attracted to public life, like Jay Leno. Your appearance may be unique, either unconventional or unimportant to you. Those of you whose sun is in a water sign (Cancer, Scorpio, or Pisces) may exercise your nurturing qualities with a large group, an extended family, or a day-care or community center.

Pisces Rising: Romantic Roles

Your creative, nurturing talents are heightened and so is your ability to project emotional drama. And, like Antonio Banderas, your dreamy eyes and poetic air bring out the protective instinct in others. You could be attracted to the arts, especially theater, dance, film, and photography, or to psychology, spiritual practice, and charity work. You are happiest when you are using your creative ability to help others. Since you are vulnerable to mood swings, it is important for you to find interesting, creative work where you can express your talents and heighten your self-esteem. Accentuate the positive. Be wary of escapist tendencies, particularly involving alcohol or drugs to which you are supersensitive, like Whitney Houston.

RISING SIGNS—A.M. BIRTHS

	1 AM	2 AM	3 AM	4 AM	5 AM	6 AM	7 AM	8 AM	9 AM	10 AM	11 AM	12 NOON
Jan 1	Lib	Sc	Sc	Sc	Sag	Sag	Sag	Cap	Cap	Aq	Pis	Ar
Jan 9	Lib	Sc	Sc	Sag	Sag	Sag	Cap	Cap	Aq	Pis	Ar	Tau
Jan 17	Sc	Sc	Sc	Sag	Sag	Cap	Cap	Aq	Aq	Pis	Ar	Tau
Jan 25	Sc	Sc	Sag	Sag	Sag	Cap	Cap	Aq	Pis	Ar	Tau	Tau
Feb 2	Sc	Sc	Sag	Sag	Cap	Cap	Aq	Pis	Pis	Ar	Tau	Gem
Feb 10	Sc	Sag	Sag	Sag	Cap	Cap	Aq	Pis	Ar	Tau	Tau	Gem
Feb 18	Sc	Sag	Sag	Cap	Cap	Aq	Pis	Pis	Ar	Tau	Gem	Gem
Feb 26	Sag	Sag	Sag	Cap	Cap	Aq	Aq	Pis	Ar	Tau	Tau	Gem
Mar 6	Sag	Sag	Cap	Cap	Aq	Pis	Pis	Ar	Tau	Gem	Gem	Can
Mar 14	Sag	Cap	Cap	Aq	Aq	Pis	Ar	Tau	Tau	Gem	Gem	Can
Mar 22	Sag	Cap	Cap	Aq	Aq	Pis	Ar	Ar	Tau	Gem	Can	Can
Mar 30	Cap	Cap	Aq	Pis	Pis	Ar	Tau	Tau	Gem	Can	Can	Can
Apr 7	Cap	Cap	Aq	Pis	Ar	Ar	Tau	Gem	Gem	Can	Can	Leo
Apr 14	Cap	Aq	Aq	Pis	Ar	Tau	Tau	Gem	Gem	Can	Can	Leo
Apr 22	Cap	Aq	Aq	Pis	Ar	Ar	Tau	Gem	Gem	Can	Leo	Leo
Apr 30	Aq	Aq	Pis	Ar	Tau	Tau	Gem	Can	Can	Can	Leo	Leo
May 8	Aq	Pis	Ar	Ar	Tau	Gem	Gem	Can	Can	Leo	Leo	Leo
May 16	Aq	Pis	Ar	Tau	Tau	Gem	Gem	Can	Can	Leo	Leo	Vir
May 24	Pis	Ar	Ar	Tau	Gem	Gem	Can	Can	Leo	Leo	Leo	Vir
June 1	Pis	Ar	Tau	Gem	Gem	Can	Can	Leo	Leo	Leo	Vir	Vir
June 9	Ar	Ar	Tau	Gem	Gem	Can	Can	Leo	Leo	Leo	Vir	Vir
June 17	Ar	Tau	Tau	Gem	Can	Can	Can	Leo	Leo	Vir	Vir	Vir
June 25	Tau	Tau	Gem	Gem	Can	Can	Leo	Leo	Leo	Vir	Vir	Lib
July 3	Tau	Gem	Gem	Can	Can	Can	Leo	Leo	Vir	Vir	Vir	Lib
July 11	Tau	Gem	Gem	Can	Can	Leo	Leo	Leo	Vir	Vir	Lib	Lib
July 18	Gem	Gem	Can	Can	Can	Leo	Leo	Vir	Vir	Vir	Lib	Lib
July 26	Gem	Gem	Can	Can	Leo	Leo	Vir	Vir	Vir	Lib	Lib	Lib
Aug 3	Gem	Can	Can	Can	Leo	Leo	Vir	Vir	Vir	Lib	Lib	Sc
Aug 11	Gem	Can	Can	Leo	Leo	Leo	Vir	Vir	Lib	Lib	Lib	Sc
Aug 18	Can	Can	Can	Leo	Leo	Vir	Vir	Vir	Lib	Lib	Sc	Sc
Aug 27	Can	Can	Leo	Leo	Leo	Vir	Vir	Lib	Lib	Lib	Sc	Sc
Sept 4	Can	Can	Leo	Leo	Leo	Vir	Vir	Lib	Lib	Lib	Sc	Sc
Sept 12	Can	Leo	Leo	Leo	Vir	Vir	Lib	Lib	Lib	Sc	Sc	Sag
Sept 20	Leo	Leo	Leo	Vir	Vir	Vir	Lib	Lib	Sc	Sc	Sc	Sag
Sept 28	Leo	Leo	Leo	Vir	Vir	Lib	Lib	Lib	Sc	Sc	Sag	Sag
Oct 6	Leo	Leo	Leo	Vir	Vir	Lib	Lib	Sc	Sc	Sc	Sag	Sag
Oct 14	Leo	Vir	Vir	Vir	Lib	Lib	Lib	Sc	Sc	Sag	Sag	Cap
Oct 22	Leo	Vir	Vir	Lib	Lib	Lib	Sc	Sc	Sc	Sag	Sag	Cap
Oct 30	Vir	Vir	Vir	Lib	Lib	Sc	Sc	Sc	Sag	Sag	Cap	Cap
Nov 7	Vir	Vir	Lib	Lib	Lib	Sc	Sc	Sc	Sag	Sag	Cap	Cap
Nov 15	Vir	Vir	Lib	Lib	Sc	Sc	Sc	Sag	Sag	Cap	Cap	Aq
Nov 23	Vir	Lib	Lib	Lib	Sc	Sc	Sag	Sag	Sag	Cap	Cap	Aq
Dec 1	Vir	Lib	Lib	Sc	Sc	Sc	Sag	Sag	Cap	Cap	Aq	Aq
Dec 9	Lib	Lib	Lib	Sc	Sc	Sag	Sag	Sag	Cap	Cap	Aq	Pis
Dec 18	Lib	Lib	Sc	Sc	Sc	Sag	Sag	Cap	Cap	Aq	Aq	Pis
Dec 28	Lib	Lib	Sc	Sc	Sag	Sag	Sag	Cap	Aq	Aq	Pis	Ar

RISING SIGNS—P.M. BIRTHS

	1 PM	2 PM	3 PM	4 PM	5 PM	6 PM	7 PM	8 PM	9 PM	10 PM	11 PM	12 MID-NIGHT
Jan 1	Tau	Gem	Gem	Can	Can	Can	Leo	Leo	Vir	Vir	Vir	Lib
Jan 9	Tau	Gem	Gem	Can	Can	Leo	Leo	Leo	Vir	Vir	Vir	Lib
Jan 17	Gem	Gem	Can	Can	Can	Leo	Leo	Vir	Vir	Vir	Lib	Lib
Jan 25	Gem	Gem	Can	Can	Leo	Leo	Leo	Vir	Vir	Lib	Lib	Lib
Feb 2	Gem	Can	Can	Can	Leo	Leo	Vir	Vir	Vir	Lib	Lib	Sc
Feb 10	Gem	Can	Can	Leo	Leo	Leo	Vir	Vir	Lib	Lib	Lib	Sc
Feb 18	Can	Can	Can	Leo	Leo	Vir	Vir	Vir	Lib	Lib	Sc	Sc
Feb 26	Can	Can	Leo	Leo	Leo	Vir	Vir	Lib	Lib	Lib	Sc	Sc
Mar 6	Can	Leo	Leo	Leo	Vir	Vir	Lib	Lib	Sc	Sc	Sc	Sc
Mar 14	Can	Leo	Leo	Vir	Vir	Vir	Lib	Lib	Lib	Sc	Sc	Sag
Mar 22	Leo	Leo	Leo	Vir	Vir	Lib	Lib	Lib	Sc	Sc	Sc	Sag
Mar 30	Leo	Leo	Vir	Vir	Vir	Lib	Lib	Sc	Sc	Sc	Sag	Sag
Apr 7	Leo	Leo	Vir	Vir	Lib	Lib	Lib	Sc	Sc	Sc	Sag	Sag
Apr 14	Leo	Vir	Vir	Vir	Lib	Lib	Sc	Sc	Sc	Sag	Sag	Cap
Apr 22	Leo	Vir	Vir	Lib	Lib	Lib	Sc	Sc	Sc	Sag	Sag	Cap
Apr 30	Vir	Vir	Vir	Lib	Lib	Sc	Sc	Sc	Sag	Sag	Cap	Cap
May 8	Vir	Vir	Lib	Lib	Lib	Sc	Sc	Sag	Sag	Sag	Cap	Cap
May 16	Vir	Vir	Lib	Lib	Sc	Sc	Sc	Sag	Sag	Cap	Cap	Aq
May 24	Vir	Lib	Lib	Lib	Sc	Sc	Sag	Sag	Sag	Cap	Cap	Aq
June 1	Vir	Lib	Lib	Sc	Sc	Sc	Sag	Sag	Cap	Cap	Aq	Aq
June 9	Lib	Lib	Lib	Sc	Sc	Sag	Sag	Sag	Cap	Cap	Aq	Pis
June 17	Lib	Lib	Sc	Sc	Sc	Sag	Sag	Cap	Cap	Aq	Aq	Pis
June 25	Lib	Lib	Sc	Sc	Sag	Sag	Sag	Cap	Cap	Aq	Pis	Ar
July 3	Lib	Sc	Sc	Sc	Sag	Sag	Cap	Cap	Aq	Aq	Pis	Ar
July 11	Lib	Sc	Sc	Sag	Sag	Sag	Cap	Cap	Aq	Pis	Ar	Tau
July 18	Sc	Sc	Sc	Sag	Sag	Cap	Cap	Aq	Aq	Pis	Ar	Tau
July 26	Sc	Sc	Sag	Sag	Sag	Cap	Cap	Aq	Pis	Ar	Tau	Tau
Aug 3	Sc	Sc	Sag	Sag	Cap	Cap	Aq	Aq	Pis	Ar	Tau	Gem
Aug 11	Sc	Sag	Sag	Sag	Cap	Cap	Aq	Pis	Ar	Tau	Tau	Gem
Aug 18	Sc	Sag	Sag	Cap	Cap	Aq	Pis	Pis	Ar	Tau	Gem	Gem
Aug 27	Sag	Sag	Sag	Cap	Cap	Aq	Pis	Ar	Tau	Tau	Gem	Gem
Sept 4	Sag	Sag	Cap	Cap	Aq	Pis	Pis	Ar	Tau	Gem	Gem	Can
Sept 12	Sag	Sag	Cap	Aq	Aq	Pis	Ar	Tau	Tau	Gem	Gem	Can
Sept 20	Sag	Cap	Cap	Aq	Pis	Pis	Ar	Tau	Gem	Gem	Can	Can
Sept 28	Cap	Cap	Aq	Aq	Pis	Ar	Tau	Tau	Gem	Gem	Can	Can
Oct 6	Cap	Cap	Aq	Pis	Ar	Ar	Tau	Gem	Gem	Can	Can	Leo
Oct 14	Cap	Aq	Aq	Pis	Ar	Tau	Tau	Gem	Gem	Can	Can	Leo
Oct 22	Cap	Aq	Pis	Ar	Ar	Tau	Gem	Gem	Can	Can	Leo	Leo
Oct 30	Aq	Aq	Pis	Ar	Tau	Tau	Gem	Can	Can	Can	Leo	Leo
Nov 7	Aq	Aq	Pis	Ar	Tau	Tau	Gem	Can	Can	Can	Leo	Leo
Nov 15	Aq	Pis	Ar	Tau	Gem	Gem	Can	Can	Can	Leo	Leo	Vir
Nov 23	Pis	Ar	Ar	Tau	Gem	Gem	Can	Can	Leo	Leo	Leo	Vir
Dec 1	Pis	Ar	Tau	Gem	Gem	Can	Can	Can	Leo	Leo	Vir	Vir
Dec 9	Ar	Tau	Tau	Gem	Gem	Can	Can	Leo	Leo	Leo	Vir	Vir
Dec 18	Ar	Tau	Gem	Gem	Can	Can	Can	Leo	Leo	Vir	Vir	Vir
Dec 28	Tau	Tau	Gem	Gem	Can	Can	Leo	Leo	Vir	Vir	Vir	Lib

CHAPTER 7

The Keys to Reading Your Horoscope: The Glyphs

Are you ready to take your astrology knowledge to the next level and read your first horoscope chart? If so, you'll encounter a new language of symbols, because horoscope charts are written in glyphs, a centuries-old pictographic language. These little "pictures" are a type of shorthand used by astrologers around the world to indicate the planets and the signs.

There's no way to avoid learning the glyphs, if you want to get deeper into astrology. Whether you download your chart from one of the many Internet sites that offer free charts or you buy one of the many interesting astrology programs, you'll find charts are always written in glyph language. Some software makes it easier for beginners by listing the planets and their signs in English alongside the chart and other programs will pop up an English interpretation as your roll your mouse over the glyph. However, in the long run, it's much easier—and more fun—to learn the glyphs yourself.

There's an extra bonus to learning the glyphs: They contain a kind of visual code, with built-in clues that will tell you not only which sign or planet each represents, but what the symbol means in a deeper, more esoteric sense. Actually the physical act of writing the symbol is a mystical experience in itself, a way to invoke the deeper meaning of the sign or planet through age-old visual elements that have been with us since time began.

Since there are only twelve signs and ten planets (not counting a few asteroids and other space objects some astrologers use), it's a lot easier than learning to read a foreign language. Here's a code cracker for the glyphs, beginning with the glyphs for the planets. To those who already know their glyphs, don't just skim over the chapter. These familiar graphics have hidden meanings you will discover!

The Glyphs for the Planets

The glyphs for the planets are easy to learn. They're simple combinations of the most basic visual elements: the circle, the semicircle or arc, and the cross. However, each component of a glyph has a special meaning in relation to the other parts of the symbol.

The circle, which has no beginning or end, is one of the oldest symbols of spirit or spiritual forces. Early diagrams of the heavens—spiritual territory—are shown in circular form. The never-ending line of the circle is the perfect symbol for eternity. The semicircle or arc is an incomplete circle, symbolizing the receptive, finite soul, which contains spiritual potential in the curving line.

The vertical line of the cross symbolizes movement from heaven to earth. The horizontal line describes temporal movement, here and now, in time and space. Combined in a cross, the vertical and horizontal planes symbolize manifestation in the material world.

The Sun Glyph ⊙

The sun is always shown by this powerful solar symbol, a circle with a point in the center. The center point is you, your spiritual center, and the symbol represents your infinite personality incarnating (the point) into the finite cycles of birth and death.

The sun has been represented by a circle or disk since ancient Egyptian times when the solar disk represented the sun god, Ra. Some archaeologists believe the great stone circles found in England were centers of sun worship. This particular version of the symbol was brought into common use in the sixteenth century after German occultist and scholar Cornelius Agrippa (1486–1535) wrote a book called *Die Occulta Philosophia,* which became accepted as the authority in the field. Agrippa collected many of the medieval astrological and magical symbols in this book, which have been used by astrologers since then.

The Moon Glyph ☽

The moon glyph is the most recognizable symbol on a chart, a left-facing arc stylized into the crescent moon. As part of a circle, the arc symbolizes the potential fulfillment of the entire circle, the life force that is still incomplete. Therefore, it is the ideal representation of the reactive, receptive, emotional nature of the moon.

The Mercury Glyph ☿

Mercury contains all three elemental symbols: the crescent, the circle, and the cross in vertical order. This is the "Venus with a hat" glyph (compare with the symbol of Venus). With another stretch of the imagination, can't you see the winged cap of Mercury the messenger? Think of the upturned crescent as antennae that tune in and transmit messages from the sun, reminding you that Mercury is the way you communicate, the way your mind works. The upturned arc is receiving energy into the spirit or solar circle, which will later be translated into action on the material plane, symbolized by the cross. All the elements are equally sized because Mercury is neutral; it doesn't play favorites! This planet symbolizes objective, detached, unemotional thinking.

The Venus Glyph ♀

Here the relationship is between two components: the circle of spirit and the cross of matter. Spirit is elevated over matter, pulling it upward. Venus asks, "What is beautiful? What do you like best? What do you love to have done to you?" Consequently, Venus determines both your ideal of beauty and what feels good sensually. It governs your own allure and power to attract, as well as what attracts and pleases you.

The Mars Glyph ♂

In this glyph, the cross of matter is stylized into an arrowhead pointed up and outward, propelled by the circle of spirit. With a little imagination, you can visualize it as the shield and spear of Mars, the ancient god of war. You can deduce that Mars embodies your spiritual energy projected into the outer world. It's your assertiveness, your initiative, your aggressive drive, what you like to do to others, your temper. If you know someone's Mars, you know whether they'll blow up when angry or do a slow burn. Your task is to use your outgoing Mars energy wisely and well.

The Jupiter Glyph ♃

Jupiter is the basic cross of matter, with a large stylized crescent perched on the left side of the horizontal, temporal plane. You might think of the crescent as an open hand, because one meaning of Jupiter is "luck," what's handed to you. You don't have to work for what you get from Jupiter; it comes to you, if you're open to it.

The Jupiter glyph might also remind you of a jumbo jet plane, with a huge tail fin, about to take off. This is the planet of travel, mental and spiritual, of expanding your horizons via new ideas, new spiritual dimensions, and new places. Jupiter embodies the optimism and enthusiasm of the traveler about to embark on an exciting adventure.

The Saturn Glyph ♄

Flip Jupiter over, and you've got Saturn. This might not be immediately apparent because Saturn is usually stylized into an "h" form like the one shown here. The principle it expresses is the opposite of Jupiter's expansive tendencies. Saturn pulls you back to earth: the receptive arc is pushed down underneath the cross of matter. Before there are any rewards or expansion, the duties and obligations of the material world must be considered. Saturn says, "Stop, wait, finish your chores before you take off!"

Saturn's glyph also resembles the sickle of old "Father Time."

Saturn was first known as Chronos, the Greek god of time, for time brings all matter to an end. When it was the most distant planet (before the discovery of Uranus), Saturn was believed to be the place where time stopped. After the soul departed from earth, it journeyed back to the outer reaches of the universe and finally stopped at Saturn, or at "the end of time."

The Uranus Glyph ♅

The glyph for Uranus is often stylized to form a capital *H* after Sir William Herschel, who discovered the planet. But the more esoteric version curves the two pillars of the H into crescent antennae, or "ears," like satellite disks receiving signals from space. These are perched on the horizontal material line of the cross of matter and pushed from below by the circle of the spirit. To many sci-fi fans, Uranus looks like an orbiting satellite.

Uranus channels the highest energy of all, the white electrical light of the universal spiritual force that holds the cosmos together. This pure electrical energy is gathered from all over the universe. Because Uranus energy doesn't follow any ordinary celestial drumbeat, it can't be controlled or predicted (which is also true of those who are strongly influenced by this eccentric planet). In the symbol, this energy is manifested through the balance of polarities (the two opposite arms of the glyph) like the two polarized wires of a lightbulb.

The Neptune Glyph ♆

Neptune's glyph is usually stylized to look like a trident, the weapon of the Roman god Neptune. However, on a more esoteric level, it shows the large upturned crescent of the soul pierced through by the cross of matter. Neptune nails down, or materializes, soul energy, bringing impulses from the soul level into manifestation. That is why Neptune is associated with imagination or "imagining in," making an image of the soul. Neptune works through feelings, sensitivity, and the mystical capacity to bring the divine into the earthly realm.

The Pluto Glyph ♀

Pluto is written two ways. One is a composite of the letters *PL*, the first two letters of the word Pluto and coincidentally the initials of Percival Lowell, one of the planet's discoverers. The other, more esoteric symbol is a small circle above a large open crescent that surmounts the cross of matter. This depicts Pluto's power to regenerate. Imagine a new little spirit emerging from the sheltering cup of the soul. Pluto rules the forces of life and death. After this planet has passed a sensitive point in your chart, you are transformed, reborn in some way.

Sci-fi fans might visualize this glyph as a small satellite (the circle) being launched. It was shortly after Pluto's discovery that we learned how to harness the nuclear forces that made space exploration possible. Pluto rules the transformative power of atomic energy, which totally changed our lives and from which there is no turning back.

The Glyphs for the Signs

On an astrology chart, the glyph for the sign will appear after that of the planet. For example, when you see the moon glyph followed first by a number and then by another glyph representing the sign, this means that the moon was passing over a certain degree of that astrological sign at the time of the chart. On the dividing lines between the houses on your chart, you'll find the symbol for the sign that rules the house.

Because sun sign symbols do not contain the same basic geometric components of the planetary glyphs, we must look elsewhere for clues to their meanings. Many have been passed down from ancient Egyptian and Chaldean civilizations with few modifications. Others have been adapted over the centuries.

In deciphering many of the glyphs, you'll often find that the symbols reveal a dual nature of the sign, which is not always apparent in the usual sun sign descriptions. For instance, the Gemini glyph is similar to the Roman numeral for two, and reveals this sign's longing to discover a twin soul. The Cancer glyph may be interpreted as resembling either the nurturing breasts or the self-protective claws of a crab, both symbols associated with the contrasting qualities of this sign. Libra's glyph embodies the duality of the spirit balanced with material reality. The Sagittarius glyph shows that the aspirant must also carry along the earthly animal nature in his quest. The Capricorn sea goat is another symbol with dual emphasis. The goat climbs high, yet is always pulled back by the deep waters of the unconscious. Aquarius embodies the double waves of mental detachment, balanced by the desire for connection with others, in a friendly way. Finally, the two fishes of Pisces, which are forever tied together, show the duality of the soul and the spirit that must be reconciled.

The Aries Glyph ♈

Since the symbol for Aries is the Ram, this glyph is obviously associated with a ram's horns, which characterize one aspect of the Aries personality—an aggressive, me-first, leaping-headfirst attitude. But the symbol can be interpreted in other ways as well. Some astrologers liken it to a fountain of energy, which Aries people also embody. The first sign of the zodiac bursts on the scene eagerly, ready to go. Another analogy is to the eyebrows and nose of the human head, which Aries rules, and the thinking power that is initiated by the brain.

One theory of this symbol links it to the Egyptian god Amun, represented by a ram in ancient times. As Amun-Ra, this god was believed to embody the creator of the universe, the leader of all the other gods. This relates easily to the position of Aries as the leader (or first sign) of the zodiac, which begins at the spring equinox, a time of the year when nature is renewed.

The Taurus Glyph ♉

This is another easy glyph to draw and identify. It takes little imagination to decipher the bull's head with long curving horns. Like its symbol the Bull, the archetypal Taurus is slow to anger but ferocious when provoked, as well as stubborn, steady, and sensual. Another association is the larynx (and thyroid) of the throat area (ruled by Taurus) and the eustachian tubes running up to the ears, which coincides with the relationship of Taurus to the voice, song, and music. Many famous singers, musicians, and composers have prominent Taurus influences.

Many ancient religions involved a bull as the central figure in fertility rites or initiations, usually symbolizing the victory of man over his animal nature. Another possible origin is in the sacred bull of Egypt, who embodied the incarnate form of Osiris, god of death and resurrection. In early Christian imagery, the Taurus Bull represented St. Luke.

The Gemini Glyph ♊

The standard glyph immediately calls to mind the Roman numeral for two (II) and the Twins symbol, as it is called, for Gemini. In almost all drawings and images used for this sign, the relationship between two persons is emphasized. Usually one twin will be touching the other, which signifies communication, human contact, the desire to share.

The top line of the Gemini glyph indicates mental communication, while the bottom line indicates shared physical space.

The most famous Gemini legend is that of the twin sons Castor and Pollux, one of whom had a mortal father while the other was the son of Zeus, king of the gods. When it came time for the mortal twin to die, his grief-stricken brother pleaded with Zeus, who agreed to let them spend half the year on earth in mortal form and half in immortal life, with the gods on Mount Olympus. This reflects a basic duality of humankind, which possesses an immortal soul yet is also subject to the limits of mortality.

The Cancer Glyph ♋

Two convenient images relate to the Cancer glyph. It is easiest to decode the curving claws of the Cancer symbol, the Crab. Like the crab's, Cancer's element is water. This sensitive sign also has a hard protective shell to protect its tender interior. The crab must be wily to escape predators, scampering sideways and hiding under rocks. The crab also responds to the cycles of the moon, as do all shellfish. The other image is that of two female breasts, which Cancer rules, showing that this is a sign that nurtures and protects others as well as itself.

In ancient Egypt, Cancer was also represented by the scarab beetle, a symbol of regeneration and eternal life.

The Leo Glyph ♌

Notice that the Leo glyph seems to be an extension of Cancer's glyph, with a significant difference. In the Cancer glyph, the lines curve inward protectively. The Leo glyph expresses energy outwardly. And there is no duality in the symbol, the Lion, or in Leo, the sign.

Lions have belonged to the sign of Leo since earliest times. It is not difficult to imagine the king of beasts with his sweeping mane and curling tail from this glyph. The upward sweep of the glyph easily describes the positive energy of Leo: the flourishing tail, the flamboyant qualities. Another analogy, perhaps a stretch of the imagination, is that of a heart leaping up with joy and enthusiasm, also very typical of Leo, which also rules the heart. In early Christian imagery, the Leo Lion represented St. Mark.

The Virgo Glyph ♍

You can read much into this mysterious glyph. For instance, it could represent the initials of "Mary Virgin," or a young woman holding a staff of wheat, or stylized female genitalia, all common interpretations. The M shape might also remind you that Virgo is ruled by Mercury. The cross beneath the symbol reveals the grounded, practical nature of this earth sign.

The earliest zodiacs link Virgo with the Egyptian goddess Isis, who gave birth to the god Horus after her husband Osiris had been killed, in the archetype of a miraculous conception. There are many ancient statues of Isis nursing her baby son, which are reminiscent of medieval Virgin and Child motifs. This sign has also been associated with the image of the Holy Grail, when the Virgo symbol was substituted with a chalice.

The Libra Glyph ♎

It is not difficult to read the standard image for Libra, the Scales, into this glyph. There is another meaning, however, that is equally relevant: the setting sun as it descends over the horizon. Libra's natural position on the zodiac wheel is the descendant, or sunset position (as the Aries natural position is the ascendant, or rising sign). Both images relate to Libra's personality. Libra is always weighing pros and cons for a balanced decision. In the sunset image, the sun (male) hovers over the horizontal earth (female) before setting. Libra is the space between these lines, harmonizing yin and yang, spiritual and material, male and female, ideal and real worlds. The glyph has also been linked to the kidneys, which are associated with Libra.

The Scorpio Glyph ♏

With its barbed tail, this glyph is easy to identify as the Scorpion for the sign of Scorpio. It also represents the male sexual parts, over which the sign rules. From the arrowhead, you can draw the conclusion that Mars was once its ruler. Some earlier Egyptian glyphs for Scorpio represent it as an erect serpent, so the Serpent is an alternate symbol.

Another symbol for Scorpio, which is not identifiable in this glyph, is the Eagle. Scorpios can go to extremes, either in soaring like the eagle or self-destructing like the scorpion. In early Christian imagery, which often used zodiacal symbols, the Scorpio Eagle was chosen to symbolize the intense apostle St. John the Evangelist.

The Sagittarius Glyph ♐

This is one of the easiest to spot and draw: an upward pointing arrow lifting up a cross. The arrow is pointing skyward, while the cross represents the four elements of the material world, which the arrow must convey. Elevating materiality into spirituality is an important Sagittarius quality, which explains why this sign is associated with higher learning, religion, philosophy, travel—the aspiring professions. Sagittarius can also send barbed arrows of frankness in the pursuit of truth, so the Archer symbol for Sagittarius is apt. (Sagittarius is also the sign of the supersalesman.)

Sagittarius is symbolically represented by the centaur, a mythological creature who is half man, half horse, aiming his arrow toward the skies. Though Sagittarius is motivated by spiritual aspiration, it also must balance the powerful appetites of the animal nature. The centaur Chiron, a figure in Greek mythology, became a wise teacher who, after many adventures and world travels, was killed by a poisoned arrow.

The Capricorn Glyph ♑

One of the most difficult symbols to draw, this glyph may take some practice. It is a representation of the sea goat: a mythical animal that is a goat with a curving fish's tail. The goat part of Capricorn wants to leave the waters of the emotions and climb to the elevated areas of life. But the fish tail is the unconscious, the deep chaotic psychic level that draws the goat back. Capricorn is often trying to escape the deep, feeling part of life by submerging himself in work, steadily ascending to the top. To some people, the glyph represents a seated figure with a bent knee, a reminder that Capricorn governs the knee area of the body.

An interesting aspect of this glyph is the contrast of the sharp pointed horns—which represent the penetrating, shrewd, conscious side of Capricorn—with the swishing tail—which represents its serpentine, unconscious, emotional force. One Capricorn legend, which dates from Roman times, tells of the earthy fertility god, Pan, who tried to save himself from uncontrollable sexual desires by jumping into the Nile. His upper body then turned into a goat, while the lower part became a fish. Later, Jupiter gave him a safe haven as a constellation in the skies.

The Aquarius Glyph ♒

This ancient water symbol can be traced back to an Egyptian hieroglyph representing streams of life force. Symbolized by the Water Bearer, Aquarius is distributor of the waters of life—the magic liquid of regeneration. The two waves can also be linked to the positive and negative charges of the electrical energy that Aquarius rules, a sort of universal wavelength. Aquarius is tuned in intuitively to higher forces via this electrical force. The duality of the glyph could also refer to the dual nature of Aquarius, a sign that runs hot and cold and that is friendly but also detached in the mental world of air signs.

In Greek legends, Aquarius is represented by Ganymede, who was carried to heaven by an eagle in order to become the cupbearer of Zeus and to supervise the annual flooding of the Nile. The sign later became associated with aviation and notions of flight. Like the other fixed signs (Taurus, Scorpio, and Leo), Aquarius is associated with an apostle, in this case St. Matthew.

The Pisces Glyph ♓

Here is an abstraction of the familiar image of Pisces, two Fishes swimming in opposite directions yet bound together by a cord. The Fishes represent the spirit—which yearns for the freedom of heaven—and the soul—which remains attached to the desires of the temporal world. During life on earth, the spirit and the soul are bound together. When they complement each other, instead of pulling in opposite directions, they facilitate the Pisces creativity. The ancient version of this glyph, taken from the Egyptians, had no connecting line, which was added in the fourteenth century.

In another interpretation, it is said that the left fish indicates the direction of involution or the beginning of a cycle, while the right fish signifies the direction of evolution, the way to completion of a cycle. It's an appropriate grand finale for Pisces, the last sign of the zodiac.

CHAPTER 8

Join the Astrology Community

Astrology fans love to share their knowledge and socialize. So why not join the community of astrologers online or at a conference? You might be surprised to find an astrology club in your local area. Connecting with other astrology fans and learning more about this fascinating subject has never been easier. In fact the many options available with just a click of your computer are mind-boggling.

You need only type the word *astrology* into any Internet search engine and watch hundreds of listings of astrology-related sites pop up. There are local meetings and international conferences where you can meet and study with other astrologers, and books and tapes to help you learn at home. You could even combine your vacation with an astrological workshop in an exotic locale, such as Bali or Mexico.

To help you sort out the variety of options available, here are our top picks of the Internet and the astrological community at large.

National Council for Geocosmic Research (NCGR)

Whether you'd like to know more about such specialties as financial astrology or techniques for timing events, or if you'd prefer the psychological or mythological approach, you'll meet the top astrologers at conferences sponsored by the National Council for Geocosmic Research. NCGR is dedicated to providing quality education, bringing astrologers and astrology fans together at conferences, and promoting fellowship. Their course structure provides a systematized study of the many facets of astrology. The organization sponsors educational workshops, taped lectures, conferences, and a directory of professional astrologers.

For an annual membership fee, you get their excellent publications and newsletters, plus the opportunity to network with other astrology buffs at local chapter events. At this writing there are chapters in twenty-six states and four countries.

To join NCGR and for the latest information on upcoming events and chapters in your city, consult their Web site: www.geocosmic.org.

American Federation of Astrologers (AFA)

Established in 1938, this is one of the oldest astrological organizations in the United States. AFA offers conferences, conventions, and a correspondence course. If you are looking for a reading, their interesting Web site will refer you to an accredited AFA astrologer.

6535 South Rural Road
Tempe, AZ 85283
Phone: (888) 301-7630 or (480) 838-1751
Fax: (480) 838-8293
Web site: www.astrologers.com

Association for Astrological Networking (AFAN)

Did you know that astrologers are still being harassed for practicing astrology? AFAN provides support and legal information, and works toward improving the public image of astrology. AFAN's network of local astrologers links with the international astrological community. Here are the people who will go to bat for astrology when it is attacked in the media. Everyone who cares about astrology should join!

8306 Wilshire Boulevard
PMB 537
Beverly Hills, CA 90211
Phone: (800) 578-2326
E-mail: info@afan.org
Web site: www.afan.org

International Society for Astrology Research (ISAR)

An international organization of professional astrologers dedicated to encouraging the highest standards of quality in the field of astrology with an emphasis on research. Among ISAR's benefits are quarterly journals, a weekly e-mail newsletter, and a free membership directory.

P.O. Box 38613
Los Angeles, CA 90038
Fax: (805) 933-0301
Web site: www.isarastrology.com

Astrology Magazines

In addition to articles by top astrologers, most have listings of astrology conferences, events, and local happenings.

Horoscope Guide
Kappa Publishing Group
6198 Butler Pike
Suite 200
Blue Bell, PA 19422-2600
Web site: www.kappapublishing.com/astrology

Dell Horoscope
Their Web site features a listing of local astrological meetings.

Customer Service
6 Prowitt Street
Norwalk, CT 06855
Phone: (800) 220-7443
Web site: www.dellhoroscope.com

The Mountain Astrologer
A favorite magazine of astrology fans, *The Mountain Astrologer* also has an interesting Web site featuring the latest news from an astrological point of view, plus feature articles from the magazine.

P.O. Box 970
Cedar Ridge, CA 95924
Web site: www.mountainastrologer.com

Astrology College

Kepler College of Astrological Arts and Sciences

A degree-granting college, which is also a center of astrology, has long been the dream of the astrological community and is a giant step forward in providing credibility to the profession. Therefore, the opening of Kepler College in 2000 was a historical event for astrology. It is the only college in the United States authorized to issue BA and MA degrees in astrological studies. Here is where to study with the best scholars, teachers, and communicators in the field. A long-distance study program is available for those interested.

Kepler College also offers online noncredit courses that anyone can take via the Kepler Community Learning Center. Classes range from two days to ten weeks in length, and the cost will vary depending upon the class taken. Students can access an online Web site to enroll in specific classes and interact with other students and instructors.

For more information, contact:

4630 200th Street SW
Suite P
Lynnwood, WA 98036
Phone: (425) 673-4292
Fax: (425) 673-4983
Web site: www.kepler.edu

Our Favorite Web sites

Of the thousands of astrological Web sites that come and go on the Internet, these have stood the test of time and are likely to still be operating when this book is published.

Astrodienst (www.astro.com)

Don't miss this fabulous international site, which has long been one of the best astrology resources on the Internet. It's a great place to view your own astrology chart. The world atlas on this site will give you the accurate longitude and latitude of your birthplace for setting up your horoscope. Then you can print out your free chart in a range of easy-to-read formats. Other attractions: a list of famous people born on your birth date, a feature that helps you choose the best vacation spot, and articles by world-famous astrologers.

AstroDatabank (www.astrodatabank.com)

When the news is breaking, you can bet this site will be the first to get accurate birthdays of the headliners. The late astrologer Lois Rodden was a stickler for factual information and her meticulous research is being continued, much to the benefit of the astrological community. The Web site specializes in charts of current newsmakers, political figures, and international celebrities. You can also participate in discussions and analysis of the charts and see what some of the world's best astrologers have to say about them. Their AstroDatabank program, which you can purchase at the site, provides thousands of birthdays sorted into categories. It's an excellent research tool.

StarIQ (www.stariq.com)

Find out how top astrologers view the latest headlines at the must-see StarIQ site. Many of the best minds in astrology comment on the latest news, stock market ups and downs, and political contenders. You can sign up to receive e-mail forecasts at the most important times keyed to your individual chart. (This is one of the best of the online forecasts.)

Astro-Noetics (www.astro-noetics.com)

For those who are ready to explore astrology's interface with politics, popular culture, and current events, here is a sophisticated site with in-depth articles and personality profiles. Lots of depth and content here for the astrology-savvy surfer.

Astrology Books (www.astroamerica.com)

The Astrology Center of America sells a wide selection of books on all aspects of astrology, from the basics to the most advanced, at this online bookstore. Also available are many hard-to-find and used books.

Astrology Scholars' Sites

See what Robert Hand, one of astrology's great teachers, has to offer on his site at www.robhand.com. A leading expert on the history of astrology, he's on the cutting edge of the latest research.

The Project Hindsight group of astrologers is devoted to restoring the astrology of the Hellenistic period, the primary source for all later Western astrology. There are fascinating articles for astrology fans on this site at www.projecthindsight.com.

Financial Astrology Sites

Financial astrology is a hot specialty, with many tipsters, players, and theorists. There are online columns, newsletters, specialized financial astrology software, and mutual funds run by astrology seers. One of the more respected financial astrologers is Ray Merriman, whose market comments on www. mmacycles.com are a must for those following the bulls and bears.

Explore Your Relationships (www.topsynergy.com)

Ever wondered how you'd get along with Brad Pitt, Halle Berry, or another famous hottie? TopSynergy offers a clever tool called a relationship analyst that will help you use astrology to analyze past, present, or possible future relationships. There's a database of celebrity horoscopes for you to partner with your own as well. It's free for unlimited use.

How to Zoom Around the Sky

If you haven't already discovered the wonders of Google Earth (www.earth.google.com), then you've been missing close-up aerial views of anyplace on the planet from your old hometown to the beaches of Hawaii. Even more fascinating for astrology buffs is the newest feature called Google Sky, a marvel of computer technology that lets you view the sky overhead from anyplace you choose. Want to see the stars over Paris at the moment? A few clicks of your mouse will take you there. Then you can follow the tracks of the sun, moon, and planets or check astronomical information and beautiful Hubble images. Go to the Google Web site to download this free program. Then get ready to take a cosmic tour around the earth and sky.

Listen to the Sounds of Your Sign

Astrology Weekly (www.astrologyweekly.com) is a Web site from Romania, with lots to offer astro surfers. Here you can check all the planetary placements for the week, get free charts, join an international discussion group, and check out charts for countries and world leaders. Of special interest is the chart generator, an easy-to-use feature that will create a natal chart. Just click on *new chart* and enter the year, month, day, time, longitude, and latitude of your birth place. Select the Placidus or Koch house system and click on *show it*. Your chart should come right up on the screen. You can then copy the link to your astrology chart, store it, and later share your chart with friends. If you don't have astrology software, this is a good way to view charts instantly. This site also has some fun ways to pass the time, such as listening to music especially chosen for your sun sign.

Stellar Gifts

If you've ever wondered what to give your astrology buddies, here's the place to find foolproof gifts. How about a mug, mouse pad, or plaque decorated with someone's chart? Would a special person like a pendant personalized with their planets? Check out www.milestonegifts.co.uk for some great ideas for putting those astrology charts to decorative use.

CHAPTER 9

The Best Astrology Software: Take Your Knowledge to the Next Level

Are you ready to begin looking at charts of friends and family? Would you like to call up your favorite celebrity's chart or check the aspects every day on your BlackBerry? Perhaps you'd like to study astrology in depth and would prefer a more comprehensive program that adapts to your needs as you learn. If you haven't discovered the wonders of astrology software, you're missing out!

Astrology technology has advanced to the point where even a computerphobe can call up a Web site on a BlackBerry browser and put a chart on the screen in seconds. It does help to have some basic knowledge of the signs, houses, planets, and especially the glyphs for the planets and the signs. Then you can practice reading charts and relating the planets to the lives of friends, relatives, and daily events, the ideal way to get more involved with astrology.

There's a program for every level of interest at all price points—starting with free. For the dabbler, there are the affordable Winstar Express, Know, and Time Passages. For the serious student, there are Astrology (free), Solar Fire, Kepler, Winstar Plus—software that does every technique on the planet and gives you beautiful chart printouts. If you're a MAC user, you'll be satisfied with the wonderful IO and Time Passages software.

However, since all the programs use the astrology symbols, or glyphs, for planets and signs, rather than written words, you should learn the glyphs before you purchase your software. Chapter 7 will help you do just that. Here are some software options for you to explore.

Easy for Beginners

Time Passages

Designed for either a Macintosh or Windows computer, Time Passages is straightforward and easy to use. It allows you to generate charts and interpretation reports for yourself or friends and loved ones at the touch of a button. If you haven't yet learned the astrology symbols, this might be the program for you. Just roll your mouse over any symbols of the planets, signs, or house cusps, and you'll be shown a description in plain English below the chart. Then click on the planet, sign, or house cusp and up pops a detailed interpretation. Couldn't be easier. A new Basic Edition, under fifty dollars at this writing, is bargain priced and ideal for beginners.

Time Passages
(866) 772-7876 (866-77-ASTRO)
Web site: www.astrograph.com

The "Know Thru Astrology" Series

This new series is designed especially for the nonastrologer. There are four programs in the series: KNOW Your Self, KNOW Your Future, KNOW Your Lover, and KNOW Your Child, each priced at an affordable $49.95 (at this writing). Though it is billed as beginner software, the KNOW series offers many sophisticated options, such as a calendar to let you navigate future or past influences, detailed chart interpretations, built-in pop-ups to show you what everything means. You'll need a PC running current Windows versions starting with Windows 98 SE, with 512 Mb RAM, and a hard drive with 170–300 Mb free space.

Matrix Software
126 South Michigan Avenue
Big Rapids, MI 49307
(800) 752-6387
Web site: www.astrologysoftware.com

Growth Opportunities

Astrolabe

Astrolabe is one of the top astrology software resources. Check out the latest version of their powerful Solar Fire software for Windows. It's a breeze to use and will grow with your increasing knowledge of astrology to the most sophisticated levels. This company also markets a variety of programs for all levels of expertise and a wide selection of computer-generated astrology readings. This is a good resource for innovative software as well as applications for older computers.

   The Astrolabe Web site is a great place to start your astrology tour of the Internet. Visitors to the site are greeted with a chart of the time you log on. And you can get your chart calculated, also free, with a mini interpretation e-mailed to you.

Astrolabe
Box 1750-R
Brewster, MA 02631
Phone: (800) 843-6682
Web site: www.alabe.com

Matrix Software

You'll find a wide variety of software at student and advanced levels in all price ranges, demo disks, lots of interesting readings. Check out Winstar Express, a powerful but reasonably priced program suitable for all skill levels. The Matrix Web site offers lots of fun activities for Web surfers, such as free readings from the I Ching, the runes, and the tarot. There are many free desktop backgrounds with astrology themes.

Matrix Software
126 South Michigan Avenue
Big Rapids, MI 49307
Phone: (800) 752-6387
Web site: www.astrologysoftware.com

Astro Computing Services (ACS)

Books, software, individual charts, and telephone readings
are offered by this company. Their freebies include astrology
greeting cards and new moon reports. Find technical astrology materials here such as *The American Ephemeris* and PC
atlases. ACS will calculate and send charts to you, a valuable
service if you do not have a computer.

Starcrafts Publishing
334 Calef Hwy.
Epping, NH 03042
Phone: (866) 953-8458
Web site: www.astrocom.com

Air Software

Here you'll find powerful, creative astrology software, plus
current stock market analysis. Financial astrology programs
for stock market traders are a specialty. There are some interesting freebees at this site. Check out the maps of eclipse
paths for any year and a free astrology clock program.

Air Software
115 Caya Avenue
West Hartford, CT 06110
Phone: (800) 659-1247
Web site: www.alphee.com

Kepler: State of the Art

Here's a program that's got everything. Gorgeous graphic images, audio-visual effects, and myriad sophisticated chart options are built into this fascinating software. It's even got an

astrological encyclopedia, plus diagrams and images to help you understand advanced concepts. This program is pricey, but if you're serious about learning astrology, it's an investment that will grow with you! Check out its features at www.astrosoftware.com.

Timecycles Research: For Mac Users

Here's where Mac users can find astrology software that's as sophisticated as it gets. If you have a Mac, you'll love their beautiful graphic IO Series programs.

Time Cycles Research
P.O. Box 797
Waterford, CT 06385
(800) 827-2240
Web site: www.timecycles.com

Shareware and Freeware: The Price Is Right!

Halloran Software: A Super Shareware Program

Check out Halloran Software's Web site, which offers several levels of Windows astrology software. Beginners should consider their Astrology for Windows shareware program, which is available in unregistered demo form as a free download and in registered form for a very reasonable price.

Halloran Software
P.O. Box 75713
Los Angeles, CA 90075
(800) 732-4628
Web site: www.halloran.com

ASTROLOG

If you're computer-savvy, you can't go wrong with Walter Pullen's amazingly complete Astrology program, which is offered absolutely free at the site. The Web address is www.astrolog.org/astrolog.htm.

Astrolog is an ultrasophisticated program with all the features of much more expensive programs. It comes in versions for all formats: DOS, Windows, Mac, and UNIX. It has some cool features, such as a revolving globe and a constellation map. If you are looking for astrology software with all the bells and whistles that doesn't cost big bucks, this program has it all!

Buying a Computer with Astrology in Mind?

The good news is that astrology software is becoming more sophisticated and fun to use. However, if you've inherited an old computer, don't despair. You don't need the fastest processor and all the newest bells and whistles to run perfectly adequate astrology software. It is still possible to find programs for elder systems, including many new exciting programs.

To take full advantage of all the options, it is best to have a system that runs versions of Windows starting with Windows 98 SE. If you're buying a new computer, invest in one with as much RAM as possible, at least 1 GB. A CD drive will be necessary to load programs or an Internet connection, if you prefer to download programs online.

Mac fans who want to run Windows astrology software should invest in dual boot computers that will operate both the Mac and the Windows XP and Vista platforms.

CHAPTER 10

Ask the Expert: A Personal Reading Could Help

In these changing times, preparing ourselves for challenges ahead becomes a top priority as new issues surface in our lives. This could be the ideal time to add an astrologer to your dream team of advisers. Horoscopes can offer general advice to all members of your sign, but a personal reading can deal with what matters most to you. It can help you sort out a problem, find and use the strengths in your horoscope, set you on a more fulfilling career path, give you insight into your romantic life, or help you decide where to relocate. Many people consult astrologers to find the optimum time to schedule an important event, such as a wedding or business meeting.

Another good reason for a reading is to refine your knowledge of astrology by consulting with someone who has years of experience analyzing charts. You might choose an astrologer with a specialty that intrigues you. Armed with the knowledge of your chart that you have acquired so far, you can then learn to interpret subtle nuances or gain insight into your talents and abilities.

How do you choose when there are so many different kinds of readings available, especially since the Internet has brought astrology into the mainstream? Besides individual one-on-one readings with a professional astrologer, there are personal readings by mail, telephone, Internet, and tape. Well-advertised computer-generated reports and celebrity-sponsored readings are sure to attract your attention on commercial Web sites and in magazines. You can even purchase a reading that is incorporated into an expensive handmade fine art book. Then there are astrologers who specialize in specific areas such as finance or medical astrology. And unfortunately, there are many questionable practitioners who range from streetwise Gypsy fortune-tellers to unscrupulous scam artists.

The following basic guidelines can help you sort out your options to find the reading that's right for you.

One-on-One Consultations with a Professional Astrologer

Nothing compares to a one-on-one consultation with a professional astrologer who has analyzed thousands of charts and can pinpoint the potential in yours. During your reading, you can get your specific questions answered and discuss possible paths you might take. There are many astrologers who now combine their skills with training in psychology and are well-suited to help you examine your alternatives.

To give you an accurate reading, an astrologer needs certain information from you: the date, time, and place where you were born. (A horoscope can be cast about anyone or anything that has a specific time and place.) Most astrologers will then enter this information into a computer, which will calculate a chart in seconds, and interpret the resulting chart.

If you don't know your exact birth time, you can usually locate it at the Bureau of Vital Statistics at the city hall of the town or the county seat in the state where you were born. If you still have no success in getting your time of birth, some astrologers can estimate an approximate birth time by using past events in your life to determine the chart. This technique is called rectification.

How to Find an Astrologer

Choose your astrologer with the same care as you would any trusted adviser, such as a doctor, lawyer, or banker. Unfortunately, anyone can claim to be an astrologer—to date, there is no licensing of astrologers or universally established professional criteria. However, there are nationwide organizations of serious, committed astrologers that can help you in your search.

Good places to start your investigation are organizations such as the American Federation of Astrologers (AFA) or the National Council for Geocosmic Research (NCGR), which offer a program of study and certification. If you live near a major city, there is sure to be an active NCGR chapter or astrology club in your area; many are listed in astrology magazines available at your local newsstand. In response to many requests for referrals, both the AFA and the NCGR have directories of professional astrologers listed on their Web sites; these directories include a glossary of terms and an explanation of specialties within the astrological field. Contact the NCGR and AFA headquarters for information. (See also Chapter 8.)

What Happens in a Reading

As a potentially lucrative freelance business, astrology has always attracted self-styled experts who may not have the knowledge or the counseling experience to give a helpful reading. These astrologers can range from the well-meaning amateur to the charlatan or street-corner Gypsy who has for many years given astrology a bad name. Be very wary of astrologers who claim to have occult powers or who make pretentious claims of celebrated clients or miraculous achievements. You can often tell from the initial phone conversation if the astrologer is legitimate. He or she should ask for your birthday time and place and then conduct the conversation in a professional manner. Any astrologer who gives a reading based only on your sun sign is highly suspect.

When you arrive at the reading, the astrologer should be prepared. The consultation should be conducted in a private, quiet place. The astrologer should be interested in your problems of the moment. A good reading is interactive and involves feedback on your part, so if the reading is not relating to your concerns, you should let the astrologer know. You should feel free to ask questions and get clarifications of any technical terms. The more you actively participate, rather than expecting the astrologer to carry the reading or come forth with oracular predictions, the more meaningful your experience will be. An astrologer should help you validate your current experience and be frank about possible negative happenings, but also suggest a positive course of action.

In their approach to a reading, some astrologers may be more literal and others more intuitive. Those who have had counseling training may take a more psychological approach. Though some astrologers may seem to have an almost psychic ability, extrasensory perception or any other parapsychological talent is not essential. A very accurate picture can be drawn from the data in your horoscope chart.

An astrologer may do several charts for each client, including one for the time of birth and a progressed chart, showing the evolution from birth to the present time. According to your individual needs, there are many other possibilities, such as a chart for a different location if you are contemplating a change of place. Relationships between any two people, things, or events can be interpreted with a chart that compares one partner's horoscope with the other's. A composite chart, which uses the midpoint between planets in two individual charts to describe the relationship, is another commonly used device.

An astrologer will be particularly interested in transits, those times when cycling planets activate the planets or sensitive points in your birth chart. These indicate important events in your life.

Many astrologers offer readings recorded on tape or CD, which is another option to consider, especially if the astrologer you choose lives at a distance from you. In this case, you'll be mailed a recorded reading based on your birth chart. This type of reading is more personal than a computer printout and can give you valuable insights, though it is not equivalent to a live dialogue with the astrologer when you can discuss your specific interest and issues of the moment.

The Telephone Reading

Telephone readings come in two varieties: a dial-in taped reading, usually recorded in advance by an astrologer, or a live consultation with an "astrologer" on the other end of the line. The recorded readings are general daily or weekly forecasts, applied to all members of your sign and charged by the minute. The quality depends on the astrologer. Be aware that these readings can run up quite a telephone bill, especially if you get into the habit of calling every day. Be sure that you are aware of the per-minute cost of each call beforehand.

Live telephone readings also vary with the expertise of the astrologer. Ideally, the astrologer at the other end of the line enters your birth data into a computer, which then quickly calculates your chart. This chart will be referred to during the consultation. The advantage of a live telephone reading is that your individual chart is used and you can ask about a specific problem. However, before you invest in any reading, be sure that your astrologer is qualified and that you fully understand in advance how much you will be charged. There should be no unpleasant financial surprises later. The best astrologer is one who is recommended to you by a friend or family member.

Computer-Generated Reports

Companies that offer computer programs (such as ACS, Matrix, and Astrolabe) also offer a variety of computer-generated horoscope readings. These can be quite comprehensive, offering a beautiful printout of the chart plus many pages of detailed information about each planet and aspect of the chart. You can then study it at your convenience. Of course, the interpretations will be general, since there is no personal input from you, and might not cover your immediate concerns. Since computer-generated horoscopes are much lower in cost than live consultations, you might consider them as either a supplement or a preparation for an eventual live reading. You'll then be more familiar with your chart and able to plan specific questions in advance. They also make a terrific gift for astrology fans. In chapter 9, there are listed several companies that offer computerized readings prepared by reputable astrologers.

Whichever option you decide to pursue, may your reading be an empowering one!

CHAPTER 11

Loving Every Sign in the Zodiac

In times of change, we crave the comfort of a loving partner more than ever. If we don't have love, we want to know how and where to find it; and if we already have a loving relationship, we want to know how to make it last forever. You can use astrology to find a lover, understand the one you have, or add excitement to your current relationship. Here are sun-sign seduction tips for romancing every sign in the zodiac.

Aries: Play Hard to Get

This highly physical sign is walking dynamite with a brief attention span. Don't be too easy to get, ladies. A little challenge, a lively debate, and a merry chase only heat them up. They want to see what you're made of. Once you've lured them into your lair, be a challenge and a bit of a daredevil. Pull out your X-rated tricks. Don't give your all—let them know there's more where that came from. Make it exciting; show you're up for adventure. Wear bright red somewhere interesting. Since Aries rules the head and face, be sure to focus on these areas in your lovemaking. Use your lips, tongue, breath, and even your eyelashes to the max. Practice scalp massages and deep kissing techniques. Aries won't wait, so when you make your move, be sure you're ready to follow through. No head games or teasing!

To keep you happy, you've got to voice your *own* needs, because this lover will be focused on *his*. Teach him how to please, or this could be a one-sided adventure.

Taurus: Appeal to All Their Senses

Taurus wins as the most sensual sign, with the most sexual stamina. This man is earthy and lusty in bed; he can go on all night. This is not a sign to tease. Like a bull, he'll see red, not bed. So make him comfortable, and then bombard all his senses. Good food gets Taurus in the mood. So do the right music, fragrance, revealing clothes, and luxurious bedlinens. Give him a massage with delicious-smelling and -tasting oils; focus on the neck area.

Don't forget to turn off the phone! Taurus hates interruptions. Since they can be very vocal lovers, choose a setting where you won't be disturbed. And don't ever rush; enjoy a long, slow, delicious encounter.

Gemini: Be a Playmate

Playful Gemini loves games, so make your seduction fun. Be their lost twin soul or confidante. Good communication is essential, so share deep secrets and live out fantasies. This sign adores variety. Nothing bores Gemini more than making love the same way all the time, or bringing on the heavy emotions. So trot out all the roles you've been longing to play. Here's the perfect partner. But remember to keep it light and fun. Gemini's turn-on zone is the hands, and this sign gives the best massages. Gadgets that can be activated with a touch amuse Gemini. This sign is great at doing two things at once, like making love while watching an erotic film. Turn the cell phone off unless you want company. On the other hand, Gemini is your sign for superhot phone sex.

Gemini loves a change of scene. So experiment on the floor, in the shower, or on the kitchen table. Borrow a friend's apartment or rent a hotel room for variety.

Cancer: Use the Moon

The key to Cancer is to get this moon child in the mood. Consult the moon—a full moon is best. Wining, dining, old-fashioned courtship, and breakfast in bed are turn-ons. Whatever makes your Cancer feel secure will promote shedding inhibitions in the sack. (Don't try any of your Aries daredevil techniques here!) Cancer prefers familiar, comfortable, homey surroundings. Cancer's turn-on zone is the breasts. Cancer women often have naturally inflated chests. Cancer men may fantasize about a well-endowed playmate. If your breasts are enhanced, show them off. Cancer will want to know all your deepest secrets, so invent a few good ones. But lots of luck delving into *their* innermost thoughts!

Take your Cancer near water. The sight and sound of the sea can be their aphrodisiac. A moonlit beach, a deserted swimming pool, a Jacuzzi, or a bubble bath are good seduction spots. Listen to the rain patter on the roof in a mountain cabin.

Leo: Offer the Royal Treatment

Leo must be the best and hear it from you often. In return, they'll perform for you, telling you just what you want to hear (true or not). They like a lover with style and endurance, and to be swept off their feet and into bed. Leos like to go first-class all the way, so build them up with lots of attention, wining and dining, and special gifts.

Never mention other lovers or make them feel second-best. A sure signal for Leo to look elsewhere is a competitive spouse. Leos take great pride in their bodies, so you should pour on the admiration. A few well-placed mirrors could inspire them. So would a striptease with beautiful lingerie, expensive fragrance on the sheets, and, if female, an occasional luxury hotel room, with champagne and caviar delivered by room service. Leo's erogenous zone is the lower back, so a massage with expensive oils would make your lion purr with pleasure.

Virgo: Let Them Be the Teacher

Virgo's standards are so sky-high that you may feel intimidated at first. The key to pleasing fussy Virgo lovers is to look for the hot fantasy beneath their cool surface. They're really looking for someone to make over. So let Virgo play teacher, and you play the willing student; the doctor-patient routine works as well. Be Eliza Doolittle to his Henry Higgins.

Let Virgo help you improve your life, quit smoking, learn French, and diet. Read an erotic book together, and then practice the techniques. Or study esoteric, erotic exercises from the Far East.

The Virgo erogenous zone is the tummy area, which should be your base of operations. Virgo likes things pristine and clean. Fall onto crisp, immaculate white sheets. Wear a sheer virginal white nightie. Smell shower-fresh with no heavy perfume. Be sure your surroundings pass the hospital test. A shower together afterward (with great-smelling soap) could get the ball rolling again.

Libra: Look Your Best

Libra must be turned on aesthetically. Make sure you look as beautiful as possible, and wear something stylishly seductive but never vulgar. Have a mental affair first, as you flirt and flatter this sign. Then proceed to the physical. Approach Libra like a dance partner, ready to waltz or tango.

Libra must be in the mood for love; otherwise, forget it. Any kind of ugliness is a turnoff. Provide an elegant and harmonious atmosphere, with no loud noise, clashing colors, or uncomfortable beds. Libra is not an especially spontaneous lover, so it is best to spend time warming them up. Libra's back is his erogenous zone, your cue to provide back rubs with scented potions. Once in bed, you can be a bit aggressive sexually. Libra loves strong, decisive moves. Set the scene, know what you want, and let Libra be happy to provide it.

Scorpio: Be an All-or-Nothing Lover

Scorpio is legendary in bed, often called the sex sign of the zodiac. But seducing them is often a power game. Scorpio likes to be in control, even the quiet, unassuming ones. Scorpio loves a mystery, so don't tell all. Keep them guessing about you, offering tantalizing hints along the way. The hint of danger often turns Scorpio on, so you'll find members of this sign experimenting with the exotic and highly erotic forms of sex. Sadomasochism, bondage, or anything that tests the limits of power could be a turn-on for Scorpio.

Invest in some sexy black leather and some powerful music. Clothes that lace, buckle, or zip tempt Scorpio to untie you. Present yourself as a mysterious package just waiting to be unwrapped.

Once in bed, there are no holds barred with Scorpio. They'll find your most pleasurable pressure points, and touch you as you've never been touched before. They are quickly aroused (the genital area belongs to this sign) and are willing to try anything. But they can be possessive. Don't expect your Scorpio to share you with anyone. It's all or nothing for them.

Sagittarius: Be a Happy Wanderer

Sagittarius men are the Don Juans of the zodiac—love-'em-and-leave-'em types who are difficult to pin down. Your seduction strategy is to join them in their many pursuits, and then hook them with love on the road. Sagittarius enjoys sex in venues that suggest movement; planes, SUVs, or boats. But a favorite turn-on place is outdoors, in nature. A deserted hiking path, a field of tall grass, or a remote woodland glade—all give the centaur sexy ideas. Athletic Sagittarius might go for some personal training in an empty gym. Join your Sagittarius for amorous aerobics, meditate together, and explore the tantric forms of sex. Lovemaking after hiking and skiing would be healthy fun.

Sagittarius enjoys lovers from exotic ethnic backgrounds, or lovers met in spiritual pursuits or on college campuses. Sagittarius are great cheerleaders and motivators, and will enjoy feeling that they have inspired you to be all that you can be.

There may be a canine or feline companion sharing your Sagittarius lover's bed with you, so check your allergies. And bring Fido or Felix a toy to keep them occupied.

Capricorn: Take Their Mind off Business

The great news about Capricorn lovers is that they improve with age. They are probably the sexiest seniors. So stick around, if you have a young one. They're lusty in bed (it's not the sign of the goat for nothing), and can be quite raunchy and turned on by X-rated words and deeds. If this is not your thing, let them know. The Capricorn erogenous zone is the knees. Some discreet fondling in public places could be your opener. Capricorn tends to think of sex as part of a game plan for the future. They are well-organized, and might regard lovemaking as relaxation after a long day's work. This sign often combines business with pleasure. So look for a Capricorn where there's a convention, trade show, or work-related conference.

Getting Capricorn's mind off his agenda and onto yours could take some doing. Separate him from his buddies by whispering sexy secrets in his ear. Then convince him you're an asset to his image and a boon to his health. Though he may seem uptight at first, you'll soon discover he's a love animal who makes a wonderful and permanent pet.

Aquarius: Give Them Enough Space

This sign really does not want an all-consuming passion or an all-or-nothing relationship. Aquarius needs space. But once they feel free to experiment with a spontaneous and exciting partner, Aquarius can give you a far-out sexual adventure.

Passion begins in the mind, so a good mental buildup is key. Aquarius is an inventive sign who believes love is a playground without rules. Plan surprise, unpredictable encounters in unusual places. Find ways to make love transcendental, an extraordinary and unique experience. Be ready to try anything Aquarius suggests, if only once. Calves and ankles are the special Aquarius erogenous zone, so perfect your legwork.

Be careful not to be too possessive. Your Aquarius needs lots of space and tolerance for friends (including old lovers) and their many outside interests.

Pisces: Live Their Fantasies

Pisces is the sign of fantasy and imagination. This sign has great theatrical talent. Pisces looks for lovers who will take care of them. Pisces will return the favor! Here is someone who can psych out your deepest desires without mentioning them. Pisces falls for sob stories and is always ready to empathize. It wouldn't hurt to have a small problem for Pisces to help you overcome. It might help if you cry on his shoulder, for this sign needs to be needed. Use your imagination when setting the scene for love. A dramatic setting brings out Pisces theatrical talents. Or creatively use the element of water. Rain on the roof, waterfalls, showers, beach houses, water beds, and Jacuzzis could turn up the heat. Experiment with pulsating jets of water. Take midnight skinny-dips in deserted pools.

The Pisces erogenous zone is the feet. This is your cue to give a sensuous foot massage using scented lotions. Let him paint your toes. Beautiful toenails in sexy sandals are a special turn-on.

Your Hottest Love Match

Here's a tip for finding your hottest love match. If your lover's Mars sign makes favorable aspects to your Venus, is in the same element (earth, air, fire, water), or is in the same sign, your lover will do what you want done! Mars influences how we act when we make love, while Venus shows what we like done to us. Sometimes fighting and making up is the sexiest fun of all. If you're the type who needs a spark to keep lust alive (you know who you are!), then look for Mars and Venus in different signs of the same quality (fixed or cardinal or mutable). For instance, a fixed sign (Taurus, Leo, Scorpio, Aquarius) paired with another fixed sign can have a sexy tug-of-war before you finally surrender. Two cardinal signs (Aries, Cancer, Libra, Capricorn) set off passionate fireworks when they clash. Mutable signs (Gemini, Virgo, Sagittarius, Pisces) play a fascinating game of cat and mouse, never quite catching each other.

Your Most Seductive Time

The best time for love is when Venus is in your sign, making you the most desirable sign in the zodiac. This only lasts about three weeks (unless Venus is retrograde) so don't waste time! And find out the time this year when Venus is in your sign by consulting the Venus chart at the end of chapter 5.

What's the Sexiest Sign?

It depends on what sign you are. Astrology has traditionally given this honor to Scorpio, the sign associated with the sex organs. However, we are all a combination of different signs (and turn-ons). Gemini's communicating ability and manual dexterity could deliver the magic touch. Cancer's tenderness and understanding could bring out your passion more than regal Leo.

Which Is the Most Faithful Sign?

The earth signs of Capricorn, Taurus, and Virgo are usually the most faithful. They tend to be more home- and family-oriented, and they are usually choosy about their mates. It's impractical, inconvenient, and probably expensive to play around, or so they think.

Who'll Play Around?

The mutable signs of Gemini, Pisces, and Sagittarius win the playboy or playgirl sweepstakes. These signs tend to be changeable, fickle, and easily bored. But they're so much fun!

CHAPTER 12

Financial Tips from the Stars

Getting the most bang from our buck will be our personal challenge this year, as we continue to learn to live within our means and balance our budgets. One of the advantages of astrology is that we can know the natural direction of the cosmic forces in advance and make financial plans accordingly.

Over the past few years, we've experienced a dramatic shift from the expansive risk taking of Pluto in Sagittarius to the conservative, thrift-promoting Pluto in Capricorn. This influence should continue for several years. Financially savvy astrologers also look to the movement of Jupiter, the planet of luck and expansion, for growth opportunities. Jupiter gives an extra boost to the sign it is passing through. Jupiter moves through Pisces, a sign that Jupiter especially favors, so Pisces and fellow water signs, Cancer and Scorpio, receive extra-lucky rays. Most of us could benefit from using some Pisces-inspired creativity, insight, and imagination especially in the area of our horoscope where Jupiter will be giving us growth opportunities. Pisces will give us the imaginative ideas; then Jupiter enters Aries briefly over the summer and for a lengthy stay next year, which should give us the courage and pioneering spirit to pursue them.

Aries

You've got a taste for fast money, quick turnover, and edgy investments, with no patience for gradual, long-term gains.

You're an impulse buyer with the nerve for risky tactics that could backfire. On the other hand, you're a pioneer who can see into the future, who dares to take a gamble on a new idea or product that could change the world ... like Sam Walton of the Wal-Mart stores, who changed the way we shop. You need a backup plan in case one of your big ideas burns out. To protect your money, get a backup plan you can follow without thinking about it. Have a percentage of your income automatically put into a savings or retirement account. Then give yourself some extra funds to play with. Your weak point is your impatience; so you're not one to wait out a slow market or watch savings slowly accumulate. When Jupiter moves into Aries temporarily this summer, you'll want to move full steam ahead. However, you may have to reevaluate your goals in the fall. Save your big moves for next year, when Jupiter reenters Aries and you can make real progress.

Taurus

You're a saver who loves to see your cash, as well as your possessions, accumulate. You have no qualms about steadily increasing your fortune. You're a savvy trader and a shrewd investor, in there for long-term gains. You have low toleration for risk; you hate to lose anything. But you do enjoy luxuries, and may need to reward yourself frequently. You might pass up an opportunity because it seems too risky, but you should take a chance once in a while. Since you're inspired by Jupiter in Pisces and Aries this year, it's time to support your long-range goals and ideals by exploring socially conscious investments, especially in the clean-energy field and the creative arts. You're especially lucky in real estate or any occupation that requires appraising and trading, as well as earth-centered businesses like organic farming and conservation.

Gemini

With Gemini, the cash can flow in and then out just as quickly. You naturally multi-task, and you are sure to have several projects going at once, as well as several credit cards, which can easily get out of hand. Saving is not one of your strong points—too boring. You fall in and out of love with different ideas; you have probably tried a round of savings techniques. Diversification is your best strategy. Have several different kinds of investments—at least one should be a long-term plan. Set savings goals and then regularly deposit small amounts into your accounts. Follow the lead of Gemini financial adviser Suze Orman and get a good relationship going with your money! With lucky Jupiter accenting your public image, there should be new career opportunities this year. Investigate careers in communications and the media.

Cancer

You can be a natural moneymaker with your peerless intuition. You can spot a winner that everyone else misses. Consider Cancer success stories like those of cosmetics queen Estee Lauder and Roxanne Quimby, of Burt's Bees, who turned her friend's stash of beeswax into a thriving cosmetics business. Who knew? So trust your intuition. You are a saver who always has a backup plan, just in case. Remember to treat and nurture yourself as well as others. Investments in the food industry, restaurants, hotels, shipping, and water-related industries are Cancer territory. You're one of the luckiest signs this year, so keep your antennae tuned for new investment opportunities.

Leo

You love the first-class lifestyle, but may not always have the resources to support it. Finding a way to fund your extravagant tastes is the Leo challenge. Some courses in money management or an expert financial coach could set you on the right track. However, you're also a terrific salesperson, and you're fabulous in high-profile jobs that pay a lot. You're the community tastemaker; you satisfy your appetite for "the best" by working for a quality company that sells luxury goods, splendid real estate, dream vacations, and first-class travel—that way you'll have access to the lifestyle without having to pay for it. This year, Jupiter brings luck through fortunate partnerships and travel.

Virgo

Your sign is a stickler for details, which includes your money management. You like to follow your spending and saving closely; you enjoy planning, budgeting, and price comparison. Your sign usually has no problem sticking to a savings or investment plan. You have a critical eye for quality, and you like to bargain and to shop to get the best value. In fact, Warren Buffet, a Virgo billionaire, is known for value investing. You buy cheap and sell at a profit. Investing in health care, organic products, and food could be profitable for you. With Jupiter in Pisces accenting partnerships, you might want to team up for investing purposes this year.

Libra

Oh, do you ever love to shop! And you often have an irresistible urge to acquire an exquisite object or a designer dress you can't really afford or to splurge on the perfect antique armoire. You don't like to settle for second-rate or bargain

buys. Learning to prioritize your spending is especially difficult for your sign, so try to find a good money manager to do
it for you. Following a strictly balanced budget is your key to
financial success. With Libra's keen eye for quality and good
taste, you are a savvy picker at auctions and antiques fairs, so
you might be able to turn around your purchase for a profit.
With Jupiter accenting the care and maintenance part of your
life, this is an excellent year to put your finances in order and
balance the budget.

Scorpio

Scorpios prefer to stay in control of their finances at all times.
You're sure to have a financial-tracking program on your computer. You're not an impulse-buyer, unless you see something
that immediately turns you on. Rely on your instincts! Scorpio
is the sign of credit cards, taxes, and loans, so you are able
to use these tools cleverly. Investing for Scorpio is rarely casual. You'll do extensive research and track your investments
by reading the financial pages, annual reports, and profit-loss
statements. Investigate the arts, media, and oil and water projects for Jupiter-favored investments this year.

Sagittarius

Sagittarius is a natural gambler, with a high tolerance for risk.
It's important for you to learn when to hold 'em, and when
to fold 'em, as the song goes, by setting limits on your risk
taking and covering your assets. You enjoy the thrill of playing the stock market, where you could win big and lose big.
Money itself is rarely the object for Sagittarius—it's the game
that counts. Since your sign rarely saves for a rainy day, your
best strategy might be a savings plan that transfers a certain
amount into a savings account. Regular bill-paying plans are
another strategy to keep you on track. Jupiter favors invest-

ing in home improvements and family-related businesses this year.

Capricorn

You're one of the strongest money managers in the zodiac, which should serve you well this year when Jupiter, the planet of luck and expansion, is blessing your house of finance. You're a born bargain hunter and clever negotiator—a saver rather than a spender. You are the sign of self-discipline, which works well when it comes to sticking with a budget and living frugally while waiting for resources to accumulate. You are likely to plan carefully for your elder years, profiting from long-term investments. You have a keen sense of value, and you will pick up a bargain and then turn it around at a nice profit. Jupiter favors the communications industry and opportunities in your local area this year.

Aquarius

There should be many chances to speculate on forward-looking ventures this year. The Aquarius trait of unpredictability extends to your financial life, where you surprise us all with your ability to turn something totally unique into a money spinner. Consider your wealthy sign mates Oprah Winfrey and Michael Bloomberg, who have been able to intuit what the public will buy at a given moment. Some of your ideas might sound far-out, but they turn out to be right on the money. Investing in high-tech companies that are on the cutting edge of their field is good for Aquarius. You'll probably intuit which ones will stay the course. You'll feel good about investing in companies that improve the environment, such as new types of fuel, or ones that are related to your favorite cause.

Pisces

Luck is with you this year! The typical Pisces is probably the sign least interested in money management. However, there are many billionaires born under your sign, such as Michael Dell, David Geffen, and Steve Jobs. Generally they have made money from innovative ideas and left the details to others. That might work for you. Find a Scorpio, Capricorn, or Virgo to help you set a profitable course and systematically save (which is not in your nature). Sign up for automatic bill paying so you won't have to think about it. If you keep in mind how much less stressful life will be and how much more you can do when you're not worried about paying bills, you might be motivated enough to stick to a sensible budget. Investment-wise, consider anything to do with water—off-shore drilling, water conservation and purifying, shipping, and seafood. Petroleum is also ruled by your sign, as are institutions related to hospitals.

CHAPTER 13

Children of 2010

Parents of several children may see a marked difference between children born in 2010 and those born more than two years ago, because the cosmic atmosphere has changed, which should imprint the personalities of this year's children.

Astrologers look to the slow-moving outer planets—Uranus, Neptune, and Pluto—to describe a generation. When an outer planet changes signs, this indicates a significant shift in energy, which is the case in 2010. In the first half of the year, Uranus and Jupiter in Pisces continue the visionary and creative influence of that sign, which will be reflected in the children born then. However, Uranus moves briefly into fiery Aries in June, which will be accompanied by Jupiter, the planet of expansion, indicating a very astrologically active summer of 2010. Children born during the warm months will reflect this with more drive and energy. After Uranus retrogrades back into Pisces in mid-August for the remainder of the year, the atmosphere becomes somewhat calmer. Neptune still passing through Aquarius and Pluto in Capricorn should add vision and practicality to the personality of this year's children. This generation will be focused on saving the planet and on making things work in order to clear the path for the future. Saturn in Libra will enter the mixture, teaching them diplomacy in getting along with others.

Astrology can be an especially helpful tool when used to design an environment that enhances and encourages each child's positive qualities. Some parents start before conception, planning the birth of their child as far as possible to harmonize with the signs of other family members. However, each baby has its own schedule, so if yours arrives a week early or late, or elects a different sign than you'd planned, recognize that the new sign may be more in line with the mission your child is here to accomplish. In other words, if you were hoping for a Libra child and he arrives during Virgo, that Virgo energy may be just what is needed to stimulate or complement your family. Remember that there are many astrological elements besides the sun sign that indicate strong family ties. Usually each child will share a particular planetary placement, an emphasis on a particular sign or house, or a certain chart configuration with his parents and other family members. Often there is a significant planetary angle that will define the parent-child relationship, such as family sun signs that form a T-square or a triangle.

One important thing you can do is to be sure the exact moment of birth is recorded. This will be essential in calculating an accurate astrological chart. The following descriptions can be applied to the sun or moon sign (if known) of a child—the sun sign will describe basic personality and the moon sign indicates the child's emotional needs.

The Aries Child

Baby Aries is quite a handful. This energetic child will walk—and run—as soon as possible, and perform daring feats of exploration. Caregivers should be vigilant. Little Aries seems to know no fear (and is especially vulnerable to head injuries). Many Aries children, in their rush to get on with life, seem hyperactive, and they are easily frustrated when they can't get their own way. Violent temper tantrums and dramatic physical displays are par for the course with this child, requiring a time-out mat or naughty chair.

The very young Aries should be monitored carefully, since he is prone to take risks and may injure himself. Aries love to take things apart and may break toys easily, but with encouragement, the child will develop formidable coordination. Aries's bossy tendencies should be molded into leadership qualities, rather than bullying, which should be easy to do with this year's babies. Encourage these children to take out aggressions and frustrations in active, competitive sports, where they usually excel. When young Aries learns to focus energies long enough to master a subject and learns consideration for others, the indomitable Aries spirit will rise to the head of the class.

Aries born in 2010 will be a more subdued version of this sign, but still loaded with energy. The Capricorn effect should make little Aries easier to discipline and more focused on achievement. A natural leader!

The Taurus Child

This is a cuddly, affectionate child who eagerly explores the world of the senses, especially the senses of taste and touch. The Taurus child can be a big eater and will put on weight easily if not encouraged to exercise. Since this child likes comfort and gravitates to beauty, try coaxing little Taurus to exercise to music, or take him or her out of doors, with hikes or long walks. Though Taurus may be a slow learner, this sign has an excellent retentive memory and generally masters a subject thoroughly. Taurus is interested in results and will see each project patiently through to completion, continuing long after others have given up. This year's earth sign planets will give him a wonderful sense of support and accomplishment.

Choose Taurus toys carefully to help develop innate talents. Construction toys, such as blocks or erector sets, appeal to their love of building. Paints or crayons develop their sense of color. Many Taurus have musical talent and love to sing, which is apparent at a young age.

This year's Taurus will want a pet or two, and a few plants of his own. Give little Taurus a small garden, and watch the natural green thumb develop. This child has a strong sense of acquisition and an early grasp of material value. After filling a piggy bank, Taurus graduates to a savings account, before other children have started to learn the value of money.

Little Taurus gets a bonanza of good luck from Jupiter in compatible Pisces, supported by Pluto in Capricorn and Saturn retrograding back into Virgo, a compatible earth sign. These should give little Taurus an especially easygoing disposition and provide many opportunities to live up to his sign's potential.

The Gemini Child

Little Gemini will talk as soon as possible, filling the air with questions and chatter. This is a friendly child who enjoys social contact, seems to require company, and adapts quickly to different surroundings. Geminis have quick minds that easily grasp the use of words, books, and telephones, and will probably learn to talk and read at an earlier age than most. Though they are fast learners, Gemini may have a short attention span, darting from subject to subject. Projects and games that help focus the mind could be used to help them concentrate. Musical instruments, typewriters, and computers help older Gemini children combine mental with manual dexterity. Geminis should be encouraged to finish what they start before they go on to another project. Otherwise, they can become jack-of-all-trade types who have trouble completing anything they do. Their disposition is usually cheerful and witty, making these children popular with their peers and delightful company at home.

This year's Gemini baby is impulsive and full of energy, with a strong Aries influence in his life. He will be highly independent and original, a go-getter. When he grows up, Gemini may change jobs several times before he finds a position that satisfies his need for stimulation and variety.

The Cancer Child

This emotional, sensitive child is especially influenced by patterns set in early life. Young Cancers cling to their first memories as well as their childhood possessions. They thrive in calm emotional waters, with a loving, protective mother, and usually remain close to her (even if their relationship with her was difficult) throughout their lives. Divorce and death—anything that disturbs the safe family unit—are devastating to Cancers, who may need extra support and reassurance during a family crisis.

They sometimes need a firm hand to push the positive, creative side of their personality and discourage them from getting swept away by emotional moods or resorting to emotional manipulation to get their way. If this child is praised and encouraged to find creative expression, Cancers will be able to express their positive side consistently, on a firm, secure foundation.

This year's Cancer baby may run against type, thanks to a meeting of Jupiter and Uranus in hyperactive Aries, which might make him much more outgoing and energetic than usual. He should have natural leadership tendencies, which should be encouraged, and the parents' challenge will be to find positive outlets for his energy.

The Leo Child

Leo children love the limelight and will plot to get the lion's share of attention. These children assert themselves with flair and drama, and can behave like tiny tyrants to get their way. But in general, they have a sunny, positive disposition and are rarely subject to blue moods.

At school, they're the types voted most popular, head cheerleader, or homecoming queen. Leo is sure to be noticed for personality, if not for stunning looks or academic work; the homely Leo will be a class clown, and the unhappy Leo can be the class bully.

Above all, a Leo child cannot tolerate being ignored for long. Drama or performing-arts classes, sports, and school politics are healthy ways for Leo to be a star. But Leos must learn to take lesser roles occasionally, or they will have some painful putdowns in store. Usually, their popularity is well earned; they are hard workers who try to measure up to their own high standards—and usually succeed.

This year's Leo should be a highly active version of the sign, with Saturn in Libra teaching lessons of balance and diplomacy in relationships, while Jupiter and Uranus in Aries amp up the energy level and Pluto in Capricorn demands focus and results. Good use of this energy could produce pioneers, fearless natural leaders who could change the world for the better.

The Virgo Child

The young Virgo can be a quiet, rather serious child, with a quick, intelligent mind. Early on, little Virgo shows far more attention to detail and concern with small things than other children. Little Virgo has a built-in sense of order and a fascination with how things work. It is important for these children to have a place of their own, which they can order as they wish and where they can read or busy themselves with crafts and hobbies. This child's personality can be very sensitive. Little Virgo may get hyper and overreact to seemingly small irritations, which can take the form of stomach upsets or delicate digestive systems. But this child will flourish where there is mental stimulation and a sense of order. Virgos thrive in school, especially in writing or language skills, and they seem truly happy when buried in books. Chances are, young Virgo will learn to read ahead of classmates. Hobbies that involve detail work or that develop fine craftsmanship are especially suited to young Virgos.

Baby Virgo of 2010 is likely to be an early talker, and will show concern for the welfare of others. This child should be a natural communicator and may show an interest in the arts or the legal profession.

The Libra Child

The Libra child learns early about the power of charm and appearance. This is often a very physically appealing child with an enchanting dimpled smile, who is naturally sociable and enjoys the company of both children and adults. It is a rare Libra child who is a discipline problem, but when their behavior is unacceptable, they respond better to calm discussion than displays of emotion, especially if the discussion revolves around fairness. Because young Libras without a strong direction tend to drift with the mood of the group, these children should be encouraged to develop their unique talents and powers of discrimination, so they can later stand on their own.

In school, this child is usually popular and will often have to choose between social invitations and studies. In the teen years, social pressures mount as the young Libra begins to look for a partner. This is the sign of best friends, so Libra's choice of companions can have a strong effect on his future direction. Beautiful Libra girls may be tempted to go steady or have an unwise early marriage. Chances are, both sexes will fall in and out of love several times in their search for the ideal partner.

Little Libra of 2010 is an especially creative, expressive child, who may have strong artistic talents. This child is endowed with much imagination, as well as social skills.

The Scorpio Child

The Scorpio child may seem quiet and shy, but will surprise others with intense feelings and formidable willpower. Scorpio children are single-minded when they want something and intensely passionate about whatever they do. One of a caregiver's tasks is to teach this child to balance activities and emotions, yet at the same time to make the most of his great concentration and intense commitment.

Since young Scorpios do not show their depth of feelings easily, parents will have to learn to read almost imperceptible signs that troubles are brewing beneath the surface. Both Scorpio boys and girls enjoy games of power and control on or off the playground. Scorpio girls may take an early interest in the opposite sex, masquerading as tomboys, while Scorpio boys may be intensely competitive and loners. When her powerful energies are directed into work, sports, or challenging studies, Scorpio is a superachiever, focused on a goal. With trusted friends, young Scorpio is devoted and caring—the proverbial friend through thick and thin, loyal for life.

Scorpio 2010 has a strong emphasis on achievement and success. Uranus and lucky Jupiter in Pisces in their house of creativity should put them on the cutting edge of whichever field they choose.

The Sagittarius Child

This restless, athletic child will be out of the playpen and off on explorative adventures as soon as possible. Little Sagittarius is remarkably well-coordinated, attempting daredevil feats on any wheeled vehicle from scooters to skateboards. These natural athletes need little encouragement to channel their energies into sports. Their cheerful friendly dispositions earn them popularity in school, and once they have found a subject where their talent and imagination can soar, they will do well academically. They love animals, especially horses, and will be sure to have a pet or two, if not a home zoo. When they are old enough to take care of themselves, they'll clamor to be off on adventures of their own, away from home, if possible.

This is a child who loves to travel, who will not get homesick at summer camp, and who may sign up to be a foreign-exchange student or spend summers abroad. Outdoor adventure appeals to little Sagittarius, especially if it involves an active sport, such as skiing, cycling or mountain climbing. Give them enough space and encouragement, and their fiery spirit will propel them to achieve high goals.

Baby Sagittarius of 2010 has a natural generosity of spirit and an optimistic, social nature. Home and family will be especially important to him, though he may have an unconventional family life. He'll have an ability to look past the surface of things to seek out what has lasting value.

The Capricorn Child

These purposeful, goal-oriented children will work to capacity if they feel this will bring results. They're not ones who enjoy work for its own sake—there must be a goal in sight. Authority figures can do much to motivate these children, but once set on an upward path, young Capricorn will mobilize his energy and talent and work harder, and with more perseverance, than any other sign. Capricorn has built-in self-discipline that can achieve remarkable results, even if lacking the flashy personality, quick brainpower, or penetrating insight of others. Once involved, young Capricorn will stick to a task until it is mastered. This child also knows how to use others to his advantage and may well become the team captain or class president.

A wise parent will set realistic goals for the Capricorn child, paving the way for the early thrill of achievement. Youngsters should be encouraged to express their caring, feeling side to others, as well as their natural aptitude for leadership. Capricorn children may be especially fond of grandparents and older relatives, and will enjoy spending time with them and learning from them. It is not uncommon for young Capricorns to have an older mentor or teacher who guides them. With their great respect for authority, Capricorn children will take this influence very much to heart.

The Capricorn born in 2010 should be a good talker, with sharp mental abilities. He is likely to be social and outgoing, with lots of friends and closeness to brothers and sisters.

The Aquarius Child

The Aquarius child has a well-focused, innovative mind that often streaks so far ahead of peers that this child seems like an oddball. Routine studies never hold the restless youngster for long; he or she will look for another, more experimental place to try out his ideas and develop his inventions. Life is a laboratory to the inquiring Aquarius mind. School politics, sports, science, and the arts offer scope for their talents. But if there is no room for expression within approved social limits, Aquarius is sure to rebel. Questioning institutions and religions comes naturally, so these children may find an outlet elsewhere, becoming rebels with a cause. It is better not to force these children to conform, but rather to channel forward-thinking young minds into constructive group activities.

This year's Aquarius will have special financial talent. Luck and talent are his and fame could be in the stars!

The Pisces Child

Give young Pisces praise, applause, and a gentle, but firm, push in the right direction. Lovable Pisces children may be abundantly talented, but may be hesitant to express themselves, because they are quite sensitive and easily hurt. It is a parent's challenge to help them gain self-esteem and self-confidence. However, this same sensitivity makes them trusted friends who'll have many confidants as they develop socially. It also endows many Pisces with spectacular creative talent.

Pisces adores drama and theatrics of all sorts; therefore, encourage them to channel their creativity into art forms rather than indulging in emotional dramas. Understand that they may need more solitude than other children may as they develop their creative ideas. But though daydreaming can be creative, it is important that these natural dreamers not dwell too long in the world of fantasy. Teach them practical coping skills for the real world.

Since Pisces are sensitive physically, parents should help them build strong bodies with proper diet and regular exercise. Young Pisces may gravitate to more individual sports, such as swimming, sailing, and skiing, rather than to team sports. Or they may prefer more artistic physical activities, like dance or ice-skating.

Born givers, these children are often drawn to the underdog (they quickly fall for sob stories) and attract those who might take advantage of their empathic nature. Teach them to choose friends wisely, to set boundaries in relationships, and to protect their emotional vulnerability—invaluable lessons in later life.

With the planet Uranus now in Pisces along with lucky Jupiter, the 2010 baby belongs to a generation of Pisces movers and shakers. This child may have a rebellious streak that rattles the status quo. But this generation also has a visionary nature, which will be much concerned with the welfare of the world at large.

CHAPTER 14

Give the Perfect Gift to Every Sign

So often we're in a quandary about what to give a loved one, someone who has everything, that hard-to-please friend, or a fascinating new person in your life, or about the right present for a wedding, birthday, or hostess gift. Why not let astrology help you make the perfect choice by appealing to each sun sign's personality. When you're giving a gift, you're also making a memory, so it should be a special occasion. The gift that's most appreciated is one that touches the heart, reminds you both of a shared experience, or shows that the giver has really cared enough to consider the recipient's personality.

In general, the water signs (Cancer, Pisces, Scorpio) enjoy romantic, sentimental, and imaginative gifts given in a very personal way. Write your loved one a poem or a song to express your feelings. Assemble an album of photos or mementos of all the good times you've shared. Appeal to their sense of fantasy. Scorpio Richard Burton had the right idea when he gave Pisces Elizabeth Taylor a diamond bracelet hidden in lavender roses (her favorite color).

Fire signs (Aries, Leo, Sagittarius) appreciate a gift presented with lots of flair. Pull out the drama, like the actor who dazzled his Aries sweetheart by presenting her with trash cans overflowing with daisies.

Air signs (Gemini, Libra, Aquarius) love to be surprised with unusual gifts. The Duke of Windsor gave his elegant Gemini duchess, Wallis Windsor, fabulous jewels engraved with love notes and secret messages in their own special code.

Earth signs (Taurus, Virgo, Capricorn) value solid, tangible gifts or ones that appeal to all the senses. Delicious gourmet treats, scented body lotions, the newest CDs, the gift of a massage, or stocks and bonds are sure winners! Capricorn Elvis Presley once received a gold-plated piano from his wife.

Here are some specific ideas for each sign:

Aries

These are the trendsetters of the zodiac, who appreciate the latest thing! For Aries, it's the excitement that counts, so present your gift in a way that will knock their socks off. Aries is associated with the head, so a jaunty hat, hair ornaments, chandelier earrings, sunglasses, and hair-taming devices are good possibilities. Aries love games of any kind that offer a real challenge, like war video games, military themes, or rousing music with a beat. Anything red is a good bet: red flowers, red gems, and red accessories. How about giving Aries a way to let off steam with a gym membership or aerobic-dancing classes? Monogram a robe with a nickname in red.

Taurus

These are touchy-feely people who love things that appeal to all their senses. Find something that sounds, tastes, smells, feels, or looks good. And don't stint on quality or comfort. Taurus know the value of everything and will be aware of the price tag. Taurus foodies will appreciate chef-worthy kitchen gadgets, the latest cookbook, and gourmet treats. Taurus is a great collector. Find out what their passion is and present them with a rare item or a beautiful storage container such as an antique jewelry box. Green-thumb Taurus would love some special plants or flowers, garden tools, beautiful plant containers. Appeal to their sense of touch with fine fabrics—high-thread-count sheets, cashmere, satin, and mohair. One of the animal-loving signs, Taurus might appreciate a retractable leash or soft bed for the dog or cat. Get them a fine wallet or checkbook cover. They'll use it often.

Gemini

Mercury-ruled Gemini appreciates gifts that appeal to their mind. The latest book or novel, a talked-about film, a CD from a hot new singer, or a high-tech gadget might appeal. A beautiful diary or a tape recorder would record their adventures. Since Geminis often do two things at once, a telephone gadget that leaves their hands free would be appreciated. In fact, a new telephone device or superphone would appeal to these great communicators. Gloves, rings, and bracelets accent their expressive hands. Clothes from an interesting new designer appeal to their sense of style. You might try giving Gemini a variety of little gifts in a beautiful box or a Christmas stocking. A tranquil massage at a local spa would calm Gemini's sensitive nerves. Find an interesting way to wrap your gift. Nothing boring, please!

Cancer

Cancer is associated with home and family, so anything to do with food, entertaining at home, and family life is a good bet. Beautiful dishes or serving platters, silver items, fine crystal and linen, gourmet cookware, cooking classes or the latest DVD from a cooking teacher might be appreciated. Cancer designers Vera Wang and Giorgio Armani have perfected the Cancer style and have many home products available, as well as their elegant designer clothing. Naturally, anything to do with the sea is a possibility: pearls, coral, or shell jewelry. Boat and water-sports equipment might work. Consider cruise wear for traveling Cancers. Sentimental Cancer loves antiques and silver frames for family photos. Cancer people are often good photographers, so consider frames, albums, and projectors to showcase their work. Present your gift in a personal way with a special note.

Leo

Think big with Leo and appeal to this sign's sense of drama. Go for the gold (Leo's color) with gold jewelry, designer clothing, or big attention-getting accessories. Follow their signature style, which could be superelegant, like Jacqueline Onassis, or superstar, like Madonna or Jennifer Lopez. This sign is always ready for the red carpet and stays beautifully groomed, so stay within these guidelines when choosing your gift. Feline motifs and animal prints are usually a hit. The latest grooming aids, high-ticket cosmetics, and mirrors reflect their best image. Beautiful hairbrushes tame their manes. Think champagne, high-thread-count linens, and luxurious loungewear or lingerie. Make Leo feel special with a custom portrait or photo shoot with your local star photographer. Be sure to go for spectacular wrapping, with beautiful paper and ribbons. Present your gift with a flourish!

Virgo

Virgo usually has a special subject of interest and would appreciate relevant books, films, lectures, or classes. Choose health-oriented things: gifts to do with fitness and self-improvement. Virgo enjoys brainteasers, crossword puzzles, computer programs, organizers, and digital planners. Fluffy robes, bath products, and special soaps appeal to Virgo's sense of cleanliness. Virgo loves examples of good, practical design: efficient telephones, beautiful briefcases, computer cases, desk accessories. Choose natural fibers and quiet colors when choosing clothes for Virgo. Virgo has high standards, so go for quality when choosing a gift.

Libra

Whatever you give this romantic sign, go for beauty and romance. Libra loves accessories, decorative objects, whatever makes him or his surroundings more aesthetically pleasing. Beautiful flowers in pastel colors are always welcome. Libras are great hosts and hostesses, who might appreciate a gift related to fine dining: serving pieces, linens, glassware, flower vases. Evening or party clothes please since Libra has a gadabout social life. Interesting books, objets d'art, memberships to museums, and tickets to cultural events are good ideas. Fashion or home-decorating magazine subscriptions usually please Libra women. Steer away from anything loud, garish, or extreme. Think pink, one of their special colors, when giving Libra jewelry, clothing, or accessories. It's a very romantic sign, so be sure to remember birthdays, holidays, and anniversaries with a token of affection.

Scorpio

Scorpios love mystery, so bear that in mind when you buy these folks a present. You could take this literally and buy them a good thriller DVD, novel, or video game. Scorpios are power players, so a book about one of their sign might please. Bill Gates, Jack Welch, Condoleezza Rice, and Hillary Clinton are hot Scorpio subjects. Scorpios love black leather, suede, fur, anything to do with the sea, power tools, tiny spy tape recorders, and items with secret compartments or intricate locks. When buying a handbag for Scorpio, go for simple shapes with lots of interior pockets. Sensuous Scorpios appreciate hot lingerie, sexy linens, body lotions, and perfumed candles. Black is the favored color for Scorpio clothing—go for sexy textures like cashmere and satin in simple shapes by designers like Calvin Klein. This sign is fascinated with the occult, so give them an astrology or tarot-card reading, beautiful crystals, or an astrology program for the computer.

Sagittarius

For these outdoor people, consider adventure trips, designer sportswear, gear for their favorite sports. A funny gift or something for their pets pleases Sagittarius. For clothing and accessories, the fashionista of this sign tends to like bright colors and dramatic innovative styles. Otherwise, casual sportswear is a good idea. These travelers usually have a favorite getaway place; give them a travel guide, DVD, novel, or history book that would make their trip more interesting. Luggage is also a good bet. Sleek carry-ons, travel wallets, ticket holders, business-card cases, and wheeled computer bags might please these wanderers. Anything that makes travel more comfortable and pleasant is good for Sagittarius, including a good book to read en route. This sign is the great gambler of the zodiac, so gifts related to their favorite gambling venue would be appreciated.

Capricorn

For this quality-conscious sign, go for a status label from the best store in town. Get Capricorns something good for their image and career. They could be fond of things Spanish, like flamenco or tango music, or of country-and-western music and motifs. In the bookstore, go for biographies of the rich and famous, or advice books to help Capricorn get to the top. Capricorns take their gifts seriously, so steer away from anything too frivolous. Garnet, onyx, or malachite jewelry, Carolina Herrera fragrance and clothing, and beautiful briefcases and wallets are good ideas. Glamorous status tote bags carry business gear in style. Capricorns like golf, tennis, and sports that involve climbing, cycling, or hiking, so presents could be geared to their outdoor interests. Elegant evening accessories would be fine for this sign, which often entertains for business.

Aquarius

Give Aquarius a surprise gift. This sign is never impressed with things that are too predictable. So use your imagination to present the gift in an unusual way or at an unexpected time. With Aquarius, originality counts. When in doubt, give them something to think about, a new electronic gadget, perhaps a small robot, or an advanced computer game. Or something New Age, like an amethyst-crystal cluster. Aquarius like innovative materials with a space-age look. They are the ones with the wraparound glasses, the titanium computer cases. This air sign loves to fly—an airplane ticket always pleases. Books should be on innovative subjects, politics, or adventures of the mind. Aquarius goes for unusual color combinations—especially electric blue or hot pink—and abstract patterns. They like the newest, coolest looks on the cutting edge of fashion and are not afraid to experiment. Think of Paris Hilton's constantly changing looks. Look for an Aquarius gift in an out-of-the-way boutique or local hipster hangout. They'd be touched if you find out Aquarius's special worthy cause and make a donation. Spirit them off to hear their favorite guru.

Pisces

Pisces respond to gifts that have a touch of fantasy, magic, and romance. Look for mystical gifts with a touch of the occult. Romantic music (a customized CD of favorite love songs) and love stories appeal to Pisces sentimentalists. Pisces is associated with perfume and fragrant oils, so help this sign indulge with their favorite scent in many forms. Anything to do with the ocean, fish, and water sports appeals to Pisces. How about a whirlpool, a water-therapy spa treatment, or a sea salt rub. Appeal to this sign with treats for the feet: foot massages, pedicures, ballet tickets, and dance lessons. Cashmere socks and metallic evening sandals are other Pisces pleasers. A romantic dinner overlooking the water is Pisces paradise. A case of fine wine or another favorite liquid is always appreciated. Write a love poem and enclose it with your gift.

CHAPTER 15

Your Pet-Scope for 2010: How to Choose Your Best Friend for Life

With Jupiter, the planet of luck and expansion, in compassionate Pisces, this is a great time to bring joy into your life by adopting an animal friend. At this writing, 63 percent of all American households have at least one pet, according to a recent survey by the American Pet Product Manufacturers Association. And we spend billions of dollars on the care and feeding of our beloved pets. Our pets are counted as part of the family, often sharing our beds and accompanying us on trips.

Whether you choose to adopt an animal from a local shelter or buy a Thoroughbred from a breeder, try for an optimal time of adoption and sun sign of your new friend. If you're rescuing an animal, however, it's difficult to know the sun sign of the animal, but you can adopt on a day when the moon is compatible with yours, which should bless the emotional relationship. Using the moon signs listed in the daily forecasts in this book, choose a day when the moon is in your sign, a sign of the same element, or a compatible element. This means fire and air signs should go for a day when the moon is in fire signs Aries, Leo, Sagittarius or air signs Gemini, Libra, or Aquarius. Water and earth signs should choose a day when the moon is in water signs Cancer, Scorpio, or Pisces or earth signs Taurus, Virgo, or Capricorn. If possible, aim for a new moon, good for beginning a new relationship.

Here are some sign-specific tips for adopting an animal that will be your best friend for life.

Aries: The Rescuer

Aries gets special pleasure from rescuing animals in distress and rehabbing them, so do check your local shelters if you're thinking of adopting an animal. As an active fire sign, you'd be happiest with a lively animal that can accompany you, and you might do well with a rescue animal such as a German shepherd or Labrador retriever. You'd also enjoy training such an animal. Otherwise look for intelligence, alertness, playfulness and obedience in your friend. Since Aries tend to have an active life, look for a sleek, low maintenance coat on your dog or cat. Cat lovers would enjoy the more active breeds such as the Siamese or Abyssinian.

An Aries sun-sign dog or cat would be ideal. Aries animals have a brave, energetic, rather combative nature. They can be mischievous, so the kittens and puppies should be monitored for safety. They'll dare to jump higher, run faster, and chase more animals than their peers. They may require stronger words and more obedience training than other signs. Give them plenty of toys and play active games with them often.

Taurus: The Toucher

Taurus is a touchy-feely sign, and this extends to your animal relationships. Look for a dog or cat that enjoys being petted and groomed, is affectionate, and adapts well to family life. As one of the great animal-loving signs, Taurus is likely to have several pets, so it is important that they all get along together. Give each one its own special safe space to minimize turf wars.

Taurus animals are calm and even tempered, but do not like being teased and could retaliate, so be sure to instruct children in the proper way to handle and play with their pet. Since this sign has strong appetites and tends to put on weight easily, be careful not to overindulge them in caloric treats and table snacks. Sticking to a regular feeding schedule could help eliminate between-meal snacking.

Taurus female animals are excellent mothers and make good breeders. They tend to be clean and less destructive of home furnishings than other animals.

Gemini: The Companion

A bright, quick-witted sign like yours requires an equally interesting and communicative pet. Choose a social animal that adapts well to different environments, since you may travel or have homes in different locations.

Gemini animals can put up with noise, telephones, music, and different people coming and going. They'll want to be part of the action, so place a pillow or roost in a public place. They do not like being left alone, however, so, if you will be away for long periods, find them an animal companion to play with. You might consider adopting two Gemini pets from the same litter.

Animals born under this sign are easy to teach and some enjoy doing tricks or retrieving. They may be more vocal than other animals, especially if they are confined without companionship.

Cancer: The Nurturer

Cancer enjoys a devoted, obedient animal who demonstrates loyalty to its master. An affectionate, home-loving dog or cat who welcomes you and sits on your lap would be ideal. The emotional connection with your pet is most important; therefore, you may depend on your powerful psychic powers when choosing an animal. Wait until you feel that strong bond of psychic communication between you both. The moon sign of the day you adopt is very important for moon-ruled Cancer, so choose a water sign, if possible.

Cancer animals need a feeling of security; they don't like changes of environment or too much chaos at home. If you intend to breed your animal, the Cancer pet makes a wonderful and fertile mother.

Leo: The Prideful Owner

The Leo owner may choose a pet that reminds you of your own physical characteristics, such as similar coloring or build. You'll be proud of your pet, keep the animal groomed to perfection, and choose the most spectacular example of the breed. Noble animals with a regal attitude, beautiful fur, or striking markings are often preferred, such as the Himalayan or red tabby Persian cat, the standard poodle, the chow chow dog. An attention getter is a must.

Under the sign of the King of Beasts, Leo-born animals have proud noble natures. They usually have a cheerful, magnanimous disposition and rule their domains regardless of their breed, holding their heads with pride and walking with great authority. They enjoy grooming, like to show off and be the center of attention. Leo animals are naturals for the show ring, thriving in the spotlight and applause. They'll thrive with plenty of petting, pampering, and admiration.

Virgo: The Caregiver

Virgo owners will be very particular about their pets, paying special attention to requirements for care and maintenance. You need a pet who is clean, obedient, intelligent, yet rather quiet. A highly active, barking or meowing pet that might get on your nerves is a no-no.

Cats are usually very good pets for Virgo. Choose one of the calm breeds, such as a Persian. Though this is a high-maintenance cat, its beauty and personality will be rewarding.

You are compassionate with animals in need, and you might find it rewarding to volunteer at a local shelter or veterinary clinic or to train service dogs.

Virgo animals can be fussy eaters, very particular about their environment. They are gentle and intelligent, and respond to kind words and quiet commands, never harsh treatment.

Virgo is an excellent sign for dogs that are trained to do service work, since they seem to enjoy being useful and are intelligent enough to be easily trained.

Libra: The Beautifier

The Libra owner responds to beauty and elegance in your pet. You require a well-mannered, but social companion, who can be displayed in all of nature's finery. An exotic variety such as a graceful curly-haired Devon Rex cat would be a show-stopper. Libra often prefers the smaller varieties, such as a miniature schnauzer, a mini-greyhound or a teacup poodle.

Pets born under Libra are usually charming, well-mannered gentlemen who love the comforts of home life. They tend to be more careful than other signs, not rushing willfully into potentially dangerous situations. They'll avoid confrontations and harsh sounds, responding to words of love and gentle corrections.

Scorpio: The Powerful

Scorpios enjoy a powerful animal with a strong character. They enjoy training animals in obedience, would do well with service dogs, guard dogs, or police animals. Some Scorpios enjoy the more exotic, edgy pets, such as hairless Sphynx cats or Chinese chin dogs. Scorpios could find rescuing animals in dire circumstances and finding them new homes especially rewarding, as Matthew McConaughey did during Hurricane Katrina.

Animals born under this sign tend to be one-person pets, very strongly attached to their owners and extremely loyal and possessive. They are natural guard animals who will take extreme risks to protect their owners. They are best ruled by love and with consistent behavior training. They need to respect their owners and will return their love with great devotion.

Sagittarius: The Jovial Freedom Lover

Sagittarius is a traveler and one of the great animal lovers of the zodiac. The horse is especially associated with your sign, and you could well be a "horse whisperer." You generally respond most to large, active animals. If a small animal, like a Chihuahua, steals your heart, be sure it's one that travels well or tolerates your absence. Outdoor dogs like hunting dogs, retrievers, and border collies would be good companions on your outdoor adventures.

Sagittarius animals are freedom-loving, jovial, happy-go-lucky types. They may be wanderers, however, so be sure they have the proper identification tags and consider embedded microchip identification. These animals tend to be openly affectionate, companionable, untemperamental. They enjoy socializing and playing with humans and other animals and are especially good with active children.

Capricorn: The Thoroughbred

Capricorn is a discriminating owner, with a great sense of responsibility toward your animal. You will be concerned with maintenance and care, will rarely neglect or overlook any health issues with your pet. You will also discipline your pet wisely, not tolerating any destructive or outrageous antics. You will be attracted to good breeding, good manners, and deep loyalty from your pet.

The Capricorn pet tends to be more quiet and serious than other pets, perhaps a lone wolf who prefers the company of its owner, rather than a sociable or mischievous type. This is another good sign for a working dog, such as a herder, as Capricorn animals enjoy this outlet for their energy.

Aquarius: The Independent Original

Aquarius owners tend to lead active, busy lives and need an animal who can either accompany them cheerfully or who won't make waves. Demanding or high-maintenance dogs are not for you. You might prefer unusual or oddball types of pets, such as dressed-up Chihuahuas who travel in your tote bag or scene-stealing, rather shocking hairless cats. Or you will acquire a group of animals who can play with one another when you are pursuing outside activities, as Oprah Winfrey does. You can relate to the independence of cats, who require relatively little care and maintenance.

Aquarius animals are not loners—they enjoy the companionship of humans or groups of other animals. They tend to be more independent and may require more training to follow the house rules. However, they can have unique personalities and endearing oddball behavior.

Pisces: The Soul Mate

This is the sign that can "talk to the animals." Pisces owners enjoy a deep communication with their pets, love having their animals accompany them, sleep with them, and show affection. Tenderhearted Pisces will often rescue an animal in distress or adopt an animal from a shelter.

Tropical fish are often recommended as a Pisces pet, and seem to have a natural tranquilizing effect on this sign. However, Pisces may require an animal that shows more affection than their fish friends.

Pisces animals are creative types, can be sensually seductive and mysterious, mischievous and theatrical. They make fine house pets, do not usually like to roam far from their owners, and have a winning personality, especially with the adults in the home. Naturally sensitive and seldom vicious, they should be treated gently and given much praise and encouragement.

CHAPTER 16

Your Pisces Personality and Potential: The Roles You Play in Life

The more you understand your Pisces personality and potential, the more you'll benefit from using your special solar power to help create the life you want. There's a life coach, personal trainer, career adviser, fashion expert, and matchmaker all built into your Pisces sun sign. Whether you want to make a radical change in your life or simply choose a new wardrobe or paint a room, your sun sign can help you discover new possibilities and make good decisions. You could tap into your Pisces power to deal with relationship issues, such as getting along with your boss or spicing up your love life. Maybe you'll be inspired by a celebrity sign mate who shares your special traits.

Let the following chapters help you move in harmony with your natural Pisces gifts. As the ancient oracle of Delphi advised, "Know thyself." To know yourself, as astrology helps you to do, is to gain confidence and strength.

You may wonder how astrologers determine what a Pisces personality is like. To begin with, we use a type of recipe, blending several ingredients. First there's your Pisces element: water. The way Pisces operates: mutable—a sign of movement, of change. Your sign's polarity: negative, feminine, yin. And your planetary ruler: Neptune, the planet of imagination. Add your sign's place in the zodiac: twelfth and last, in the house of spirituality, of selflessness, of charity. Finally, stir in your symbol, the Fish swimming in opposite directions, indicating duality.

This cosmic mix influences everything we say about Pisces. Wouldn't a water sign with a Neptune ruler have an aqua blue signature color? Is your personality likely to be creative, a bit dreamy? Very likely.

But all Pisces are not alike! Your individual astrological personality contains a blend of many other planets, colored by the signs they occupy, plus factors such as the sign coming over the horizon at the exact moment of your birth. However, the more Pisces planets in your horoscope, the more likely you'll recognize yourself in the descriptions that follow. On the other hand, if many planets are grouped together in a different sign, they will color your horoscope accordingly, sometimes making a low-key, mellow sun sign come on much stronger. So if the Pisces traits mentioned here don't describe you, there might be other factors flavoring your cosmic stew. (Look up your other planets in the tables in this book to find out what they might be!)

The Pisces Man: The Romantic Hero

The Pisces man has been characterized too often as a romantic adventurer with no roots in reality. However, in the last decade Pisces men have ridden the highest waves of success. Computer wizards Michael Dell and Steve Jobs, entertainment mogul David Geffen and media's Rupert Murdoch are a few examples of the Pisces man who shows that he can be a shark as well as a charming goldfish, a surfer of life with an uncanny sense of when and how to catch the best wave.

The Pisces man often puzzles more predictable signs with a chameleon-like personality that seems to take on the colorations of each environment. You have an amazing ability to adapt to different situations and people, socializing with the jet set one day and hanging out at a working-class bar the next, reveling in a constantly changing cast of characters.

What makes you so adaptable is your sensitivity, which some Pisces go to great lengths to hide, with good reason. Your compassion also attracts many who take advantage of your good nature. And, since Pisces picks up moods from your surroundings, negative influences from these people can be disastrous. It is often a Pisces challenge to find a way to help others without being drained and martyred yourself.

Once you find a place where your talents are appreciated, you can be extremely successful. Your intuitive ability to spot trends, your creative imagination, and your ability to second-guess the competition work in your favor. But, before you settle down, you may go through a period of drifting and soul-searching until you determine who you are and where you are going. Sadly, some Pisces men fall under the influence of drugs and alcohol during this time, unless they have strong outside support. With positive, constructive influences, you'll use your varied experiences as grist for creative ideas or find work that gives you the variety you crave, like writer Tom Wolfe or film director Spike Lee.

In a Relationship

The positive Pisces man makes a loving partner who will keep the romance going long after the wedding. You are very susceptible to female charms, but you'll remain faithful if your wife gives you oceans of emotional support and steadily builds your self-esteem. Not the take-over type, you need constant stroking and reassurance. However, the woman who imposes her will on you or tries to control you will find you slip through her fingers. If she can strike the right balance of strong support and gentle stroking, you'll be an appreciative, sensual, and romantic lover for life!

The Pisces Woman: The Romantic Heroine

The Pisces woman is likely to have a life story worthy of a novel. She embodies a combination of glamour, talent, and empathy that seems to attract dramatic scenarios. The most receptive, compassionate, imaginative sign of the zodiac, Pisces often dives beneath the waters of the emotions. You are attracted to the underdog. One of your paradoxes is that by helping the sick or needy, you miraculously gain prestige, power, and financial stability for yourself—if you don't become so involved in the troubles of others that you actually absorb them. Many Pisces, like Elizabeth Taylor and Drew Barrymore, come out of the depths of difficult experiences to emerge victorious and stronger than ever.

Your symbol, the Fish swimming in opposite directions while tied together, gives clues about your contradictions. You are really many women in one, and what fascinating characters you all are! Here is the ravishing beauty who swears like a dockworker, the socialite who runs off with her bodyguard, the sophisticated talk-show hostess with half a dozen children, the wholesome former Miss America dethroned by past scandal who reemerged a popular star, the desperately impoverished teenager who became an ambassador. Never predictable, Pisces hides much strength and resourcefulness under an ultrafeminine exterior. Deceptively fragile and vulnerable, you're really quite capable of fending for yourself and reinventing yourself after fate has dealt you a blow.

One Pisces challenge is to use your great compassion and sensitivity in a productive way. Your sympathy encompasses everyone who is suffering, and you'll often champion causes that others reject as too controversial, such as Elizabeth Taylor's work on behalf of AIDS. But you must learn to discriminate in order to protect yourself against those who would play upon your sympathies. By building up your own self-esteem, and by learning to discern the really needy from those who merely drain your energy, you can truly help others and reward yourself with a feeling of accomplishment.

It is especially important for Pisces to find an outlet for your powerful emotions, preferably one that rewards your self-expression with financial security. Gloria Vanderbilt, once the poor little rich girl, made her own fortune after forty as a fashion designer. Model and spokeswoman Cindy Crawford is another Pisces who capitalized on her beauty and talent. Extremely compassionate, you can enter and absorb a role, which makes you an excellent actress. Pisces women also do well in sports (Jackie Joyner-Kersee), where they can lose themselves in physical activity.

Along with success stories are the inevitable tearjerker tales of Pisces whose scandalous ups and downs, marriages, and bouts with alcohol and drugs are chronicled in the tabloids. When you are drowning in your emotions, you can be easily threatened, jealous, possessive, a clinging vine. Or your feelings may get the better of you physically, creating illnesses and addictions. You become fulfilled when you can express your feelings in some artistic or creative way. This quickly puts you on the road to confidence, self-esteem, and financial independence.

In a Relationship

Even the most liberated and independent of this sign tends to become reactive in romance. You easily perceive what your partner wants and switch into the appropriate role, often being both wife and mistress to the one you love. Because you are so willing to indulge a man's fantasies, you've been called the most dangerous "other woman" of the zodiac. However, many men prefer not to marry their Pisces paramours, choosing them as a diversion from their confining domestic life.

You need a mate who appreciates your many talents and helps you put them to constructive use. Though you may prefer to leave practical matters to your partner so you can focus on your creative talents, you have a surprisingly practical side, which is quite able to balance the budget. Negatively, you're not above using a bit of emotional manipulation, playing the martyr or victim to get your way.

Pisces in the Family

The Pisces Parent

Having children brings out the loving, supportive side of Pisces and can become the anchor Pisces needs to stop drifting and set goals. Your intuitive sensitivity to young children's needs and developing feelings gives them gentle, nonjudgmental support, while your creativity makes learning and playtime special. Yours is the sign most capable of unconditional love, and you are particularly nurturing to a child who is needy or handicapped in some way. Typical of the caring nature of Pisces is the story of the famous actress who chose to adopt a crippled child and help it regain health. On the negative side, you should cultivate detachment and objectivity in order to deal with the emotional ups and downs of your child. A fulfilling marriage will assure that you will not overinvest emotionally in the child and that you will be willing to let go when the time comes for independence.

The Pisces Stepparent

In the challenging position of stepparent, Pisces has personality assets to cope with a ready-made family. As one of the most adaptable and compassionate signs, you can easily open your heart to stepchildren and empathize with their feelings. You'll be especially supportive of your mate in the period of transition and willingly give up some of your own priorities to smooth over this delicate situation. Using your natural sense of drama and glamour, you can easily fascinate this young audience and channel their feelings into creative activities. Since these children need your love and understanding, you will give it wholeheartedly. But you may also have to assert your authority from time to time to gain their respect as well as their love.

The Pisces Grandparent

Pisces grandparents can share a magical world of fantasy with the grandchildren. When you enter their world, you become like a child again yourself. You're their special permissive playmate who never competes with parents for disciplinary rights. You are the accomplice who joins children in mischievous pranks! Through opening their minds to fantasy, you're their best teacher—the one who teaches them that it's okay to daydream and to explore their fantasies in play, for the most creative ideas happen when you're playing. You'll live in their memories because you've touched their hearts and awakened their imagination.

CHAPTER 17

Pisces Fashion and Decor Tips: Elevate Your Mood with Pisces Style!

In this year of serious concerns, why not put joy and imagination into your life by creating a harmonious environment and expressing your sun sign's natural flair in everything you do and wear? There are colors, sounds, fashion, and decor tips that fit Pisces like the proverbial glove and that could brighten every day. Even small changes in decor could make you feel "home at last." A simple change of color in your walls or curtains, your special music in the air, and a wardrobe makeover inspired by a Pisces designer or celebrity are natural mood elevators that boost your confidence and energy level. Even your vacations might be more fun if you tailor them to your natural Pisces inclinations. Try these tips to enhance your lifestyle and express the Pisces in you.

Pisces Fashion Secrets

Pisces, the sign of glamour and illusion, understands the power of clothing to enable you to play many roles in life. Rather than limit yourself to one look, you can switch with ease from crisp, efficient office clothes to romantic evening wear or casual sporty weekend clothes. But you are most in your element when you wear glamorous clothes with a theatrical flair. Juliette Binoche, the French star of *Chocolat,* is the perfect example of the ultrafeminine Pisces style. Or Sharon Stone, who can look like a mermaid in simple sequins, or wear a Gap T-shirt to a formal party with a few diamonds added for sparkle, or play another role in tweeds. Keep your weight down so you can wear the dramatic styles you love best.

Theatrical makeup is associated with Pisces. Many Pisces have soulful eyes, which are likely to be your best features. Use makeup cleverly to play up your lids and lashes. Experiment with false eyelashes and groom your brows carefully. If you wear glasses, have several different frames to change with your mood.

Since the feet belong to Pisces, shoes should be your special fashion indulgence. Play up your dancing feet with sexy strappy sandals or decorated pumps. Collect boots for all occasions. Since uncomfortable shoes can torture Pisces more than other signs, invest in stylish walking shoes to protect your posture. Even your glamorous evening shoes can be made more wearable with padded inserts.

Don't forget the invisible power of perfume, which should have a special place in your wardrobe, since fragrance is another Pisces specialty, especially the essential oils. Choose a signature scent and remember that the sense of smell has the longest memory.

Pisces Colors

Complement your Pisces personality by wearing colors creatively. All the colors of the sea—iridescent fish scales, coral, sea foam green, and the deep aquamarine of tropical waters complement the dreamy side of your personality. The blue and white of the Greek islands and the elegant neutral grays of a storm-tossed sea would be good choices.

Your Pisces Fashion Role Models

For fashion inspiration, Pisces designers Alexander McQueen, Kenzo, and Nannette Lepore do clothes to fantasize about. Or steal some style from Pisces supermodels: Cindy Crawford, Eva Herzigova, and Nadja Auermann. Perennial fashion icons born under Pisces include Gloria Vanderbilt, Ivana Trump, and Lee Radziwill, while Sharon Stone, Eva Longoria, Eva Mendes, and Drew Barrymore show the Pisces theatrical style.

Pisces Home Makeover Tips

Your home is the ideal place to express your Pisces personality. If your rooms don't suit you, you probably don't feel as comfortable as you should in your environment, which could adversely affect your health and well-being. Since solitude and security are especially important to fulfilling your Pisces creative potential, you need a safe haven to live out Pisces dreams and fantasies. Even if you share your home with others, there should be a quiet place where you can meditate, practice yoga, listen to music, and dream.

As a mutable water sign, you are very susceptible to the mood of your surroundings. If it's chaotic, you can feel jittery and unfocused. If it's too pristine, you can feel uncreative. The trick is to find the middle ground. All it takes is a beautiful rug, exotic pillows, and pools of mood lighting to do the trick. Add some mirrors and a few fabulous throws to toss over the furniture and perhaps an aquarium or small fountain to bring in your water element.

Pisces should pay special attention to comfort underfoot and the condition of your floor. Wonderful floor tiles, polished wood, and exotic carpets can make your home special as well as define each area. Pisces often shares a habitat with animal friends, so find some decorative baskets and scratch posts for your pets (and buy a powerful vacuum cleaner).

In your kitchen, provide for liquid refreshment and nourishment as well as touches of theater and fantasy. A well-stocked wine rack, a good blender or juicer, and a water purifier are important for water signs. Stock some exotic spices and delicacies to add drama to your meals. Pans suitable for cooking and serving seafood as well as decorative fish-shaped dishes could be displayed prominently.

Tap into your dreams and fantasies when you design your bedroom. Create a soothing atmosphere with water colors, ocean motifs, sensual fabrics. Go all out for a spectacular bed, with sumptuous coverings and piles of pillows. Pisces loves to spend time in bed and to bring work into the bedroom, which calls for cleverly hidden telephones and telecommunications lines and a table that can hold bedside refreshment. But maintain an atmosphere of rest and relaxation when propped on pillows, tapping on your laptop.

Your bath should be a room for self-pampering, where you indulge in lotions and bubbly potions, a showerhead with multiple pulse settings, and a Jacuzzi, if possible. You're a water sign, so your bath should be therapeutic and restorative.

Pisces Sounds

Dreamy, emotional music by Chopin or Ravel stirs your soul. Baroque music such as Handel's "Water Music" and Vivaldi's "Four Seasons" stimulates creative work. New Age meditative music and dance music, especially ballet themes, put you in a relaxed mood. Pisces voices include Seal, Nat King Cole, James Taylor, Harry Belafonte, Johnny Cash, and opera stars Kiri Te Kanawa and Renata Scotto. The mystical sounds from many lands now available as world music would be especially intriguing to Pisces, with your love of exotica.

Pisces Getaways

You're always ready for a getaway, especially one to a magical place with romance and fantasy appeal, and if the spot is near water, so much the better! Venice, Portugal, and Normandy fill the bill perfectly. Spiritual Pisces should seek out power spots such as Glastonbury, England, where King Arthur is said to be buried; the Mayan ruins of Tulum, on the coast of Mexico; the surfing beaches and mystical mountains of Hawaii. Or you might scuba dive in search of Atlantis off the coast of Bimini.

In the United States, head for the crashing surf of Monterey, the Maine coast, or the coral reefs of the Virgin Islands. Romantic Vermont is an inland Pisces-ruled place for snow lovers and ice skaters.

For an important trip, pack all your bags well in advance, when your concentration is best. The more advance planning the better when you're traveling for business. To make your trip run smoothly, tap into the Virgo side of your nature (your polar opposite) by making lists and checking them off methodically. Be sure you have double sets of directions, the proper insurance, and enough money to get you through the initial adaptation to a foreign city, when dreamy Pisces may be soaking up impressions rather than focusing on practical details. Keep a special travel folder with all your maps and papers organized together. That way you'll be free to go with the flow and truly enjoy your trip.

CHAPTER 18

The Pisces Way to Stay Healthy and Age Well

This year we'll be focused on staying healthy to avoid the high costs of health care and to cope with stressful events. Some signs have an easier time than others committing to a health and diet regimen. Pisces needs a creative approach to health and exercise—one that offers plenty of variety so you won't get bored or distracted. And this year, with Jupiter expanding your sign, you'll tend to expand your waistline, so extra attention to your diet will be needed. Astrology can clue you in to the specific Pisces tendencies that contribute to good or ill health. Follow these sun-sign tips to help yourself become the healthiest Pisces possible.

The Addictive Eater

Pisces is a sign of no boundaries, therefore one of the most difficult to discipline diet-wise. You can get hooked on a fattening food like French fries (or alcohol), a habit like coffee with lots of sugar and a sweet roll, and easily gain weight. What's more, your water-sign body may have a tendency to bloat, holding extra pounds of water weight at certain times, especially around the full moon.

The key for you, as with so many others, is commitment and support. Don't try to go it alone. Get a partner, a doctor, a group, or one of the online diet-related sites to help. Since you're influenced by the atmosphere around you, choose to be with slim healthy friends and those who will support your efforts. Avoid those seemingly well-meaning diet saboteurs who say just one cookie won't do any harm. A seafood-based diet could be the right one for you. Your Pisces sisters—Queen Latifah, Liza Minnelli, and Camryn Manheim—have slimmed down, and so can you!

Detox Your System

Health-wise, supersensitive Pisces, associated with the lymphatic system, reacts strongly to environmental toxins and emotional stress. It's no accident that we often do spring cleaning during the Pisces months. Start your birthday off right by detoxing your system with a liquid diet or supervised fast. This may also help with water retention, a common Pisces problem. Lymphatic drainage massage is especially relaxing and beneficial to Pisces.

Don't Forget Your Feet!

The feet are Pisces territory. Consider how often you take your feet for granted and how miserable life can be when your feet hurt. Since our feet reflect and affect the health of the entire body, devote some time to pampering them. Check your walking shoes or buy ones designed specifically for your kind of exercise. If your arches are high, custom-molded orthotic inserts could make a big difference in your comfort and performance. Though you may love your sexy stiletto heels, they can take a toll on your posture and bone structure. Save them for special occasions.

Just as the sign of Pisces contains traces of all the previous signs, the soles of our feet contain nerve endings that connect with all other parts of our body. This is the theory behind reflexology, a therapeutic foot massage that treats all areas of the body by massaging the soles of the feet. For the sake of your feet, as well as your entire body, consider treating yourself to a session with a local practitioner of this technique.

Exercise in Your Water Element

Exercise is not a favorite Pisces activity, unless it is a creative activity like dance or ice-skating, or is related to your water element, such as water aerobics or swimming. Generally, you fare best in a solo activity that is graceful and artistic. A caring coach or exercise instructor who gives you personal attention can make a difference in your motivation.

Walking regularly releases tension, gets you outdoors, and can be a way to socialize with friends away from the temptation of food and drink. If you live near the ocean or a beautiful lake, make this a place for your daily walk. If you live in a city, do local errands on foot and find a local park where you can take a daily stroll. Invite someone you love or would like to get to know better to share this time with you. Owning an active pet forces you to get out and explore the neighborhood several times a day, so why not adopt an adorable pooch from your local shelter?

Stay Forever Young

Elder Pisces is happiest when pursuing creative activities, such as filmmaking, painting, writing, or a hobby or craft in which you can express your imagination. Fortunately, artistic talents often improve with age, allowing Pisces great fulfillment in your senior years. If traveling on vacation or planning a retirement home, choose a cruise or a location near the ocean or a scenic lake. Places near water are particularly healthful for Pisces. Water sports, especially swimming and water aerobics, can maintain your health. Avoid addictive substances, and stick to a balanced diet of organic foods, including plenty of fish. Pay special attention to the condition of your feet, which become more vulnerable as you age, and be sure to wear the appropriate shoes for each activity.

CHAPTER 19

Add Pisces Star Power to Your Career: What It Takes to Succeed in 2010

In today's tight job market, you'll need to pull out all the stops to land a great job. Lucky Pisces, you'll get a terrific boost from Jupiter, the planet of expansion, in 2010, and it is bound to help you futher your career goals. If you want to change jobs or get an advanced degree to enhance your skills, go for it! You're sure to succeed if you emphasize the special talents that only Pisces has to offer, especially in the creative fields. If you develop and nurture these talents, you'll be more likely to find a career you truly enjoy, as well as one that rewards you financially. Here's to your success!

Where to Look for Your Perfect Job

The key to Pisces success is to find a place where your sensitivity and creativity work for you rather than against you. Avoid rigid, structured companies and overbearing employers who simply exploit your talents. Office power games can sap your energy and divert your talent in unproductive directions. Instead, put your sensitive antennae to work psyching out the competition, divining the consumer mood, and understanding the hidden agendas of your coworkers.

Though Pisces-friendly jobs are usually in creative fields, that is not always the case. Pisces can use special insight in high finance, publishing, science, and medicine. Special Pisces-influenced areas are the oil, perfume, footwear, and film industries. Alcohol and drugs are also Pisces-ruled, but work in those areas will require self-discipline, as Pisces is very susceptible to alcohol and drug abuse. The caring and healing professions capitalize on your natural empathy with clients, offering many opportunities in psychotherapy, nursing, and home health care. Glamour fields of fashion and beauty, as well as theater in any form, are always Pisces havens.

Live Up to Your Leadership Potential

The Pisces boss has uncanny intuition, the kind of instinct that can't be taught in business school. You grasp the thoughts and trends in the air as if by magic. Extremely creative, you may prefer to work alone and do your real thinking in solitude. You are very compassionate and caring of your subordinates, and oddly, they are protective of you in return, sometimes shielding you from office politics. Though they may be baffled by your unpredictable moods (sometimes your sweet temper can turn mean as a shark) and your vague sense of direction (be sure to put your orders in writing), they adore you for your caring concern and respect your outstanding talent.

Pisces's secret is your sensitivity, put to good use. It can help you psyche out the competition, divine the consumer mood, and understand the hidden agendas of coworkers. Teamed with your water sign's creativity, it's a formidable combination. There are many inspiring examples of successful Pisces, such as billionaire Michael Dell, who dropped out of college to start Dell Computers, a pioneer in direct-to-customer computer sales. At age twenty-seven, he became the youngest CEO of a Fortune 500 company in history. Steven Jobs, co-founder of Apple Computers, developed the Macintosh with an easy-to-use graphic interface that made it the first user-friendly computer. Now he has moved Apple to lead high-tech entertainment with the iPod. Sanford Weill and Walter Annenberg are legendary Pisces entrepreneurs who flourished in the worlds of finance and publishing, respectively.

How to Work with Others

As an emotional water sign, you do your best work when you are not tied down to a routine or made to punch a time clock. This doesn't mean that you are undisciplined. You'll turn out extraordinary work in a job where your talents are appreciated and where you have creative freedom. You are not one to step on toes to get ahead, or fight to keep your position, so an atmosphere of intense competition can upset your delicate sense of balance and distract you from the work you do best. You must learn to focus on the job at hand and tune out chaotic vibrations.

Because you can adapt to many situations easily and are extremely versatile, you may take time to discover your professional potential, floating from job to job, often going far adrift of your original direction. But perceptions gained from these diverse experiences only enhance your talent and professional value. You'll amaze others with your success and stamina when you finally find a job that fully engages your abilities.

The Pisces Way to Get Ahead

Get behind the steering wheel of your life. Use your special Pisces talents and abilities to bring you the highest return on your investment of time and energy. Look for a positive, supportive working environment with plenty of creative opportunity. Then play up these Pisces attributes:

- Creativity
- Insight
- Tact
- Charm
- Empathy
- Intuition
- Talent
- Good timing

CHAPTER 20

Learn from Pisces Celebrities

You know how much fun it is when you find a famous person who shares your sun sign—and even your birthday! Why not turn your brush with fame into an education in astrology? Celebrities who capture the media's attention reflect the current planetary influences, as well as the unique star quality of their sun sign. Who's in this year may be out next year. You can learn from the hottest stellar spotlight stealers what the public is responding to and what this says about our current values.

If one of your famous sign mates intrigues you, explore his personality further by looking up his other planets using the tables in this book. You may even find his horoscope posted on astrology-related Internet sites like www.astrodatabank. com or www.stariq.com, which have charts of world events and headline makers. Then apply the effects of Venus, Mars, Saturn, and Jupiter to his sun-sign traits. It's a way to get up close and personal with your famous friend, maybe learn some secrets not revealed to the public.

You're sure to discover many traits that you share with your famous Pisces sign mates. Perhaps you prefer the bohemian style of Drew Barrymore and Queen Latifah. Or you've coped with adversity like Elizabeth Taylor, Liza Minnelli, and Chelsea Clinton. Do you have the Pisces business savvy of Rupert Murdoch, Steve Jobs, and Michael Dell? Let their success inspire you to make the most of your own sun-sign talents.

Get to know these famous Pisces better and learn what makes their stars shine brightly.

Pisces Celebrities

Smokey Robinson (2/19/40)
Prince Andrew (2/19/60)
Benicio Del Toro (2/19/67)
Gloria Vanderbilt (2/20/25)
Sidney Poitier (2/20/25)
Ivana Trump (2/20/49)
Patricia Hearst (2/20/54)
Cindy Crawford (2/20/66)
Kurt Cobain (2/20/67)
Rihanna (2/20/68)
Rue McClanahan (2/21/34)
Tyne Daly (2/21/43)
David Geffen (2/21/43)
Kelsey Grammer (2/21/55)
Mary-Chapin Carpenter (2/21/58)
William Baldwin (2/21/63)
Jennifer Love Hewitt (2/21/79)
Charlotte Church (2/21/86)
Edna St. Vincent Millay (2/22/1892)
Julius Erving (2/22/50)
Kyle MacLachlan (2/22/59)
Kristin Davis (2/22/65)
Drew Barrymore (2/22/75)
Peter Fonda (2/23/39)
Michael Dell (2/23/54)
Dakota Fanning (2/23/94)
Edward J. Olmos (2/24/47)
Steve Jobs (2/24/55)
Paula Zahn (2/24/56)
George Harrison (2/25/43)
Sally Jessy Raphael (2/25/43)
Téa Leoni (2/25/66)
Johnny Cash (2/26/32)
Michael Bolton (2/26/53)
Erykah Badu (2/26/72)
Joanne Woodward (2/27/30)
Elizabeth Taylor (2/27/32)
Ralph Nader (2/27/34)

Chelsea Clinton (2/27/80)
Josh Groban (2/27/81)
Bugsy Siegel (2/28/1906)
Bernadette Peters (2/28/48)
Dinah Shore (3/1/17)
Ron Howard (3/1/54)
Dr. Seuss (3/2/1904)
Desi Arnaz (3/2/17)
Mikhail Gorbechev (3/2/31)
Jon Bon Jovi (3/2/62)
Daniel Craig (3/2/68)
Miranda Richardson (3/3/58)
Jackie Joyner-Kersee (3/3/62)
Julie Bowen (3/3/70)
Jessica Biel (3/3/82)
Samantha Eggar (3/5/39)
Eva Mendes (3/5/74)
Kevin Connolly (3/5/74)
Niki Taylor (3/5/75)
Rob Reiner (3/6/47)
Stedman Graham (3/6/51)
Tom Arnold (3/6/59)
Shaquille O'Neal (3/6/72)
Willard Scott (3/7/34)
Tammy Fay Messner (3/7/42)
Michael Eisner (3/7/42)
Rachel Weisz (3/7/71)
Cyd Charisse (3/8/23)
Lynn Redgrave (3/8/43)
Camryn Manheim (3/8/61)
Kathy Ireland (3/8/63)
Freddie Prinze Jr. (3/8/76)
James Van Der Beek (3/8/77)
Raul Julia (3/9/40)
Faith Daniels (3/9/57)
Juliette Binoche (3/9/64)
Chuck Norris (3/10/42)
Sharon Stone (3/10/58)
Prince Edward (3/10/64)
Shannon Miller (3/10/77)

Carrie Underwood (3/10/83)
Lawrence Welk (3/11/1903)
Rupert Murdoch (3/11/31)
Benji and Joel Madden (3/11/79)
Gianni Agnelli (3/12/42)
Liza Minnelli (3/12/46)
James Taylor (3/12/48)
Neil Sedaka (3/13/39)
William H. Macy (3/13/50)
Dana Delany (3/13/67)
Albert Einstein (3/14/1879)
Michael Caine (3/14/33)
Billy Crystal (3/14/47)
Prince Albert of Monaco (3/14/58)
Fabio (3/15/61)
Mark McGrath (3/15/68)
Eva Longoria (3/15/75)
Jerry Lewis (3/16/26)
Sanford Weill (3/16/33)
Bernardo Bertolucci (3/16/40)
Kate Nelligan (3/16/51)
Lauren Graham (3/16/67)
Brooke Burns (3/16/78)
Patrick Duffy (3/17/49)
Kurt Russell (3/17/51)
Gary Sinise (3/17/55)
Rob Lowe (3/17/64)
Brittany Daniel (3/17/76)
Charley Pride (3/18/38)
Queen Latifah (3/18/70)
Vanessa L. Williams (3/18/63)
Ursula Andress (3/19/36)
Glenn Close (3/19/47)
Bruce Willis (3/19/55)
Mr. Rogers (3/20/28)
Jerry Reed (3/20/37)
William Hurt (3/20/50)
Spike Lee (3/20/57)
Theresa Russell (3/20/57)
Holly Hunter (3/20/58)

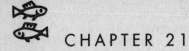

CHAPTER 21

Your Pisces Relationships with Every Other Sign: The Green Lights and Red Flags

Are you looking for insight into a relationship? Perhaps it's someone you've met online, a new business partnership, a rooommate, or the proverbial stranger across a crowded room. After an initial attraction, you may be wondering if you'll still get along down the line. Or why supposedly incompatible signs sometimes have a magical attraction to each other. If things aren't working out, astrology could give you some clues as to why he or she is "not that into you."

Astrology has no magic formula for success in love, but it does offer a better understanding of the qualities each person brings to the relationship and how your partner is likely to react to your sun-sign characteristics. Knowing your potential partner's sign and how it relates to yours could give you some clues about what to expect down the line.

There is also the issue of the timing of a new relationship. From an astrological perspective, the people you meet at any given time provide the dynamic that you require at that moment. If you're a sensitive creative Pisces, you might benefit from a more objective Aquarius or a go-getter Aries companion at a certain time in your life.

The celebrity couples in this chapter can help you visualize each sun-sign combination. You'll note that some legendary lovers have stood the test of time, while others blazed, then broke up, and still others existed only in the fantasy world of film or television (but still captured our imagination).

Traditional astrological wisdom holds that signs of the same element are naturally compatible. For Pisces, that would be fellow water signs Cancer and Scorpio. Also favored are signs of complementary elements, such as water signs with earth signs (Taurus, Virgo, Capricorn). In these relationships communication supposedly flows easily, and you'll feel most comfortable together.

As you read the following matches, remember that there are no hard-and-fast rules; each combination has perks as well as peeves. So when sparks fly and an irresistible magnetic pull draws you together, when disagreements and challenges fuel intrigue, mystery, passion, and sexy sparring matches, don't rule the relationship out. That person may provide the diversity, excitement, and challenge you need for an unforgettable romance, stimulating friendship, or a successful business partnership!

Pisces/Aries

THE GREEN LIGHTS:

Pisces love to be swept off their feet and Aries is happy to comply! Pisces is someone who can appreciate Aries dynamism without feeling the least bit threatened by Aries power. On the contrary, Aries energizes you! This sign gets Pisces moving! Aries will be number one with Pisces, who'll have wonderful, romantic ideas to contribute. Aries tempts Pisces to swim in new waters . . . to follow that dream!

THE RED FLAGS:

Aries wants what it wants when it wants it. And this sign doesn't care who has other plans. Supersensitive Pisces feelings can be a problem here. Pushy, bossy, or inconsiderate partners turn you into a martyr or a monster who could rain on the Aries parade. Balancing positive and negative energies is the key. Aries needs brakes to slow down and consider the consequences of their actions; in turn, Pisces needs a charge to get up and running.

Pisces Freddie Prinze Jr. and Aries Sarah Michelle Gellar

Pisces/Taurus

THE GREEN LIGHTS:

You both love the good things in life and can indulge each other sensually and sexually. The Taurus focus adds stability and direction to Pisces, while your Pisces creativity is lovingly encouraged by Taurus. Taurus and Pisces are both nurturers who love to take care of each other. Your energies are complementary—there will be few fights here.

THE RED FLAGS:

Taurus wants Pisces to produce, not just dream, and will try to corral the slippery Fish. Pisces can't be bossed or caged, and may leave Taurus with the dotted line unsigned!

SIGN MATES:

Pisces Eva Longoria and Taurus Tony Parker
Pisces Javier Bardem and Taurus Penelope Cruz

Pisces/Gemini

THE GREEN LIGHTS:

You both are dual personalities in mutable, freedom-loving signs. You fascinate each other with ever-changing facets. You keep each other from straying by providing constant variety and new experiments to try together.

THE RED FLAGS:

At some point, you'll need a frame of reference for this relationship to hold together. Since neither likes structure, this could be a problem. Overstimulation is another monster that can surface. Pisces sensitive feelings and Gemini hyperactive nerves could send each other searching for soothing, stabilizing alternatives. The relentless socializing of Gemini could send Pisces scurrying to calmer waters.

SIGN MATES:

Pisces Ivana Trump and Gemini Donald Trump
Pisces soul singer Seal and Gemini supermodel Heidi Klum

Pisces/Cancer

THE GREEN LIGHTS:

You both love to swim in emotional waters, where your communication flows easily. Cancer protective attention and support help Pisces gain confidence and direction. Pisces gives Cancer dreamy romance and creative inspiration. A very meaningful relationship develops over time.

THE RED FLAGS:

You two emotionally vulnerable signs know where the soft spots are and can really hurt each other! Pisces has a way of slipping through the clingy Cancer clutches, possibly to dry out after too much emotion. Learn to give each other space. Find creative projects to defuse moods.

SIGN MATES:

Pisces James Taylor and Cancer Carly Simon

Pisces/Leo

THE GREEN LIGHTS:

Highly sensitive Pisces admires the Leo radiant confidence. You will gain stability under the warm and encouraging protection of Leo. Leo will gain an adoring admirer in Pisces, as you easily show affection and satisfy Leo's constant craving for romance. This is a noncompetitive mutual admiration society where you promote each other enthusiastically.

THE RED FLAGS:

Pisces also loves to flirt. Unlike Leo, Pisces is not basically monogamous. A stickler for loyalty, Leo may try to keep Pisces dancing attendance by strong-arm tactics. Pisces operates best in free-flowing waters—you swim off when you sense a hook!

SIGN MATES:

Pisces Téa Leoni and Leo David Duchovny

Pisces/Virgo

THE GREEN LIGHTS

Virgo supplies what Pisces often needs most—clarity and order—while Pisces creative imagination takes Virgo into fascinating new realms away from the ordinary. If you can reconcile your opposing points of view, you'll have much to gain from this relationship.

THE RED FLAGS:

There are many adjustments for both signs here. Virgo could feel overwhelmed with your Pisces emotions and seeming lack of control and frustrated when makeover attempts fail. Pisces could feel bogged down with Virgo worries and deflated by negative criticism. Try to support, not change, each other.

Pisces Antonio Sabato, Jr., and Virgo Virginia Madsen

Pisces/Libra

THE GREEN LIGHTS:

You're one of the most creative couples. Libra keeps the delicate Pisces ego on keel, while Pisces provides the romance and attention Libra craves. You are ideal collaborators. Pisces appreciates Libra aesthetic judgment. Libra refines Pisces ideas without dampening your creative spirit or deflating your ego.

THE RED FLAGS:

Pisces swims in the emotional waters where Libra gets seasick. Libra indecisiveness sends Pisces looking elsewhere for an anchor. Fluctuating moods rock the boat here, unless you find a way to give each other stability and support. Turn to calm reason, avoiding emotional scenes, to solve problems.

SIGN MATES:

Pisces Prince Andrew and Libra Sarah "Fergie" Ferguson
Pisces Chris Martin of Coldplay and Libra Gwyneth Paltrow

Pisces/Scorpio

THE GREEN LIGHTS:

When these two signs click, nothing gets in their way. Your Pisces desire to merge completely with a beloved is just the all-or-nothing message Scorpio has been waiting for. These two will play it to the hilt, often shedding previous spouses or bucking public opinion (like Elizabeth Taylor and Richard Burton).

THE RED FLAGS:

Both signs are possessive, yet neither likes to be possessed. Scorpio could easily mistake your Pisces vulnerability for weakness—a big mistake. Both signs fuel each other's escapist tendencies when dark moods hit. Learning to merge without submerging one's identity is an important lesson for this couple.

SIGN MATES:

Pisces Kurt Russell and Scorpio Goldie Hawn

Pisces/Sagittarius

THE GREEN LIGHTS:

You spark each other creatively and romantically. Pisces imagination and Sagittarius innovation work well on all levels. Variety, mental stimulation, and spiritual understanding—plus an appreciation of exotic places—could draw and keep you together.

THE RED FLAGS:

Pisces can turn from a gentle tropical fish to a vengeful shark when Sagittarius disregards tender Pisces feelings. Sagittarius goes for direct attacks, and could feel that self-protective Pisces hides truths far beneath the surface.

SIGN MATES:

Pisces William H. Macy and Sagittarius Felicity Huffman

Pisces/Capricorn

THE GREEN LIGHTS:

Capricorn organizational abilities and worldly know-how impress, helping Pisces find a clear direction. Pisces romance, tenderness, and knowledge of the art of love bring out the gypsy in Capricorn—a fair exchange.

THE RED FLAGS:

What spells security for Capricorn could look like a gilded cage to Pisces, who doesn't play by the same rules. If you both can make allowances for radical differences, you'll find you can go far together. Don't try to make each other over!

SIGN MATES:

Pisces Penny Lancaster and Capricorn Rod Stewart

Pisces/Aquarius

THE GREEN LIGHTS:

You two neighboring signs can be best buddies. You both need plenty of space and freedom, though in different ways. You'll have great tolerance for each other's eccentricities. You can inspire each other to be original, unpredictable, and romantic. You can explore unknown waters together.

THE RED FLAGS:

Intense emotions feed you Pisces Fish, but make Aquarius swim away. Aquarius detachment could cause Pisces to look for warmer seas. Pisces needs one-on-one intimacy and reassurance, while Aquarius are people who need people in groups. You'll both have to leave your elements to make this work.

SIGN MATES:

Pisces Joanne Woodward and Aquarius Paul Newman
Pisces Stedman Graham and Aquarius Oprah Winfrey

Pisces/Pisces

THE GREEN LIGHTS:

Who understands your inner complexity better than one of your own? Here's the psychic soul mate you've been waiting for—finally someone who's as sensitive and sensual as you are! You'll love the good life together, and you will spark each other creatively.

THE RED FLAGS:

This romance can sink if you both get into a negative mood at the same time. There you are, caught in the undertow without a lifeguard! Avoid escaping into alcohol or food binges. Plan a strategy to defuse black moods with lighthearted friends and shared creative projects.

SIGN MATES:

Pisces Elizabeth Taylor and Rex Harrison in *Cleopatra*

CHAPTER 22

The Big Picture for Pisces in 2010

Welcome to 2010! This is your year for building alliances in your daily work and to be diligent in maintaining your health and well-being, and there's a service-oriented quality to the year.

Your coruler, Jupiter, enters your sign on January 17, zooms through it, enters Aries on June 6, retrogrades on July 23, and remains in Pisces for the rest of the year. By January 2011, it has entered Aries again. What all this means for you is that while Jupiter is in Pisces, your life is expanding in unprecedented ways. In fact, Jupiter hasn't been in your sign since 1998. You may want to look back to that year for hints about the kind of expansion that may be in store for you. Possibilities? You get married, move, change jobs, have a child, get a major promotion at work, go back to school—in other words, expansion can happen in any area of your life.

Once Jupiter enters Aries and your second house, you'll get a taste of the possibilities for your finances before Jupiter begins to retrograde and returns to your sign. The time for Jupiter's magic on your finances will be in 2011. That said, here are the possibilities: Your earnings and expenses expand; you'll be able to come up with innovative ways to make money, and these methods could be connected to publishing, education, foreign cultures, or spiritual themes, all areas that Jupiter rules.

If you're a writer, you'll love Jupiter's transit through Pisces, because it should expand your publishing venues and will expand the types of things you write.

Uranus has been in your sign since 2003, shaking up your personal life and shaking you out of your ruts and routines. And on May 27, Uranus finally moves on, into Aries and your second house of finances. It will be there until August 13, when it has retrograded back into Pisces. But it will give you a taste of how Uranus will impact your finances in 2011. While Jupiter and Uranus travel together in either Pisces or Aries, expansion and excitement take place suddenly and unexpectedly. While both are in Aries, you'll have a chance to think way outside the box in terms of how you earn your living.

Saturn, the planet that rules our physical existence, structures, bones, and teeth begins the year retrograde in Libra, in your eighth house. That is probably good news for you, because it means it finally left Virgo, your opposite sign, where it may have created restrictions and delays in your romantic and business partnerships. But you won't be quite free of that, because by May 30 it has retrograded back into Virgo. By July 21, it enters Libra again, where it will remain until October 2012. If you handled things well while Saturn was transiting Virgo, then you may not even notice when it retrogrades back into that sign. But you'll have to pay close attention to things like taxes and insurance, mortgages and loans while it's in Libra.

Pluto begins the year in Capricorn, in your eleventh house, where it has been since late 2008 and where it will be until early 2024. It will actually enter Aquarius in 2023, but due to a retrograde motion will retreat into Capricorn, then move forward again. Pluto is the great transformer, and during its transit of your eleventh house, you'll undergo a complete revision in your friendships, dreams, and aspirations. Since Capricorn is an earth sign compatible with your water-sign sun, this transit should prove to be quite positive and profound for you. It will put you more in control of your life. It's possible that people you have known in previous lives will surface. Your psychic abilities will increase.

All these changes will be subtle because Pluto moves so slowly. In 2010, for instance, the planet travels from three to five degrees of Capricorn, hardly anything at all. Pluto turns retrograde on April 6 and doesn't turn direct again until September 13. During this retrograde period, pay close attention to everything that happens. Note repeating patterns. Follow synchronicities; listen to your intuition.

Neptune—the planet that symbolizes illusions, idealism, all forms of escapism, and higher selves—continues its journey through Aquarius, your twelfth house. By now this transit is no stranger to you. It has been in Aquarius since 1998. There can be psychic experiences with Neptune, so continue to explore your gut feelings, impulses, and dreams. When Neptune turns retrograde between May 31 and November 6, it essentially enters a period of dormancy. Its energy will be turned inward, so you may be scrutinizing your own unconscious quite closely.

Mercury begins the year retrograde in Capricorn, a carryover from 2009 that may mess up your social plans during the first two weeks of the year. But on January 15 it turns direct in Capricorn, where Venus is at that time, and suddenly everything looks much rosier, particularly your love life!

Romance and Creativity

There are two notable time periods this year that favor romance and creative endeavors. Between February 11 and March 7, Venus is in your sign, marking one of the most romantic and creative periods for you all year. While Venus is in your sign, your sex appeal, charisma, and general self-confidence are bolstered significantly. You get another boost later in the year, between August 6 and September 8, while Venus transits fellow water sign Cancer. This should increase the possibility of romance, will enhance all you do for fun and pleasure, and will deepen your creativity.

The second great time period for romance and sex falls between September 14 and October 28, while Mars is transiting fellow water sign Scorpio. During this transit, your sexuality will be heightened and your emotions quite intense.

Career

The best career dates this year occur when Mars transits Sagittarius and your tenth house, between October 28 and December 7. Good backup dates fall between January 17 and June 6, while Jupiter transits your sign. The first period should bring about a lot of communication with bosses and peers, increased networking, and perhaps some business travel. Other people will be receptive to your ideas. You'll be very aggressive and hardworking during this period, and the major risk you run is being too assertive or blunt. Otherwise, though, this transit gives you plenty of energy and determination to get to wherever you want to be.

Another great time falls around the new moon in your sign on March 15. This moon happens just once a year and sets the tone for the next twelve months. It should usher in new opportunities for your personal life and for many other areas of your life as well. You'll feel more appreciated, more recognized, more . . . applauded!

Best Times For

Buying or selling a home: April 25 to May 19, while Venus is transiting Gemini and your fourth house.

Family reunions: Same dates as above.

Financial matters: June 6 to July 23, while Jupiter is moving direct through Aries and your second house. Also excellent: Jupiter's transit in Pisces from January 17 to June 6. This transit tends to expand options in your personal life, but can impact any area.

Signing contracts: When Mercury is moving direct! Especially good between March 1 and March 17, while Mercury is moving direct through your sign.

Overseas travel, publishing, and higher-education endeavors: September 8 to October 8, and November 18 to November 29, while Mercury is moving direct through Scorpio and your ninth house.

Mercury Retrogrades

Every year, Mercury—the planet of communication and travel—turns retrograde three times. During this period, it's wise not to sign contracts (unless you don't mind renegotiating when Mercury is moving direct), to check and recheck travel plans, and to communicate as succinctly as possible. Refrain from buying any big-ticket items or electronics during this time too. Often, computers and appliances go on the fritz, cars act up, data is lost—you get the idea. Be sure to back up all files before the dates below:

April 17–May 11: Mercury retrograde in Taurus, your third house of communication, relatives, neighborhood, and community.

August 20–September 12: Mercury retrograde in Virgo, your opposite sign and seventh house of partnerships.

December 10–December 30: Mercury retrograde in Capricorn, your eleventh house of friendships.

Eclipses

Solar eclipses tend to trigger external events that bring about change according to the sign and the house in which they fall. Lunar eclipses trigger inner, emotional events according to the sign and house in which they fall. Any eclipse marks both beginnings and endings. The solar and lunar eclipse in a pair fall in opposite signs.

If you were born under or around the time of an eclipse, it's to your advantage to take a look at your birth chart to find out exactly where the eclipses will impact you.

Most years feature four eclipses—two solar, two lunar, with the set separated by about two weeks. In 2009, there was a lunar eclipse in Cancer on December 31, so the first eclipse in 2010 is a solar eclipse in the opposite sign, Capricorn, in your eleventh house. This year, three of the eclipses occur either in Cancer or in Capricorn. Below are the dates for this year's eclipses:

January 15: solar, Capricorn. New opportunities to achieve your dreams. New opportunities with friendships and group affiliations.

June 26: lunar, Capricorn. Inner stuff now, but the same area as the January 15 eclipse is affected.

July 11: solar, Cancer, your fifth house of romance and creativity. New opportunities surface in this area.

December 21: lunar, Gemini, your fourth house of the home, family, your roots. Emotions swirl in this area.

Luckiest Day of the Year

There's at least one day a year when the sun and Jupiter link up in some way. This year, March 2 looks to be that day, with a nice backup on July 26.

Now let's find out what's in store for you, day by day.

CHAPTER 23

Eighteen Months of Day-by-Day Predictions: July 2009 to December 2010

Moon sign times are calculated for Eastern Standard Time and Eastern Daylight Time. Please adjust for your local time zone.

JULY 2009

Wednesday, July 1 (Moon in Libra to Scorpio 1:20 a.m.) Uranus turns retrograde in your sign. The impact of this movement is subtle, but over the next few months, you'll be taking a closer look at your personal life. Where have you become habitual in your responses or beliefs? Strive for change.

Thursday, July 2 (Moon in Scorpio) Your personal beliefs in several areas are highlighted. If you happen to be traveling overseas, your trip isn't strictly for pleasure. You're on a quest of some kind.

Friday, July 3 (Moon in Scorpio to Sagittarius 11:12 a.m.) Mercury enters Cancer until July 17. During the next two weeks, you and partners will be discussing the finer details of your relationship. Also, there will be a lot of conversation about a creative project. If you're a writer, this transit brings a quick flow to your endeavors.

Saturday, July 4 (Moon in Sagittarius)   You've got the big picture concerning a career issue or professional relationship. Even though it's the July Fourth weekend, you may sneak off to tend to some work project. Your sense of humor definitely saves the day!

Sunday, July 5 (Moon in Sagittarius to Capricorn 11:08 p.m.)   Venus enters Gemini, your fourth house, where it will be until July 31. This transit should add pizzazz to your love life at home. You may also feel compelled to beautify your surroundings in some way. If you're not involved, you probably will be by the time Venus finishes its transit of Cancer and your fifth house. That transit begins on July 31 and ends on August 26.

Monday, July 6 (Moon in Capricorn)   Take a close look at your goals. Are they an expression of who you really are or have you adopted them because of peer or parental pressure? It's important to be true to yourself. Don't fall for a sob story!

Tuesday, July 7 (Moon in Capricorn)   The lunar eclipse in Capricorn triggers emotions related to friends and your own wishes and dreams. Saturn forms a close and harmonious angle to this moon, so you find the proper vehicle for expressing what you feel. The event to watch for comes on July 21, with a solar eclipse in Cancer.

Wednesday, July 8 (Moon in Capricorn to Aquarius 12:04 p.m.)   If you're ready for a new relationship, put out your intention to the universe. List the qualities you're seeking in a close relationship. Be focused, but don't worry about how it will happen.

Thursday, July 9 (Moon in Aquarius)   Keep your feelings to yourself. When the moon is firmly in your sign on Saturday, you'll be ready to broadcast what you feel and think. Work behind the scenes is emphasized. You're getting recharged right now, so relax.

Friday, July 10 (Moon in Aquarius)   Early tomorrow, the moon enters your sign, signaling a busy couple days ahead of you. You're prepped and ready for whatever the next few days bring. Listen to others, but make your own decisions.

Saturday, July 11 (Moon in Aquarius to Pisces 12:44 a.m.)   Mars enters Gemini, joining Venus in your fourth house, and the moon joins Uranus in your sign. These combinations of planets should lead to an exciting day, although there could be some stress involved too. It depends on how well you respond to change and the quick flux of events.

Sunday, July 12 (Moon in Pisces)   Whenever Venus and Mars are in the same sign and house, as they are now, your love life and your sexuality are heightened. If you're not involved, you will be soon, if that's what you want.

Monday, July 13 (Moon in Pisces to Aries 11:40 a.m.) Keep a lid on your temper. Don't fight or argue with others even if there's disagreement. With any conflict, say what you have to say, and then walk away. Show your appreciation for the parts of your life that are running smoothly. The more you cultivate appreciation, the greater the chances that you attract more to appreciate.

Tuesday, July 14 (Moon in Aries)   Take care of your bills; don't procrastinate. You're working up to the solar eclipse in Cancer on July 21, which will be like a double new moon. So clear the clutter from your desk and closets, and clean out the cobwebs in your own mind. These gestures signal the universe that you're ready for all the opportunities the solar eclipse will bring.

Wednesday, July 15 (Moon in Aries to Taurus 6:30 p.m.) Assimilate yesterday's events and emotions, and get on with business. You may get together with siblings or neighbors, perhaps for some sort of community project. You may be hurrying to meet a deadline pertaining to a research paper or project or to a book or novel that you're writing.

Thursday, July 16 (Moon in Taurus)   You resist what you must and insist on doing things your way. It's exactly what is needed in this situation, so don't apologize or backpedal. Remain firm and committed to your own path. If the issue involves a relationship, you may want to be more flexible and really listen to what your partner says.

Friday, July 17 (Moon in Taurus to Gemini 11:42 p.m.) Mercury enters Leo, your sixth house. Until August 2, you're involved in conversations and discussions concerning work. This could involve bargaining with employees, planning some sort of trip or project with coworkers, or working on a writing project.

Saturday, July 18 (Moon in Gemini)   A situation at home may need your attention. Perhaps a parent or a child needs help with something. If you're part of the sandwich generation—with young children at home and also responsible for elderly parents—you may be the one who needs help! Enlist the advice of experts.

Sunday, July 19 (Moon in Gemini)   Take things a step at a time. By early tomorrow, the moon will be in a fellow water sign, and you'll feel more positive about everything. You may be completing a home-improvement project.

Monday, July 20 (Moon in Gemini to Cancer 12:52 a.m.) The moon joins Mars in Cancer, your fifth house. This powerful combination brings romance, love, and sexuality together in one very nice package! If you're not involved, this energy could find expression in creative endeavors or in just plain ol' fun!

Tuesday, July 21 (Moon in Cancer)   The solar eclipse in Cancer promises excitement. Even though one relationship or creative project may be ending, the solar eclipse should attract opportunities in romance and creativity, and with children. In fact, if you have been wanting to start a family, this eclipse could make it happen.

Wednesday, July 22 (Moon in Cancer to Leo 12:28 a.m.)
You're the star at work. Be sure to dress for success and to act decisively and with self-confidence. Even if you may not feel particularly self-confident, others will perceive you that way because you speak with authority.

Thursday, July 23 (Moon in Leo)   Strive for diplomacy in your dealings with others. With Jupiter still in your twelfth house, you probably have a clear idea of other people's motives—as well as your own—so don't use that knowledge against anyone. File the information away, and deal with what is visible.

Friday, July 24 (Moon in Leo to Virgo 12:24 a.m.)   If the devil lies in the details, today should be dedicated to details. Whether you're dealing with a professional or a personal issue, your path to understanding the situation lies in what may not be obvious. While you're tending to details, make appointments with health-care professionals for the maintenance of your physical well-being.

Saturday, July 25 (Moon in Virgo)   If you've finished a project already, take another look and, revise, review, and rewrite. Be as picky as you want in your scrutiny. Better to turn in something you love than to turn in something toward which you only feel lukewarm.

Sunday, July 26 (Moon in Virgo to Libra 2:26 a.m.)   It's wise to draw on the expertise of the people around you. While your knowledge is impressive, you may not be an expert in what you're dealing with. Let your intuition loose; it will bring you the people you need.

Monday, July 27 (Moon in Libra)   Take the lead. It could be that the people around you are locked in indecisiveness or simply not available. Approach everyone with forthrightness. It will make things easier in the long run, and the others involved will appreciate your honesty.

Tuesday, July 28 (Moon in Libra to Scorpio 7:57 a.m.)   Research and investigative work are your strong points. You're trying to get to the bottom of a situation or relationship, and once you turn your intuition loose on this issue, you find what you need.

Wednesday, July 29 (Moon in Scorpio)   In a couple days, Venus enters Cancer and your fifth house, signaling the beginning of the most romantic and creative time for you this year. You may be feeling the effects of this impending transit already. Someone new could show up in your life tomorrow, and you'll suddenly be looking at the world through the eyes of an innocent.

Thursday, July 30 (Moon in Scorpio to Sagittarius 5:10 p.m.)   You may be too flexible, too willing to bend to other people's wishes and demands. This issue involves your career or a professional relationship. Tread carefully.

Friday, July 31 (Moon in Sagittarius)   Venus enters Cancer and your fifth house and stays there until August 26. This transit brings opportunities in romance, with creative endeavors, and with activities that make your heart sing. Your self-confidence and sex appeal soar.

AUGUST 2009

Saturday, August 1 (Moon in Sagittarius)   With the moon in your tenth house, you're planning for the week ahead. You socialize at some point and strive to maintain your broader perspective about your career and path in life. There's a lot of flirtation going on with someone special.

Sunday, August 2 (Moon in Sagittarius to Capricorn 5:09 a.m.)   Mercury enters Virgo, your seventh house and remains there until August 25. During this period, you have numerous discussions with romantic and business partners. You tend to be more detail-oriented too, even when it irritates you to be so.

Monday, August 3 (Moon in Capricorn) The moon joins Capricorn in your eleventh house. You may be conscious about spending and power issues related to money and friends. For every dollar you spend, stash another dollar into your savings.

Tuesday, August 4 (Moon in Capricorn to Aquarius 6:08 p.m.) You may be planning a trip for your family or with a group of friends. Check out the usual travel search engines and pick a spot on the globe. Then see what kinds of fares are being offered and figure out the cheapest way of getting there.

Wednesday, August 5 (Moon in Aquarius) The lunar eclipse in Aquarius brings up emotional issues related to the past. You gain insights into your own unconscious, and your insights expand and broaden your life in some way. Mars forms a harmonious angle to this moon, suggesting lots of activity around this date.

Thursday, August 6 (Moon in Aquarius) What would you like to be doing tomorrow when the moon enters your sign? Rather than thinking in terms of obligations and what you should be doing, go with the flow of your emotions and see where it leads.

Friday, August 7 (Moon in Aquarius to Pisces 6:35 a.m.) You feel the shift in energies as soon as you wake up. You may feel a visceral tug toward a particular person or experience. Rather than rationalize the feeling, go with it. Resistance isn't on your agenda.

Saturday, August 8 (Moon in Pisces) If you have an encounter with an animal, think about the deeper meaning. What is the animal's behavior? What myths and fairy tales and legends surround this animal? What are its mating habits? All of this information may hold clues about what the encounter means on a deeper level.

Sunday, August 9 (Moon in Pisces to Aries 5:24 p.m.) If you're having financial troubles, try visualizing yourself with a

219

check for whatever sum you want. Back the visualization with emotion. Create a spread sheet where you enter that amount of money. Experiment. Have fun. Then get out of the way, and let the universe bring you the money you want.

Monday, August 10 (Moon in Aries)   You may pursue something that you know should be left alone. Perhaps it's the result of a feeling of jealousy, possessiveness, or passion. Back off, and think things over. Tomorrow, you'll be glad that you did.

Tuesday, August 11 (Moon in Aries)   Pioneering is something you probably did a lot of in previous lives. And when you trailblaze, it feels familiar, as if you know the terrain. You're forging new emotional synapses in your love life.

Wednesday, August 12 (Moon in Aries to Taurus 1:51 a.m.)   Aesthetic pleasure is the hallmark. You appreciate being surrounded by beauty, so wherever you are, that's what you strive to do. Seems as if your choices are wide-open.

Thursday, August 13 (Moon in Taurus)   Yesterday's revisions are today's new ideas. You may want to spend a few minutes grounding yourself. Whether it's through meditation or some other technique, it enables you to get in touch with your most genuine feelings and desires.

Friday, August 14 (Moon in Taurus to Gemini 7:27 a.m.) Indulge your restlessness by changing your routine in some way. There are a million ways to do something or to think about a given topic. Explore your options.

Saturday, August 15 (Moon in Gemini)   You're into body language—not your own, but that of a family member. What the person says with his or her body reveals just about everything you need to know. You're so intuitive that you don't need a repeat performance.

Sunday, August 16 (Moon in Gemini to Cancer 10:14 a.m.) One of the best ways to understand the patterns that operate in your own life is to take note of how lunar transits affect you. When the moon enters Cancer, for example, how do you feel? What kinds of experiences do you have? Does your love life pick up? Does your creative adrenaline really get going?

Monday, August 17 (Moon in Cancer)   You're in the mood for creating. Ideas flow fast and furiously, and you have to be sure you capture all of them. Ideas are like books that you save for rainy days. Have a file for them on your computer that you can consult when your creativity seems flat.

Tuesday, August 18 (Moon in Cancer to Leo 10:57 a.m.) The day after tomorrow there will be a new moon in Virgo, your sixth house. Prepare for it now by listing the opportunities and experiences related to your work routine and health you would like to have. A new job? Include it. More pay? Include it. You get the idea.

Wednesday, August 19 (Moon in Leo)   You could be challenged at work. Someone annoys you or pesters you in some way. You react with hostility, and from there, of course, things only snowball. Or, at any rate, that's one version of events. But if you're aware of what the energy is, you can change it and the situation by toning down your reaction.

Thursday, August 20 (Moon in Leo to Virgo 11:01 a.m.) The new moon in Virgo should attract opportunities related to work, health, and interactions with the larger world. Mars forms a harmonious angle to this new moon, indicating a lot of activity that ushers in opportunities. Travel could be involved too.

Friday, August 21 (Moon in Virgo)   The moon in your seventh house usually may lead to some sort of tension between you and a partner. It's not serious, but it should be addressed as soon as it happens. If you just let it slide, the tension may fester, and the repercussions will multiply.

Saturday, August 22 (Moon in Virgo to Libra 12:12 p.m.) Activities revolve around balance, relationships, and socializing. You may have to revise the terms of a mortgage or loan, perhaps through refinancing. You could be delving into areas like reincarnation and communication with the dead.

Sunday, August 23 (Moon in Libra)   Can you put off making a decision for a few more days? Wait until the moon is in a fellow water sign. In fact, Tuesday would be the day to make your decision. Mars enters Cancer that day, galvanizing everything you do for fun and amusement.

Monday, August 24 (Moon in Libra to Scorpio 4:17 p.m.)   This afternoon, the moon enters fellow water sign Scorpio, and you're after the absolute bottom line. And if you can't get that, you're not interested. Your business interests may be expanding to overseas markets.

Tuesday, August 25 (Moon in Scorpio)   Mercury enters Libra, your eighth house, and Mars enters Cancer. The first transit brings taxes and insurance matters up front and center in your life until October 28. During this period, Mercury will be retrograde from September 6 to 29. So sign contracts and travel on either side of that date. The transit of Mars lasts until October 16 and heightens your sexuality, your creative drive, and romance.

Wednesday, August 26 (Moon in Scorpio)   Venus enters Leo, your sixth house, where it remains until September 20. During this period, your work life should run smoothly, and an office flirtation could launch a relationship. But be careful about mixing business with pleasure.

Thursday, August 27 (Moon in Scorpio to Sagittarius 12:16 a.m.)   The moon enters your tenth house and fire signs figure prominently in events. An Aries, a Leo, or a Sagittarius is helpful in career matters. Someone in your family shares ideas that you can use professionally.

Friday, August 28 (Moon in Sagittarius)   The day calls for greater flexibility on your part. It's due to a career matter that may not be going quite as you hoped. The situation is easily rectified, by adjusting your attitude and seeing things from the other person's point of view.

Saturday, August 29 (Moon in Sagittarius to Capricorn 11:45 a.m.) You may hook up with your support group. Whether it's a group of writers, actors, artists, or people who follow a particular political and spiritual belief, you come away refreshed and recharged. You have the creative inspiration and drive to pursue your dreams.

Sunday, August 30 (Moon in Capricorn) You have a lot of friends and even more acquaintances, part of your network. The party may be at your place today. So go all out. But don't overdo it. Tomorrow is a workday.

Monday, August 31 (Moon in Capricorn) Hidden issues surface. They involve your own motives or those of someone else. If you don't like what you discover, strive to change it by focusing your intentions on what you want to happen.

SEPTEMBER 2009

Tuesday, September 1 (Moon in Capricorn to Aquarius 12:43 a.m.) Yesterday's hidden issues become today's conversation. You're trying to puzzle through what you learned and may need some help figuring it all out. Ask an air sign for help—a Gemini, a Libra, or an Aquarius.

Wednesday, September 2 (Moon in Aquarius) You rarely lack for ideas. How can you make them practical? How can you implement them in your life and work? Tomorrow, when the moon has moved into your sign, you'll gain clarity on this issue.

Thursday, September 3 (Moon in Aquarius to Pisces 12:59 p.m.) A relationship that begins this close to the full moon in your sign will be unusual, to say the least. However, if you're involved already, tomorrow's full moon simply brings

223

clarity to your feelings. Today, the person you meet is someone you have known in previous lives.

Friday, September 4 (Moon in Pisces)   The full moon in your sign may require an attitude adjustment on your part in terms of a romantic relationship. You gain insight and clarity into a personal issue. Events probably unfold without warning, taking you by surprise.

Saturday, September 5 (Moon in Pisces to Aries 11:15 p.m.)   Money is your focus. You may be trying to earn more of it and feel somewhat frustrated by your lack of progress. Focus on the abundance in your life, whatever form it takes. And nurture the art of appreciation. Mercury turns retrograde tomorrow in Libra. Back up your computer files!

Sunday, September 6 (Moon in Aries)   Mercury turns retrograde in Libra and stays that way until September 29. Don't apply for mortgages or loans under this retrograde. In fact, don't make any investment decisions. Just lie low financially.

Monday, September 7 (Moon in Aries)   You'll feel like going on a spending spree. Instead, hit the thrift shops. Keep your expenses low. At the end of the month, you'll be glad you did. If your values are attacked by someone, just turn around and walk away.

Tuesday, September 8 (Moon in Aries to Taurus 7:19 a.m.)   Try not to become trapped by your own perceptions. Just because you think you're right doesn't mean that you are. Listen to another person's point of view. Then make up your mind later this month.

Wednesday, September 9 (Moon in Taurus)   You may be tapped to work on a neighborhood beautification project. You'd like to volunteer, but time may be a factor. Before you commit, consider this. A relative may figure into activities.

Thursday, September 10 (Moon in Taurus to Gemini 1:18 p.m.)   The moon enters your fourth house, stirring up activity and emotions, and triggering a need for more information. You and one of your parents iron out differences in your relationship.

Friday, September 11 (Moon in Gemini)   Pluto turns direct in your eleventh house. You'll feel the impact over time, as issues with friends begin to straighten out. This transit, though, is a very long one, so don't expect immediate effects. You may have to compromise to reach an agreement with a family member.

Saturday, September 12 (Moon in Gemini to Cancer 5:20 p.m.)   The moon joins Mars in Cancer, in your fifth house. This combination of planets should really rev up your creative adrenaline. Time to get serious about doing what you love and making your living at it. This combo also heightens your sexuality, and you're actively seeking love and romance.

Sunday, September 13 (Moon in Cancer)   Intuitively, you're in very high gear. So go with your hunches and don't allow your left brain to shout over what you know to be true. Since it's the weekend, get out and do what you love. Another water sign may be part of the picture—a Cancer, a Pisces, or a Scorpio.

Monday, September 14 (Moon in Cancer to Leo 7:40 p.m.)   There's something a bit different about the day. As the moon makes its transition from Cancer to Leo, you can feel the shift in energies. You're suddenly feeling more flamboyant, showy, ready to strut your stuff.

Tuesday, September 15 (Moon in Leo)   Let the air fill your senses, and then take your goodwill out into the larger world. There are gaps in other people's lives that beg to be filled. Today is about service to others. Figure out where you can be of help, and then volunteer.

Wednesday, September 16 (Moon in Leo to Virgo 8:56 p.m.)   If you feel you're being taken advantage of, speak up. Whether it involves a business or personal partnership, you're entitled to your opinion. Don't hold in what you feel. Deal with things as they are, not as you wish things to be.

Thursday, September 17 (Moon in Virgo)   You may want to plan something special for this weekend for your partner, especially with tomorrow's new moon in Virgo coming up. If you're not involved, do something special for yourself!

Friday, September 18 (Moon in Virgo to Libra 10:26 p.m.) The new moon in Virgo attracts business and personal partners. If you're not involved, you will be soon. If you're involved already, this new moon indicates the relationship may be taken to a higher level. In business, you attract exactly the right person you need at this point in time.

Saturday, September 19 (Moon in Libra)   Your spiritual or political beliefs take center stage. You may feel conflicted about your beliefs in some way, and this conflict attracts a confrontation that forces you to clarify what you believe.

Sunday, September 20 (Moon in Libra)   Venus enters Virgo, your seventh house, a transit that lasts until October 14. This should be a very romantic and even creative period for this year. If you're involved, this transit may have the two of you moving in together or getting married. If you're not involved, hold on to your hat. Things are about to get very interesting!

Monday, September 21 (Moon in Libra to Scorpio 1:52 a.m.) This moon sharpens your edges and gives you penetrating insight into other people's motives and agendas. Your intense feelings toward someone deepen. You're a seeker of truth.

Tuesday, September 22 (Moon in Scorpio)   With Mercury still retrograde, you may be scrambling to set things right with a partner, family member, or friend. You might consider putting everything in an e-mail. Sometimes, it's helpful to get your feelings on paper.

Wednesday, September 23 (Moon in Scorpio to Sagittarius 8:44 a.m.)   It's a career day, and you are prepped and ready. There may be travel related to your career and work. But you're even ready for that, with your bag packed and Mercury retrograde. Just remain flexible. Your schedule will change.

Thursday, September 24 (Moon in Sagittarius)   You're in an expansive, buoyant mood, and it spills over, infusing people around you. Suddenly, you're the center of attention, with colleagues and bosses clamoring for you. People figure you have the answers!

Friday, September 25 (Moon in Sagittarius to Capricorn 7:19 p.m.)   You enjoy this earth-sign moon. It helps to ground your ideas, to make you more practical in your approach to life and living. It also helps to solidify your relationship with a particular group of friends.

Saturday, September 26 (Moon in Capricorn)   You hook up with your support group. This could be just a group of friends with whom you meet periodically for lunch or a group of writers, actors, or political activists—whatever your passion is.

Sunday, September 27 (Moon in Capricorn)   If your dreams and goals are in flux, fine-tune them. You may want to look back over the past five years to see how far you've come. If you're not satisfied with where you are, make a one-year plan.

Monday, September 28 (Moon in Capricorn to Aquarius 8:07 a.m.)   Tomorrow, Mercury turns direct. You'll start feeling the energy—a kind of difference in your communications with people. You may retreat for a while to do research and creative work.

Tuesday, September 29 (Moon in Aquarius)   Mercury turns direct. This is always cause for celebration, but today it really is. You can move forward with your holiday travel plans. Touch base with clients and friends. Get ready for the moon to move into your sign tomorrow.

Wednesday, September 30 (Moon in Aquarius to Pisces 8:27 p.m.) You're ready for a power day. You may attract the attention of another water sign and feel a deep tug of attraction, particularly if this person is a Scorpio. It's safe to apply for that mortgage or loan.

OCTOBER 2009

Thursday, October 1 (Moon in Pisces) To enhance this power day, consider conducting some sort of ritual to celebrate who you are. You may want to meditate for a few minutes at some point just to underscore your intuitive nature and to find out where your imagination may take you.

Friday, October 2 (Moon in Pisces) Your dream recall is terrific. Whether it's an afternoon nap or your regular sleep at night, keep a notebook and pen handy. Your dreams are likely to provide insights into issues that concern you, they may cough up visions of the future, and they could even take you straight into a past life.

Saturday, October 3 (Moon in Pisces to Aries 6:21 a.m.) Finances are your top priority. You're anticipating a large expense in some area, and you may be stashing away money for that purchase. But with the holidays rapidly approaching, you may have to dig into your savings for a gift for someone special in your life.

Sunday, October 4 (Moon in Aries) The full moon in Aries clarifies a financial issue. It also may have you feeling pretty restless, perhaps even directionless. That feeling won't last long.

Monday, October 5 (Moon in Aries to Taurus 1:34 p.m.) It's a communication day. Whether you're writing or talking, you're very clear and precise in what you say. Others appreciate your ability to express yourself. You may be digging in your heels about something related to your neighborhood or community.

Tuesday, October 6 (Moon in Taurus)   You can sell anything to anyone. Even if you're not in sales, you can sell an idea or concept. You'll surprise yourself!

Wednesday, October 7 (Moon in Taurus to Gemini 6:47 p.m.)   This evening, home will be your focus. Plan something special with your family, even if it's just a dinner out. Your parents could be a part of this scenario. On some level, you're collecting information that you'll use later this month.

Thursday, October 8 (Moon in Gemini)   Yesterday, you dealt with foundations. Today you deal with what you can see, hear, and feel. Things are up close and personal, and your imagination fills in the gaps. Before you jump to any conclusions, open the group to discussion.

Friday, October 9 (Moon in Gemini to Cancer 10:48 p.m.) Tonight, you don't have to dig very far for inspiration. Your muse is close enough to whisper in your ear. But you have to commit to the time. Take advantage of this energy for the next two days. You might be able to finish your manuscript or portfolio, or you might land the audition of your dreams!

Saturday, October 10 (Moon in Cancer)   You're especially sensitive to the moods of others. If you have kids, you'll have to resist smothering them with love and attention, especially if they're teens. Mars is in Cancer for another six days. The combination creates an intuitive flow that you can dip into whenever you want.

Sunday, October 11 (Moon in Cancer)   Your impulses lead you in important directions creatively. You may want to brainstorm with a partner or friend, or write down your ideas. Get them down so that on days when you don't feel as creative, you can use them.

Monday, October 12 (Moon in Cancer to Leo 2:03 a.m.) Jupiter turns direct in Aquarius, your twelfth house. It will now be easier for you to integrate your worldview and spiritual beliefs into your life. And you'll start with your work routine. How can you improve this situation?

Tuesday, October 13 (Moon in Leo)   You and your partner can enjoy each other's company without petty differences intervening. In fact, you may want to get off together this evening for some activity you both enjoy.

Wednesday, October 14 (Moon in Leo to Virgo 4:46 a.m.) Venus enters Libra, your eighth house, and doesn't move on again until November 7. During this period, applications for mortgages and loans go well. You could get a break on tax or insurance matters. If a relationship begins under this transit, balance will be key to its success.

Thursday, October 15 (Moon in Virgo)   You may be more self-critical or critical of others. It's vital that you back off on the criticism. It will only create discord and unhappiness. Instead, practice the art of appreciation.

Friday, October 16 (Moon in Virgo to Libra 7:30 a.m.) Mars enters Leo and your sixth house, where it will be through the end of the year. It will be retrograde from December 20 on into 2010. During this transit, your work routine will undergo change. You may be more concerned about your appearance.

Saturday, October 17 (Moon in Libra)   You're happiest when harmony prevails. So don't do anything to rock the boat. Keep your criticism to yourself, and focus on self-perfection. Your artistic interests take center stage later in the day.

Sunday, October 18 (Moon in Libra to Scorpio 11:23 a.m.) The new moon in Libra ushers in opportunities in social relationships, mortgages, taxes, and insurance. You could have the chance to explore the deeper questions in life too—something at which every Pisces excels.

Monday, October 19 (Moon in Scorpio)   Try not to overreact. Even though your emotions are intense, and you could be somewhat jealous or taken aback by a partner's actions or words, don't let things get out of hand. Tomorrow, as they say, is another day. Even better, wait until the moon is in Capricorn to get things off your chest.

Tuesday, October 20 (Moon in Scorpio to Sagittarius 5:50 p.m.)   The gregarious Sagittarius moon has you focused on career matters, but with great humor and optimism. Your mood spreads throughout the office like a beneficial virus, and makes the day far more enjoyable to everyone in your environment.

Wednesday, October 21 (Moon in Sagittarius)   You gain prestige and support just when you need it. Colleagues are behind you a hundred percent. Bosses are paying close attention. Some travel may be involved in the day's events—something other than your regular commute.

Thursday, October 22 (Moon in Sagittarius)   Your love life should be moving full speed ahead, with Mars in Cancer making you more aware of the importance of roots, family, and stability. Start submitting manuscripts and portfolios, and scheduling auditions.

Friday, October 23 (Moon in Sagittarius to Capricorn 3:40 a.m.)   In your research, insist on getting the full picture, not just bits and pieces. This may require some intensive investigation over the Internet. If you need other facts and figures, consult an expert in the field.

Saturday, October 24 (Moon in Capricorn)   There is power within a group of individuals coming from the same place. Whether the group's interest is politics or spirituality or something else altogether, you stand united. Change begins when it gathers momentum.

Sunday, October 25 (Moon in Capricorn to Aquarius 3:08 p.m.)   A kick-back kind of day. You may want to get off by yourself. If it's fall where you are, take a hike, a walk, or a bike ride. If it's warm where you are, head to the pool or the beach, if that's possible. You need to recharge by relaxing.

Monday, October 26 (Moon in Aquarius)   You could be virtual traveling, in preparation for a trip. With Mercury entering Scorpio and your ninth house on October 28, your destination could be overseas. Find out what you can about the country you're going to visit. A traveler is never overprepared.

Tuesday, October 27 (Moon in Aquarius)   You and a partner spend the day together. Regardless of where this together time takes place, it renews your spirits and your relationship. Sometimes, you simply have to get out of the routine of your ordinary life and rediscover the magic you are certain exists beneath the surface.

Wednesday, October 28 (Moon in Aquarius to Pisces 3:46 a.m.)   Mercury enters Scorpio and remains there until November 15. During this time, your emotional focus shifts to your belief system. It may be that you've absorbed beliefs from family and friends. Untangle the web.

Thursday, October 29 (Moon in Pisces)   Saturn enters Libra—a major transit that lasts for about two and a half years. Since the moon is in your sign, you may be too caught up in your own stuff to realize the importance of this transit.

Friday, October 30 (Moon in Pisces to Aries 1:57 p.m.)   If you find yourself in a blue funk, it may be because you're absorbing the energy of people around you. Turn in early so you can save energy for the weekend ahead.

Saturday, October 31 (Moon in Aries)   Happy Halloween! You could be shopping to show your appreciation for someone you love. Be sure to make the gift specific to that person. A generic gift just won't cut it.

NOVEMBER 2009

Sunday, November 1—Daylight Saving Time Ends (Moon in Aries to Taurus, 7:45 p.m.)   Conversations with relatives are likely today; perhaps they'll concern the upcoming holidays. Whose house will the celebrations be at this year? Behind the scenes, there may be some soul-searching going on concerning a relationship.

Monday, November 2 (Moon in Taurus) The full moon in Taurus brings insights concerning a relative, a communication project, or your neighborhood and community. Your beliefs may come up against those of someone close to you. News is also possible, particularly if you're a writer or in the communication business.

Tuesday, November 3 (Moon in Taurus to Gemini 11:53 p.m.) Get organized. You'll need to as the moon enters Gemini late tonight. Persevere to get things done. You're in the right place at the right time, but you have to believe you are. Without that underlying belief in yourself, it's all just words.

Wednesday, November 4 (Moon in Gemini) Neptune turns direct in Aquarius. Once again, the effects of this movement are subtle because Neptune crawls through the zodiac. But you should be in a much better spot now to integrate your ideals and idealism into your life. Remember, too, that Jupiter is also in the same sign and house, expanding your inner world.

Thursday, November 5 (Moon in Gemini) After your organization spree, you may want to take time to retreat. Maybe you take the day off from work and usher the family out of town for a long weekend. You're dealing with the foundation of who you are.

Friday, November 6 (Moon in Gemini to Cancer 2:43 a.m.) The moon represents feminine yin energy, the mother, your emotional security. Your emotional security lies in two primary areas: your creative output and your love life. Your mother or another nurturing female plays a role in activities.

Saturday, November 7 (Moon in Cancer) Venus enters Scorpio, your ninth house. During this transit, which lasts until December 1, romance abroad is likely. And if you're not traveling overseas, you could meet someone from another country who interests you. If you're involved already, you and your partner may head overseas for a trip that has some deeper purpose. Sounds like the beginning of a quest.

Sunday, November 8 (Moon in Cancer to Leo 5:23 a.m.) Look beyond the immediate. Nurture yourself in the same way that you nurture others. Set your goals, and get to work. Mars is also in Leo and your sixth house, galvanizing you to achieve and accomplish.

Monday, November 9 (Moon in Leo)   It's a service day. You're taking care of your own business, but you also may be doing a good deed for someone else. This is the sort of thing you do because you are moved by the other person's situation or plight.

Tuesday, November 10 (Moon in Leo to Virgo 8:31 a.m.) The moon enters your opposite sign, shifting your emotional focus to a business or romantic partnership. It's wise to pay attention to the kind of details you might miss ordinarily because they seem mundane. But the mundane is the day's saving grace!

Wednesday, November 11 (Moon in Virgo)   You have the ability to make friends with anyone, even people who don't like you. It's not just your charm and wit, but your ability to reach inside other people and extract their innate goodness. Put this skill to work.

Thursday, November 12 (Moon in Virgo to Libra 12:23 p.m.) Relationships are the focus. You may need balance in this area of your life, but aren't sure how to achieve it. Enlist the help of a Gemini, a Libra, or an Aquarius. They're great with ideas, and ideas are exactly what you need now.

Friday, November 13 (Moon in Libra)   A romance blossoms. And while that's going on, you may sign up for a seminar in an esoteric topic that interests you.

Saturday, November 14 (Moon in Libra to Scorpio 5:25 p.m.)   Here's that intense Scorpio moon. But you're ready for it. Your creative adrenaline is pumping fast and furiously, you're on top of the holiday preparations, and you've got your activities lined up.

Sunday, November 15 (Moon in Scorpio)   Mercury enters Sagittarius, your tenth house. During this transit, which ends on December 5, you'll have ample opportunities to pitch your ideas and gather support for your pet projects. You may even be traveling for work. Even if your focus isn't on your professional life, use this transit to push forward in your career.

Monday, November 16 (Moon in Scorpio)   Today's new moon in Scorpio ushers in opportunities related to education, overseas travel, or an expansion of your business interests overseas. You may be doing more research and investigative work of some kind. Neptune forms a close and challenging angle to this new moon, suggesting that you should be careful about deceptive scams.

Tuesday, November 17 (Moon in Scorpio to Sagittarius 12:23 a.m.)   The moon joins Mercury in Sagittarius, your tenth house. The combination of energies makes this the ideal day to pitch ideas, submit manuscripts, schedule auditions, or put the finishing touches on a portfolio. Your security lies in your satisfaction with your career.

Wednesday, November 18 (Moon in Sagittarius)   You're very responsive to the needs of colleagues and coworkers. You're more in the public view, perhaps due to travel or public relations or even public speaking. Your relationship with a boss goes well.

Thursday, November 19 (Moon in Sagittarius to Capricorn 10:01 a.m.)   Conclude projects and reflect on how to expand your base. Your friends may hold vital clues to how you can do this. Perhaps it's simply a matter of broadening your network.

Friday, November 20 (Moon in Capricorn)   Capricorn excels at long-range planning, so use the lunar energies to examine your goals. How can you best attain these goals? Do you need more education or greater opportunities? Would it be in your best interest to move to a different area?

Saturday, November 21 (Moon in Capricorn to Aquarius 10:11 p.m.)   The moon joins Neptune and Jupiter in your twelfth house. This trio of planets heightens everything you do behind the scenes. Your understanding of your own unconscious is broadening and deepening.

Sunday, November 22 (Moon in Aquarius)   Time to ease up on your routine. Kick back with a favorite book or movie, or get together with a group of friends and celebrate the upcoming holidays early. Tomorrow you'll have plenty of time for your Thanksgiving preparations.

Monday, November 23 (Moon in Aquarius)   Keep your feelings to yourself. Tomorrow, you'll be glad that you did. You're working on uncovering your own motives and inhibitions. Your imagination and intuition are valuable guides in this area. Tomorrow, the moon enters your sign, so you're preparing for another power day.

Tuesday, November 24 (Moon in Aquarius to Pisces 11:08 a.m.)   With the moon entering your sign this morning, you're feeling physically vital and upbeat. Approach everything with an unconventional attitude. Don't hesitate to think outside the box. Unconventional thinking takes you much farther than the status quo.

Wednesday, November 25 (Moon in Pisces)   Your Thanksgiving preparations are done, and you're ready to rock and roll! Whether the festivities are at your place or someone else's, you've got the food prepared, you're in the proper frame of mind for appreciation, and you're ready to enjoy yourself.

Thursday, November 26 (Moon in Pisces to Aries 10:11 p.m.)
Happy Thanksgiving! Your values certainly come into play.

You look around at the people with whom you share your life and realize that the outer world is a perfect expression of your inner world. So, if the day is great for you, how can you attract more of this good feeling into your life?

Friday, November 27 (Moon in Aries)   It's the biggest shopping day of the year in the U.S. So when someone suggests going to the local mall for a jump on holiday shopping, you may want to think twice about it—unless you love crowds.

Saturday, November 28 (Moon in Aries)   You're on a mind trip that could take you into unexplored terrains. It's as if you're aware of the invisible world that moves to the right and left of you, but your eyes are straight ahead. Live in the moment.

Sunday, November 29 (Moon in Aries to Taurus 5:35 a.m.) You tackle a community or neighborhood project. This could include writing or some other type of mass communication, perhaps through a Web site.

Monday, November 30 (Moon in Taurus)   As you get ready to enter the last month of the year, take stock of where you have been this year and where you would like to be next year. Lay down your goals. It's not too early to think about New Year's resolutions!

DECEMBER 2009

Tuesday, December 1 (Moon in Taurus to Gemini 9:24 a.m.) Venus enters Sagittarius and your tenth house, and Uranus turns direct. Even if you're not fully into professional matters, this Venus transit, which lasts until December 25, is fantastic for your career. Travel could also be involved. For romance, it may indicate a relationship with a colleague or someone you meet through work. Uranus's movement should help straighten out your personal life!

Wednesday, December 2 (Moon in Gemini)   The full moon in Gemini brings lots of activity at home. You gain insight into a family issue. With both Mars and Saturn forming wide but harmonious angles to this moon, your insights are funneled into the proper structure.

Thursday, December 3 (Moon in Gemini to Cancer 11:01 a.m.)   The moon stirs up your emotions concerning a relationship or a creative endeavor. Use the emotions in a positive way, and then you're on a roll. You could feel somewhat possessive about kids or loved ones. You may have to back off some.

Friday, December 4 (Moon in Cancer)   You could be feeling somewhat nostalgic for a relationship, a certain time in your life, a parent, or a place that you lived. These feelings can be transformed into creative fodder. You may want to spend some time with your kids. You've earned the time off!

Saturday, December 5 (Moon in Cancer to Leo 12:08 p.m.)   Mercury enters Capricorn, your eleventh house. This transit, which ends on December 25, should bring plenty of invites for holiday festivities. You may be involved in some sort of group activity that has a long-range plan too.

Sunday, December 6 (Moon in Leo)   Your health and how to maintain it occupies you. Maybe it's time to hit the gym, take that yoga class you've been promising yourself, or join an aerobics class. If you shop, it's with the new you in mind!

Monday, December 7 (Moon in Leo to Virgo 2:07 p.m.) The moon enters your opposite sign. Now that Saturn has finally moved out of Virgo and into Libra, there's a lightness in most of your partnerships that has been absent the past few years. Enjoy it.

Tuesday, December 8 (Moon in Virgo)   Women play an important role—anyone from friends to a female relative. Don't allow others to manipulate your feelings. You know who you are and where you're going and what you feel right this second.

Wednesday, December 9 (Moon in Virgo to Libra 5:48 p.m.)   The moon joins Saturn in your eighth house. There's a certain heaviness to this combination, but it also provides the right structure for the exploration of metaphysics.

Thursday, December 10 (Moon in Libra)   Romance with a coworker could blossom. If you're involved already, you and a partner may undertake a project together. Think back to a time when you felt really happy and buoyant. Then try to conjure those emotions if you feel low.

Friday, December 11 (Moon in Libra to Scorpio 11:32 p.m.)   The highlights involve publishing and education. If you're headed for college next year, you may be preparing to take SATs or GREs, or you may be involved in extracurricular activities that look good on applications.

Saturday, December 12 (Moon in Scorpio)   Your research is taking unexpected turns, but you're anticipating the adventure. It's like a treasure hunt, and even if you don't find the treasure, the search and the journey are what matter.

Sunday, December 13 (Moon in Scorpio)   Whatever you learn is something you can put to work immediately. It may be connected to your deeper beliefs and how those beliefs create your reality from the inside out.

Monday, December 14 (Moon in Scorpio to Sagittarius 7:25 a.m.)   You may feel somewhat conflicted. You have obligations at home and at work. Given the upcoming holidays, your best bet is to take the day off and finish up your holiday shopping. Then play catch-up with clients and colleagues by phone or e-mail.

Tuesday, December 15 (Moon in Sagittarius)   Tomorrow's new moon in Capricorn will set the stage for your career in the New Year. So start thinking about what you would like for

239

yourself professionally over the next year. Take steps to set a plan into action at work.

Wednesday, December 16 (Moon in Sagittarius to Capricorn 5:32 p.m.)   The new moon in Capricorn ushers in opportunities for career options. You may find a new job, get a raise or a promotion, or move to another location within your company. It's also possible that you'll become self-employed. It all depends on what you want.

Thursday, December 17 (Moon in Capricorn)   You do some things for money, and other things for the love of it. Today it's a combination of those energies. But you may be wondering how you can earn money doing what you love. Ask a Taurus.

Friday, December 18 (Moon in Capricorn)   Until December 20, every planet is moving in direct motion. That means they're all functioning the way they should be. So for this weekend, take advantage of that energy, and do something special with the special people in your life.

Saturday, December 19 (Moon in Capricorn to Aquarius 5:39 a.m.)   You're finalizing your holiday plans. Whether you're going out of town or having the festivities at home, there are plenty of details to tend to. In addition, your inner world continues to expand, offering insights into issues that concern you.

Sunday, December 20 (Moon in Aquarius)   Mars turns retrograde in Leo. The timing on this is probably good, what with the holidays taking your mind off work. But until mid-March, when Mars turns direct, you may be revisiting work issues and situations that you thought were resolved.

Monday, December 21 (Moon in Aquarius to Pisces 6:42 p.m.)
With the moon entering your sign, you're in high spirits, and with good reason. People are either arriving at your place, or you and your partner and family are leaving town. If you're single or uncommitted, you've got plenty on your plate.

Tuesday, December 22 (Moon in Pisces)   Your thoughts and feelings are in alignment. That angst you often feel is blessedly absent. Your physical vitality is strong; your intuition is right on target. Take time to listen to others. There are plenty of stories to hear!

Wednesday, December 23 (Moon in Pisces)   If someone you know has a birthday, be sure that person isn't celebrating alone. Bring the person to your place, or have a surprise party. In a sense, this is your holiday gift for the person—you're helping her or him to create memories that will last.

Thursday, December 24 (Moon in Pisces to Aries 6:40 a.m.) The spotlight is on independence. You're on fire with ideas and plans. You may want to keep them to yourself. You sometimes puzzle the people around you, and these plans will have them totally baffled.

Friday, December 25 (Moon in Aries)   Merry Christmas! Venus enters Capricorn and your eleventh house, making it likely that in 2010, you'll have plenty of social invitations coming your way. Some may be from friends you haven't seen for a while.

Saturday, December 26 (Moon in Aries to Taurus 3:27 a.m.) Mercury turns retrograde in Capricorn. This movement may change your New Year's Eve plans, so remain flexible and open, and don't be surprised if a party gets canceled at the last minute or if someone tosses a party at the last minute.

Sunday, December 27 (Moon in Taurus)   The moon entered your third house yesterday and you know the score on this moon! It's stubborn, it likes to have its own way, and it doesn't give in easily. But that's exactly what're required from you. Dealings with relatives may be getting a bit more challenging.

Monday, December 28 (Moon in Taurus to Gemini 8:15 p.m.)   The moon enters your fourth house, stimulating your home and family life. There could be some miscommunications, particularly with Mercury moving retrograde. Be sure everyone is on the same page before you attempt a dinner discussion!

Tuesday, December 29 (Moon in Gemini)   The gathering and dissemination of information is at the top of your agenda. There's no telling what the information is about—with your active imagination, it could be about virtually anything. But you're surrounded by your supporters.

Wednesday, December 30 (Moon in Gemini to Cancer 9:46 p.m.)   How nice that your year will end with the moon in your fifth house of romance, creativity, and fun. It certainly is a nice send-off to 2009 and a great way to greet 2010.

Thursday, December 31 (Moon in Cancer)   The lunar eclipse in Cancer brings up feelings and emotions concerning romance, children, and all your creative endeavors. You may be looking back over 2009 with whoever is sharing your New Year's Eve.

HAPPY NEW YEAR!

JANUARY 2010

Friday, January 1 (Moon in Cancer to Leo 10:42 p.m.)
Even though it's New Year's Day, your thoughts are on work. You may even be involved in some work, perhaps to get a jump on things on Monday. If you haven't written up your New Year's resolutions, do it today, while the year is still fresh and filled with promise.

Saturday, January 2 (Moon in Leo)   Mercury began the year retrograde in Capricorn, and that won't change until January 15. It may mess up your social calendar until then. Hopefully, you backed up your computer files before the retrograde began in December. Hold off on purchasing any big-ticket items until after January 15.

Sunday, January 3 (Moon in Leo to Virgo 10:53 p.m.)   Your focus shifts to others—specifically your spouse or partner, either in romance or in business. The two of you may be scrutinizing the fine points of your relationship. Try not to do too much navel gazing. You run the risk of miring the relationship in constant critique mode.

Monday, January 4 (Moon in Virgo)   If you're feeling self-critical today, blame the Virgo moon. There's no point in taking yourself to task for something that happened in the past. Your point of power lies in the present, so it's best to use the moment to turn your feelings and thoughts in a more positive direction.

Tuesday, January 5 (Moon in Virgo)   You may feel somewhat vulnerable about a relationship. The reality is probably much different, with the relationship on solid footing. But no one can convince you of that. It's a conclusion you have to arrive at on your own. In the end, it all comes down to belief.

Wednesday, January 6 (Moon in Virgo to Libra 12:59 a.m.)   The social Libra moon enjoys all things artistic and beautiful, and wants everyone to be happy. You may not be able to make everyone happy, but you certainly can beautify your own surroundings. You may want to download onto your iPod music that soothes your soul.

Thursday, January 7 (Moon in Libra)   You're seeking balance today among your various responsibilities. But balance may be the very thing that eludes you. At least you're aware of it and of your need for time to yourself, away from the demands of other people.

Friday, January 8 (Moon in Libra to Scorpio 6:01 a.m.)   In some way, an investigation of your spiritual beliefs comes into play today. You may be looking into ways to expand your product or services or those of your company to foreign markets. This moon forms a harmonious angle to Jupiter in Capricorn, so there's an expansiveness about events today.

Saturday, January 9 (Moon in Scorpio)   The Scorpio moon helps you make decisions more easily. It enhances your intuition, and you're able to tap in to the deeper parts of your own psyche today. Whether you're searching for new ideas or simply looking for answers to various issues, this moon helps you to accomplish your goal.

Sunday, January 10 (Moon in Scorpio to Sagittarius 2:10 p.m.)   The moon enters your tenth house, the career sector of your chart. For the next two and a half days, whether you're at work or not, your focus is on professional matters and relationships. Your own flexibility and ability to go with the flow may surprise you and everyone around you.

Monday, January 11 (Moon in Sagittarius)   Looking for the big picture today? You've got it, as it exists in your career and professional life. It's as if something clicks in the back of your mind, and you suddenly grasp what you're doing, what you're supposed to be doing, and why.

Tuesday, January 12 (Moon in Sagittarius)   You've got plenty of drive and ambition today, but you're a bit restless as well. Perhaps that's the part of your feelings you should indulge. Knock off early from work, if you can, and head out of town. It doesn't have to be a long drive. The point is the journey. Does it open your head?

Wednesday, January 13 (Moon in Sagittarius to Capricorn 12:54 a.m.)   Saturn turns retrograde in Libra today and remains that way until May 30. During this retrograde period, it's best not to apply for mortgages or loans, since there may be delays or restrictions imposed. The Capricorn moon brings structure and focus to your social life and your friendships.

Thursday, January 14 (Moon in Capricorn)   On January 17, Jupiter will enter your sign, and between then and June 6, when it enters Aries, you're in for a delightfully lucky ride! Reread the big-picture section for your sign. The focus today is on your friendships and any group to which you belong. You may decide to work more closely with a political party or some other group that supports your interests.

Friday, January 15 (Moon in Capricorn to Aquarius 1:17 p.m.)   Two events occur today—a solar eclipse in Capricorn, and Mercury turns direct in Capricorn. The eclipse should attract new friends and new ways for you to achieve your wishes and dreams. Venus is exactly conjunct to the eclipse degree, indicating there could be a new romantic relationship or a new creative project in the offing.

Saturday, January 16 (Moon in Aquarius)   Now that Mercury is moving direct, things in your life should begin to pick up steam again. Right now you're focused on tying up projects so that you'll be ready for the moon entering your sign on Monday. Clean out your closet, your garage, or any spot where stuff accumulates. Symbolically, you're making room for the new.

Sunday, January 17 (Moon in Aquarius)   Jupiter enters your sign, certainly a cause for celebration. Think of this transit as the Midas touch. It expands everything in your life, offering you new opportunities to broaden your intellect, your creativity, and your understanding of the larger world. About the only drawback to be aware of is that Jupiter can cause excess too. Excessive spending, for instance. Weight gain. So be mindful and present during this transit.

Monday, January 18 (Moon in Aquarius to Pisces 2:18 a.m.) Venus enters Aquarius and your twelfth house, where it will be until February 11. This transit could lead you into a secretive romance or a relationship where the two of you prefer spending your time alone together. With the moon entering your sign today, you're on a power roll until Wednesday afternoon, so pick and choose your activities carefully. Take on projects and issues that are challenging, and resolve them between today and Wednesday. Your chances of success are much higher now.

Tuesday, January 19 (Moon in Pisces)   If a relationship begins while Venus is in Aquarius, it's because the other person has seduced your mind first. Retrograde Mars in Leo is opposed to Venus now, which can create tension between you and this new romantic interest. But isn't it a little early for tension? Try to go with the flow.

Wednesday, January 20 (Moon in Pisces to Aries 2:37 p.m.)   You may be worrying about money for the next few days. It's a good idea to be clear on your priorities and to try to arrange your financial life according to those priorities. In other words, if you have a child in college and that child is one of your main priorities, then the child's education ranks up there with your financial priorities.

Thursday, January 21 (Moon in Aries)   Resist the urge to speculate or gamble right now. Best to take an honest look at your financial picture and base your decisions on things as they exist and not as you wish they existed. That said, never hesitate to visualize and imagine yourself in more prosperous circumstances.

Friday, January 22 (Moon in Aries)   A trailblazer, an entrepreneur, someone who thinks outside the box—that's you today. Even if these qualities don't seem to fit you, reach for them. You'll get the day's work done more quickly and be ready to gear up for the weekend, when the moon will be in compatible earth sign Taurus.

Saturday, January 23 (Moon in Aries to Taurus 12:41 a.m.)   If you're a writer or in any facet of the communication business, you'll enjoy today. The Taurus moon stimulates that part of you that enjoys a free flow of ideas, thoughts, or opinions. It also brings an emotional certainty about what you're writing and communicating.

Sunday, January 24 (Moon in Taurus)   You may be sprucing up your neighborhood or beautifying your community in some way. If it's a project for which you volunteered, stick with it to the end. If it's a project into which you were drafted, you may not feel the same joy as you would otherwise.

Monday, January 25 (Moon in Taurus to Gemini 7:12 a.m.) Home and hearth are the day's focus. Your parents, children, partner, or someone else within your family environment may need your support or advice today. Whatever your obligations at home, you could feel torn between them and your obligations at work.

Tuesday, January 26 (Moon in Gemini) Network and get in touch with clients, friends, and family members through e-mail. If you blog or have a Web site, it may be time for an update. Ditto for your company, if it has a Web site. You may want to look into new software for some particular project that you're involved in.

Wednesday, January 27 (Moon in Gemini to Cancer 10:02 a.m.) Romance, creativity, and nurturing are part of the day's package. The Cancer moon deepens your natural intuition and encourages you to nurture your imagination. Use both to make decisions about relationships that are important to you.

Thursday, January 28 (Moon in Cancer) Your options are wide-open today. Rather than forcing yourself to make a decision to go in one direction or another, just sit on the fence until you feel compelled to make a choice. A time favorable for that kind of thing is when the moon is in fixed sign Scorpio.

Friday, January 29 (Moon in Cancer to Leo 10:10 a.m.) There are degrees of knowing. Sometimes, you know immediately what you should do in a given situation. Other times, your heart screams one thing, your head another. But today, you're apt to do what makes you feel best.

Saturday, January 30 (Moon in Leo) Today's full moon in Leo brings news about a work situation, issue, or relationship. If you've applied for another job or put in for a promotion, then today—or a few days on either side—could be when you hear. Mars is within a degree of this moon, suggesting a lot of activity, movement, showmanship.

Sunday, January 31 (Moon in Leo to Virgo 9:23 a.m.)   With the moon entering your opposite sign, your focus shifts to a partner in either business or romance. You and a partner may, for instance, be trying a new exercise or health routine or a new diet together. Connect the dots. That's where you'll find your answers.

FEBRUARY 2010

Monday, February 1 (Moon in Virgo)   With the moon in your opposite sign today, February begins with a focus on others. Specifically, the others can be your friend, if you're a young person, or a business and romantic partner, if you're an adult. It's possible that you and your partner need to sit down and discuss the finer points of the relationship—and each other's expectations.

Tuesday, February 2 (Moon in Virgo to Libra 9:42 a.m.) You have to adjust your attitude concerning resources you share with others somewhat. These individuals can be anyone from roommates to spouses to parents and children. You're seeking an elusive balance, and you may need to engage others as part of a team effort to straighten things out.

Wednesday, February 3 (Moon in Libra)   Your artistic self really emerges today. Regardless of how you use your creative talents, you find inspiration in the works of certain artists, writers, photographers, or filmmakers. So if you need a jump-start to the creative process today, rent your favorite film, visit a museum, or hurry to your nearest bookstore.

Thursday, February 4 (Moon in Libra to Scorpio 12:56 p.m.) You may want to virtual travel today in anticipation of an overseas trip you're planning or would like to take. This trip won't be strictly for enjoyment. There's a quest element to it, a need to find something, to experience something. So follow your heart on this one.

Friday, February 5 (Moon in Scorpio)   Your essential dilemma often centers around being torn in two different directions. Your heart wants to go in one direction, your head in another. So you end up not making any choice at all. But today, thanks to the fixed quality of the Scorpio moon, you know exactly in which direction you should go, which choice to make. Doesn't it feel good?

Saturday, February 6 (Moon in Scorpio to Sagittarius 8:04 p.m.)   The moon enters the career section of your chart. Even if you feel vulnerable about your professional standing today, you grasp the big picture, the larger implications of how you feel. Isn't it possible that another job might be more satisfying for you?

Sunday, February 7 (Moon in Sagittarius)   In a few days, Venus will enter your sign, beginning one of the most romantic and creative periods for you all year. You may be feeling the effects of this already, perhaps in a flirtation at work or within your own neighborhood. If you have no interest in involvement at this time, you should turn Venus's energy toward a creative project of some kind.

Monday, February 8 (Moon in Sagittarius)   The Mars retrograde forms a harmonious angle to the Sagittarius moon, and bolsters your thrust to set your agenda in your career. If you're working for someone else, you may want to take steps toward setting up your own business. If you don't have any idea what kind of business that might be, brainstorm with someone you trust. Start looking for gaps in the market that you might fill.

Tuesday, February 9 (Moon in Sagittarius to Capricorn 6:45 a.m.)   A friend or a group to which you belong may be on your mind today. You're wondering how you can help your friend or what you can do to become more involved in the group. Whether it's a church or spiritual group or a group that supports your interests, your involvement is important to you.

Wednesday, February 10 (Moon in Capricorn)   Mercury enters Aquarius and your twelfth house and will be there until March 1. During this transit, you'll be exploring the workings of your own psyche. What motivates you? What issues or beliefs do you have that may be holding you back? Meditation and even therapy would be beneficial, if you're so inclined.

Thursday, February 11 (Moon in Capricorn to Aquarius 7:25 p.m.)   Venus enters your sign today and will be there until March 7. Use this period to take on anything you have placed on a back burner. Make your pitches, set your professional agenda, move in with your partner, get engaged or married, or submit your manuscripts and portfolios. This is *your* time to triumph.

Friday, February 12 (Moon in Aquarius)   The moon joins Mercury in your twelfth house. Not only is your conscious mind focused within, but emotionally you're seeking understanding of something from the past. Perhaps it's time to treat yourself to a past-life regression.

Saturday, February 13 (Moon in Aquarius)   Today's new moon in Aquarius ushers in opportunities to work behind the scenes. Neptune forms a close conjunction to the degree of this moon, indicating that your compassion and ideals come into play. Your dreams should be especially vivid now. Keep a notebook and pen close to your bed.

Sunday, February 14 (Moon in Aquarius to Pisces 8:24 a.m.)   Happy Valentine's Day! And how perfect that the moon is in your sign and it's another power day. Combined with Jupiter, also in your sign, you've got the world at your feet. Take your pick of projects, relationships, or situations. Jupiter brings luck and serendipity to whatever you choose.

Monday, February 15 (Moon in Pisces)   Whenever the moon is in your sign, particularly with expansive Jupiter *and*

Venus, take on projects and issues that you've avoided. You'll have a broader, more comprehensive view that will enable you to make a more informed decision. Your intuition is nothing short of remarkable today, so definitely act on your hunches.

Tuesday, February 16 (Moon in Pisces to Aries 8:31 p.m.)
You may be brainstorming with a friend or a family member about how to earn more money. The first step is to figure out where you're spending the money you earn now. Maybe it's time to create a budget. Make it realistic and include hidden costs—like your monthly video rentals or bookstore purchases.

Wednesday, February 17 (Moon in Aries)   You're on fire with an idea you have. Write it down, discuss it with someone you trust, and then try to figure out how to put this idea to work in your life. Don't try to do everything yourself. Delegate. Others can do the job.

Thursday, February 18 (Moon in Aries)   With Mercury still in Aquarius, you can combine its visionary abilities with your innate intuition and try to view the future. What trends will be hot next year? What kinds of books and movies will prove popular? How far can you take what you discover?

Friday, February 19 (Moon in Aries to Taurus 6:56 a.m.)
The Taurus moon suits you nearly as well as the moon in your own sign. Today, this moon grounds you emotionally and enables you to explore your conscious mind—what it contains, where it got the facts it owns, and how those mental wheels turn and churn with every new experience you have.

Saturday, February 20 (Moon in Taurus)   A relative or even a neighbor plays into the day's events. This individual may have words of wisdom that you should hear or vice versa. It depends on the dynamics of your relationship. It could be that your neighbor has someone special he or she would like you to meet.

Sunday, February 21 (Moon in Taurus to Gemini 2:47 p.m.)
By early this afternoon, the texture of life has changed. You're

after information of some kind, and you won't stop until you find it. You may have to travel to track down whatever you're looking for, so be sure to take a family member along. The outing will be fun for both of you.

Monday, February 22 (Moon in Gemini)   Communication rules the day. Whether it's written or verbal, keep your communications straightforward and succinct. Even though Mercury isn't retrograde, the risk of being misunderstood just isn't worth the possible fallout.

Tuesday, February 23 (Moon in Gemini to Cancer 7:29 p.m.) This fellow water-sign moon brings romance and creativity back into your life. It's also about fun and pleasure. The Cancer moon is the universe's monthly gift to you. So take your pick: a day to kick back, chill, and do whatever makes you happy.

Wednesday, February 24 (Moon in Cancer)   How do you nurture yourself and others? Today you have an opportunity to do some nurturing. Children—yours or someone else's— may be the receivers of that nurturing. Or it could be your creative children who are nurtured. One way or another, you embrace someone.

Thursday, February 25 (Moon in Cancer to Leo 9:09 p.m.) Employees or coworkers are your focus today. There could be a situation at work that requires your intervention. And if you're not in a position to intervene, you can certainly find the person who is. Or you can turn your considerable intuitive ability onto the situation and figure out what should be done.

Friday, February 26 (Moon in Leo)   You have a chance to strut your stuff today—and not in a boastful way. You're recognized by coworkers and peers for something you have done or achieved. It warms your soul. As it should. Pat yourself on the back for a job well done.

Saturday, February 27 (Moon in Leo to Virgo 8:53 p.m.)   If the devil is in the details, then today you're combing through the fine print, perhaps in some sort of insurance or tax document or in something related to health. Your spouse or partner could use some help on a project or issue, and you're there for that person.

Sunday, February 28 (Moon in Virgo)   Today's full moon in Virgo should bring news concerning a business or romantic partnership. Saturn forms a wide conjunction to this moon, and Pluto trines it, which means the news is serious and you're in the power seat.

MARCH 2010

Monday, March 1 (Moon in Virgo to Libra 8:32 p.m.)   Mercury enters your sign and will be there until March 17. This is a wonderful period for pitching your ideas or selling just about anything to anyone. Your conscious mind is exceptionally intuitive during this period, and you're able to divine other people's motives and personalities easily. If you're a writer, this transit signals that you're on a roll.

Tuesday, March 2 (Moon in Libra)   With both Mercury and Venus in your sign now, any relationship that begins under these two transits will be romantic, intuitive, and perhaps even psychic. Your communication will be strong too. It will be easier for you to make decisions as long as you don't allow romance to cloud your head!

Wednesday, March 3 (Moon in Libra to Scorpio 10:12 p.m.) You'll feel the change in the air late tonight, when the moon enters Scorpio. Suddenly, you'll be very clear and determined about what to do and when to do it. With three planets now in fellow water signs, there'll be an intuitive flow to whatever you do.

Thursday, March 4 (Moon in Scorpio)   You're so connected to your environment and the people around you that you absorb their moods and thoughts. It's important to associate only with positive, upbeat people today and tomorrow. Don't get sucked in by a sob story.

Friday, March 5 (Moon in Scorpio)   With the moon in your ninth house, you may be delving more deeply into your own belief system. What beliefs, for instance, do you hold that you've adopted from family and friends? Which beliefs are your own? What are your core beliefs? How do these beliefs create your experiences?

Saturday, March 6 (Moon in Scorpio to Sagittarius 3:37 a.m.)   The moon enters the career sector of your chart and forms a beneficial angle to retrograde Mars. The combination makes you more conscious of appearances. You could be compelled to beautify your surroundings in some way today. Fresh flowers or indoor plants are an inexpensive way to do this.

Sunday, March 7 (Moon in Sagittarius)   Venus enters Aries and forms a terrific angle to both Mars and the moon. This trio of fire signs acts as your booster rocket, and urges you to tie up stuff that has languished on a back burner somewhere. Finish up that résumé, get those photos loaded onto your computer, or touch base with people whose e-mails have been collecting in your in-box.

Monday, March 8 (Moon in Sagittarius to Capricorn 1:15 p.m.)   Your career goals rise to the forefront today, appropriate for a Monday! And with Jupiter still in your sign, you're thinking big. Perhaps bigger than you ever have. If the vastness of your plans intimidates you, just remember that you're the scriptwriter of your own life!

Tuesday, March 9 (Moon in Capricorn)   A friend or a group of friends may want to brainstorm today. Perhaps the group of you have considered starting your own business and are now getting together to put a plan together. You're excited about whatever this is and eager to embrace all the possibilities.

Wednesday, March 10 (Moon in Capricorn)   Mars turns direct in Leo, in your sixth house, where it will be until June 7. This transit infuses your daily work routine with enormous energy and enthusiasm. You may be working longer hours, but you have the physical stamina and support system to do so. Coworkers applaud your dedication.

Thursday, March 11 (Moon in Capricorn to Aquarius 1:44 a.m.)   The moon joins Neptune in your twelfth house. This transit often brings up old stuff, so delve into yourself today; sink deeply into your own psyche. Use your intuition to uncover your true motives.

Friday, March 12 (Moon in Aquarius)   With Venus in Aries and the financial sector of your chart and the moon in Aquarius and your twelfth house, you may be able to tap into the true source of prosperity consciousness. Meditation will help in this regard, if only to teach you to keep your mind still and rooted in the present moment.

Saturday, March 13 (Moon in Aquarius to Pisces 2:44 p.m.)   Early this afternoon, you're aware of a palpable shift in energy as the moon enters your sign. It's not earth-shattering, but you suddenly feel more tuned in and on top of things. It's your power day—use it wisely.

Sunday, March 14—Daylight Saving Time Begins (Moon in Pisces)   You may just want to chill out, read a book, watch a movie, or do some of the things that your busy life often crowds out. It's a perfect day to study a divination system. Choose a system that resonates with you: tarot, I Ching, or even astrology.

Monday, March 15 (Moon in Pisces)   Today's new moon in Pisces is your special moon. It comes around just once a year and sets the tone for the next twelve months. This moon should usher in many opportunities in your personal life: a job, a relationship, a move, a home, or the birth of a child. It depends on where you have been placing your energy. Mercury and Uranus form close conjunctions to this moon, suggesting a sudden change of events, lots of talk and discussion, or a possible contract and travel.

Tuesday, March 16 (Moon in Pisces to Aries 3:32 a.m.)
The moon joins Venus in Aries. Mars, now moving direct in

Leo, forms a beneficial angle to these two planets. The results? Your sexuality is heightened, your love life improves, and you gain insights into what's really important to you.

Wednesday, March 17 (Moon in Aries)   Mercury enters Aries, joining Venus and the moon in your second house. This combination of planets brings plenty of discussion about money and values. It's terrific for sales, and excellent for writing and any kind of communication.

Thursday, March 18 (Moon in Aries to Taurus 1:30 p.m.) People around you will notice that your decisions today are made easily, flawlessly, with stunning prediction. Don't you just love it when others see you in your best light?

Friday, March 19 (Moon in Taurus)   Your relatives get in touch, perhaps to plan a family reunion this summer. You may not be able to commit to anything this far ahead, and that's fine. Don't allow anyone to pressure you. Follow your instincts.

Saturday, March 20 (Moon in Taurus to Gemini 9:29 p.m.) The moon enters Gemini, the only other sign besides yours that is represented by two of something. And today that duality may be apparent to your family and other people in your personal environment. So even though others may feel you've been cloned, you're enjoying multitasking!

Sunday, March 21 (Moon in Gemini)   Communication and networking are your focus today. Most of what goes on in this sphere takes place within your family or neighborhood structure. Possibilities? You get in touch with a sibling with whom you don't get along and try to mend fences. You talk to a Realtor about listing your home or contact a Realtor about viewing a home. You and your kids have a heart-to-heart.

Monday, March 22 (Moon in Gemini)   If you remember that Jupiter expands everything, you'll understand why you may be obsessed with an idea today. And if not an idea, then a book, a movie, or a conversation you had with someone. The obsession involves ideas or communication. Your obsession should be history by tomorrow.

Tuesday, March 23 (Moon in Gemini to Cancer 3:16 a.m.) The moon enters Cancer and your fifth house, bringing focus to a romance, a creative project, or simply what you do for fun and pleasure. Jupiter forms a positive angle to this moon, increasing your feelings of well-being, your general optimism, and your belief that just about anything is possible.

Wednesday, March 24 (Moon in Cancer) Think of these Cancer moon days as the universe's gift to you, the time of the month when you can do whatever you want, as long as it doesn't harm anyone else. So define what brings you joy and pleasure, and pursue it.

Thursday, March 25 (Moon in Cancer to Leo 6:40 a.m.) The moon enters your sixth house. This brings your focus directly on your daily work routine. You may have to race to make a deadline. You also may have to rush on an issue concerning a coworker or an employee.

Friday, March 26 (Moon in Leo) If there's an upside to this moon for you, it's that you realize there's a part of you that needs to be recognized or appreciated for who you are. But the bottom line is that you must learn to appreciate yourself before others can appreciate you.

Saturday, March 27 (Moon in Leo to Virgo 7:58 a.m.) The moon enters your opposite sign, and suddenly, it's detail time! Read the fine print, pay attention to how the dots in your own life are connected, and leave no possibility unexplored in research and investigation.

Sunday, March 28 (Moon in Virgo) Your partner— business or romantic—may have different ideas and opinions about the nature of your relationship. Perhaps it's a good time to sit down and discuss what you both feel. If the differences are great, then seek common ground.

Monday, March 29 (Moon in Virgo to Libra 8:22 a.m.) Today's full moon in Libra illuminates resources you share with others. You want very much to be helpful, to do the right and judicious thing, and Saturn's wide conjunction to this moon demands that you fulfill your obligations. A difficult angle from Pluto suggests a power struggle, but the struggle may be your own.

Tuesday, March 30 (Moon in Libra) It's a good time to beautify your environment in some way. The Libra moon loves and appreciates pretty stuff: fresh flowers, a new piece of intriguing art or music, or even a new coat of brightly colored paint on your office walls.

Wednesday, March 31 (Moon in Libra to Scorpio 9:42 a.m.) Venus enters compatible earth sign Taurus, where it will be until April 25. This transit could bring love and romance to your doorstep. You may find that you're attracted to someone in your neighborhood. This person could be someone you meet through a sibling or a neighbor.

APRIL 2010

Thursday, April 1 (Moon in Scorpio) This moon helps to solidify what you feel emotionally and intuitively. It should be easier for you to make decisions, but you'll have to guard against feeling that you're right and everyone else is wrong. Your sexuality should be quite a bit stronger too.

Friday, April 2 (Moon in Scorpio to Sagittarius 1:54 p.m.) Mercury joins Venus in Taurus, in your third house, and will be there until June 10. Between now and April 17, when it turns retrograde, you and a romantic or creative partner will be discussing the particulars of your relationship or your creative vision or both. Your discussions will be broad and may change the way you approach a romantic relationship and your creative projects.

Saturday, April 3 (Moon in Sagittarius) The moon entered your tenth house yesterday. This house symbolizes the career area, but also represents your public face. Today, others see you as the person who has the answers. Are you ready for that kind of responsibility?

Sunday, April 4 (Moon in Sagittarius to Capricorn 10:08 p.m.) You're on a roll with social activities. You and a group of friends who hold similar beliefs are gathered together to achieve something, even if you don't have any idea what it is yet. The goal may actually be simpler than you think: to enjoy one another's company. What a concept!

Monday, April 5 (Moon in Capricorn) Take the time today to do anything that requires deep and profound investigation. Don't hesitate to dig around in whatever you're doing. Pluto turns retrograde tomorrow and won't turn direct again until September 13, so it won't be functioning at capacity.

Tuesday, April 6 (Moon in Capricorn) Pluto turns retrograde in Capricorn. Between now and September 13, when it turns direct again, you may be taking a deeper and more probing look at your friendships. What are you looking for in a friend? Do you have expectations of your friends? You may also be scrutinizing your professional goals and asking the same types of questions.

Wednesday, April 7 (Moon in Capricorn to Aquarius 9:51 a.m.) Whenever the moon enters Aquarius, it's a good time to make symbolic gestures that make it clear to the universe that you're clearing space for the new. So clean your closets, your garage, your attic, your office, and your desk in order to experience new things, situations, people, and relationships.

Thursday, April 8 (Moon in Aquarius) On April 17, Mercury will turn retrograde in Taurus, your third house of communication. So start backing up your computer files now. Have multiple backups—a flash drive, perhaps, and an external hard drive. Nothing wrong with redundancy!

Friday, April 9 (Moon in Aquarius to Pisces 10:48 p.m.) Tonight, the moon enters your sign, a kind of blissful change after today's busy schedule. And since the moon will be in your sign over the weekend, be sure to get together with people you enjoy and to do things that you enjoy. Most Pisces individuals are creative in some way, so part of what you do should involve your creative abilities.

Saturday, April 10 (Moon in Pisces)   With Jupiter, Uranus, and the moon all in your sign, there should be plenty of excitement today. The kind of excitement depends on whether you're in search of mental, emotional, creative, or spiritual insight. All are possible. Just about anything lies within your reach today.

Sunday, April 11 (Moon in Pisces)   If you're one of those people who waits until the eleventh hour to get your tax stuff ready, then today is the day to do it. You're in an expansive mood—the best frame of mind for this sort of work. As you put your figures together, be appreciative for all that you have. Don't dwell on what you may have to pay out.

Monday, April 12 (Moon in Pisces to Aries 10:31 a.m.) Spurred on, perhaps, by your tax preparations, today you may be looking for new ways to earn money. Whether it's a second job or a different job, you should be working at something you enjoy. Too many of us work just to pay bills.

Tuesday, April 13 (Moon in Aries)   Don't hesitate to think outside the box today. This sort of thinking is exactly what is called for now. You're prioritizing what's important to you—a vital step in reaching out for new experiences, jobs, people, and belief systems.

Wednesday, April 14 (Moon in Aries to Taurus 7:55 p.m.) Today's new moon in Aries should attract financial opportunities. Whether this means a job, a raise, or something else altogether, remain vigilant so that you can seize the opportunity when it presents itself. Neptune forms a harmonious angle to this moon, indicating that your ideals play a part in whatever this opportunity is.

Thursday, April 15 (Moon in Taurus)   Tax day. Mail off your return and be done with it! You and a neighbor or a sibling could be involved in an exchange of e-mails or calls about some issue or situation of concern to you both. You hold your ground. Good. It's exactly what you should do.

Friday, April 16 (Moon in Taurus)   This moon forms a harmonious angle to Uranus and Jupiter in your sign and to your sun sign. The combination of energies practically guarantees that whatever you take on today ends successfully. Your intuition and imagination are quite strong, so be sure to check in with your inner voice before making decisions. Back up your computer files today. Mercury turns retrograde tomorrow!

Saturday, April 17 (Moon in Taurus to Gemini 3:09 a.m.)
Mercury turns retrograde in Taurus, in the communication section of your chart. Between now and May 11, be sure to communicate clearly and succinctly with other people. Don't get into discussions that could lead to arguments, because you may say things you'll regret later. Travel plans during this time? If you've bought your ticket, the best you can do is to remain flexible!

Sunday, April 18 (Moon in Gemini)   Connections made through networking are valuable. Whether your network consists primarily of friends or of Internet and e-mail buddies, you can draw on the support and ideas of these individuals to flesh out a project, idea, or creation.

Monday, April 19 (Moon in Gemini to Cancer 8:40 a.m.)
The moon enters the romance section of your chart, and Venus in Taurus forms a harmonious angle. Nice energy for the beginning of a romance, creative project, or renewed communication with a child or children. If you're involved already, this combination of energies strengthens your ties with your partner and could encourage the two of you to work on a joint creative project.

Tuesday, April 20 (Moon in Cancer)   When the moon is in a fellow water sign, as it is today, you feel more in touch with who you are, with your emotions and needs, and with your own unconscious. So use this awareness of the inner workings of your own being to bring clarity to a creative project or to a relationship that is important to you.

Wednesday, April 21 (Moon in Cancer to Leo 12:43 p.m.) You may need to spend time today with coworkers or employees to iron out differences or issues that are important to everyone involved. You may be the mediator, because intuitively you can see the many sides of the issue and situation.

Thursday, April 22 (Moon in Leo)   Don't hesitate to toot your own horn. You actually may not have to, because the people around you appreciate what you're doing, admire your abilities, and like you personally. But it never hurts to know this, right?

Friday, April 23 (Moon in Leo to Virgo 3:25 p.m.)   The moon joins retrograde Saturn in Virgo, in your seventh house. Any delays you're currently experiencing in romantic or business partnerships may prey on you today, eat away at your mood, and erode your optimism. If you find yourself in that frame of mind, immediately reach for a thought that makes you feel better. Once you recognize these patterns in yourself, they're much easier to reverse.

Saturday, April 24 (Moon in Virgo)   Intuitively, you know what's going on. But you may have to connect the left-brain dots, to tend to details, to really convince yourself. Practice the art of listening. What is really being said?

Sunday, April 25 (Moon in Virgo to Libra 5:18 p.m.)   Venus enters Gemini and your fourth house, where it will be until May 19. Your love life at home should improve significantly. You may feel the need to beautify your home in some way too. But with Mercury retrograde, hold off on buying new furniture or other big-ticket items. Use simplicity for beautification—fresh flowers or bold colors for your walls.

Monday, April 26 (Moon in Libra)   Other people's resources are your focus today. Usually, this means a spouse's income, but it can be virtually anyone with whom you share finances, resources, time, or energy. You're seeking balance in this area, but the balance has to come from within.

Tuesday, April 27 (Moon in Libra to Scorpio 7:30 p.m.)
With the moon in fellow water sign Scorpio, the intuitive flow in your life is stronger, more pervasive. And this flow may be urging you to travel overseas, where your perceptions change, and you feel renewed. Just be sure you travel after Mercury turns direct on May 11.

Wednesday, April 28 (Moon in Scorpio)   Today's full moon in Scorpio lights up a belief that you hold. Is it really your belief or one you have adapted from parents, friends, or an authority figure? Is this belief holding you back in some way? Purge such beliefs and watch your life turn around!

Thursday, April 29 (Moon in Scorpio to Sagittarius 11:36 p.m.)   The moon enters the career sector of your chart. You've got a million things to do, and you may be unable to decide what should be tackled first. Select the item that's easiest to resolve or complete. Then move on to the more challenging items.

Friday, April 30 (Moon in Sagittarius)   Feeling restless? Feeling like you would enjoy being on the open road? Then go for it. Take the weekend off, and head out for parts unknown. Just be aware that Mercury's retrograde may bring surprise twists in your plans!

MAY 2010

Saturday, May 1 (Moon in Sagittarius)   With Mercury still retrograde, back up your computer files several times a day. Be sure to double-check all correspondence and e-mail. Be thoughtful in your conversations with others so there's no wiggle room for miscommunication.

Sunday, May 2 (Moon in Sagittarius to Capricorn 7:00 a.m.)
There could be a gathering at your place today, friends and perhaps family members getting together to celebrate spring. You're in a jovial, upbeat, expansive mood, and it's infectious. People are attracted to you. They feel better in your presence.

Monday, May 3 (Moon in Capricorn)   The Capricorn moon is focused, directed, a builder. So what are *you* building today? It could be something as complex as an inner world into which you can retreat when you feel the need for solitude. Or it could be something as simple as building emotional defenses that help you to deal more effectively with an aggressive individual.

Tuesday, May 4 (Moon in Capricorn to Aquarius 5:52 p.m.)
You've got the leading edge today. Whether you're using your visionary qualities in your professional or personal life (on in both), people sense you understand what they do not and seek you out for advice and answers. You may not have all the answers, but you have enough to satisfy even the skeptics.

Wednesday, May 5 (Moon in Aquarius)   You may retreat into yourself and try to figure out some complex emotional puzzle. But there's really nothing to figure out. You know what you feel and why you feel it. Your problem is that you may not be able to express it. So write it out, and come back to it when the moon is in your sign.

Thursday, May 6 (Moon in Aquarius)   Complete projects, tie up loose ends, and finalize plans. You're making space for new experiences, feelings, and situations. You share your life with other people, so you may want to reach out to someone you trust and run ideas and solutions past this person. Seek out feedback from others.

Friday, May 7 (Moon in Aquarius to Pisces 6:34 a.m.)   The moon enters your sign early this morning, and you awaken with a sense of purpose, determined to make excellent use of the next two and a half days. How can you capitalize on this strength and resolve that you feel? How can you best use your talents?

Saturday, May 8 (Moon in Pisces) A power day. With both Jupiter and Uranus back in your sign again, you don't even have to go looking for excitement. *It* finds *you.* And the excitement invariably broadens your horizons in some way, and you experience synchronistic connections with other people. Diving into the labyrinthine mystery of life isn't a bad way to spend a Saturday!

Sunday, May 9 (Moon in Pisces to Aries 6:30 p.m.) Mars in Leo forms a beneficial angle to the Aries moon, and acts as your booster rocket. If you thought you were going to chill today, think again. You've got energy to burn, and you're moving full speed ahead. Anyone who can't keep up gets left in the dust.

Monday, May 10 (Moon in Aries) You're all over the place today, eager to do this or that. Take a deep breath and focus. Find one project or issue, and work on that. If you don't want to finish it, just launch things and have someone else finish up.

Tuesday, May 11 (Moon in Aries) Mercury turns direct today in Taurus, in your third house. Anything that has been stalled or delayed should now start moving forward again. Proceed with your travel plans, tie up contract negotiations, and sign on the dotted line!

Wednesday, May 12 (Moon in Aries to Taurus 3:49 a.m.) The moon joins Mercury in Taurus, in your third house, a nice combination for communication, particularly now that Mercury is moving in direct motion. You and a sibling or a neighbor could be talking about making improvements in your neighborhood or community, perhaps through a volunteer program.

Thursday, May 13 (Moon in Taurus) Today's new moon in Taurus should be absolutely splendid for you. New opportunities for education, writing, and travel surface. These opportunities will emerge swiftly and unexpectedly, which requires you to be alert. Uranus, Jupiter, and Saturn form beneficial angles to this new moon, indicating that the opportunities are serious and grounded.

Friday, May 14 (Moon in Taurus to Gemini 10:19 a.m.)
Home is where the heart is—isn't that how the saying goes? Well, today home is also about where the information is— information pouring in, being disseminated, discussed, debated. Sounds like a family powwow or a political campaign!

Saturday, May 15 (Moon in Gemini)　　The Gemini moon is gregarious and social, when the situation calls for it, and today you're a party animal, at least in terms of whatever that means for you. It could mean a big party at your place, or it could mean a gathering of close friends at your place. However it unfolds, avoid confrontation and argument.

Sunday, May 16 (Moon in Gemini to Cancer 2:47 p.m.)
You should be feeling pretty mellow for the next few days. The Cancer moon tends to make you dreamier than usual, with your imagination unleashed and wandering through other dimensions. On your imaginative journeys, try to bring back fodder for your creative projects.

Monday, May 17 (Moon in Cancer)　　Romance, creativity, kids, and what you do for fun and pleasure—that's the MO for today. If you've been feeling overworked and unappreciated, then take today for yourself. Do whatever stokes your passions or whatever makes you laugh. Then be ready to return to your routine tomorrow.

Tuesday, May 18 (Moon in Cancer to Leo 6:07 p.m.)　　Refreshed from yesterday's time-out, you're prepared for the day's assault. Whether it's issues with coworkers or employees or just that your desk overflows with stuff that needs attention, take things one step at a time, one item at a time, one breath at a time.

Wednesday, May 19 (Moon in Leo)   Venus enters Cancer and your fifth house, where it will be until June 14. This period is one of the most romantic, creative, and fun-filled all year. If you're not involved when this transit begins, you probably will be before it ends. If you've wanted to start a family, then this transit encourages you to get busy!

Thursday, May 20 (Moon in Leo to Virgo 8:59 p.m.)   Your partner, business or romantic, takes precedence today. He or she may need your input, advice, or opinion on a personal issue. You're an apt listener, and while you listen, you often pick up subliminal messages intuitively. Act and give advice according to what you honestly feel.

Friday, May 21 (Moon in Virgo)   You don't have to bend over backward to please anyone. The only thing required of you is to be present in each moment, to live that moment as though it is your last. By doing this, you bring yourself and your life into alignment with forces greater than you. It's all about connecting the dots.

Saturday, May 22 (Moon in Virgo to Libra 11:50 p.m.)   It's time to find out once and for all where you stand. You may be reluctant to push for an answer, but you feel as if you can't continue not knowing. But before you send that e-mail or make that phone call, be absolutely sure you have reached your limits.

Sunday, May 23 (Moon in Libra)   Balance and equality, beauty and harmony—that's what you're striving for today. You may find it in an unusual way on a path you have never explored. Before you throw up your hands and make some lame excuse about how you have no interest in this particular path, take a few tentative steps along it. Ask questions. Explore. Be open-minded.

Monday, May 24 (Moon in Libra)   To satisfy your artistic side, drop by a museum today and take in the latest exhibit. It doesn't matter which museum or which exhibit, as long as it's a form of art that interests you. Take solace as you walk among the creations of the masters. You too have this ability.

Tuesday, May 25 (Moon in Libra to Scorpio 3:18 a.m.)   If you're headed to college or graduate school in the fall, today is the perfect time to submit paperwork. You may want to make a list of supplies and other items you think you'll need, and come up with a rough estimate of what it all will cost.

Wednesday, May 26 (Moon in Scorpio)   Feeling the itch to travel? Have you been spending more and more time on travel sites? Count the pennies in your piggy bank and decide where you can feasibly go and how much it will cost. Look on some of the discounted travel sites. It's possible to find all kinds of excellent deals.

Thursday, May 27 (Moon in Scorpio to Sagittarius 8:16 a.m.)   Today's full moon in Sagittarius brings career news. Whatever this news is, it's unexpected and definitely exciting. Uranus, which enters Aries today, forms a wide and beneficial angle to this moon and is likely to attract unusual individuals.

Friday, May 28 (Moon in Sagittarius)   In the big-picture section for your sign, be sure to read about what Uranus's transit into Aries means for you. With the moon still in Sagittarius, and both Uranus and Mars in fire signs, you're cranked up with enthusiasm today about a moneymaking plan. Don't make any commitments today. Wait until the moon is in your sign or in Capricorn or Taurus, the grounded earth signs.

Saturday, May 29 (Moon in Sagittarius to Capricorn 3:44 p.m.)   By this afternoon, you find it easier to make decisions and to stick to what you decide. You may have quite a singular focus, which will distract you from something that may be sapping your energy.

Sunday, May 30 (Moon in Capricorn)   Saturn finally turns direct, in Virgo, your opposite sign, where it will be until July 21. You should have a pretty clear idea what this transit means for you, since Saturn was in Virgo between 2007 and

2009. If you fulfilled your obligations and responsibilities during its transit, this transit probably won't impact you much. Some possibilities: delays or restrictions concerning a partnership (romantic or business) and a need to shoulder more responsibility in a relationship.

Monday, May 31 (Moon in Capricorn)   Neptune turns retrograde in Aquarius, your twelfth house. The impact won't be that great because Neptune moves so slowly. But you'll notice that between now and November 6, when Neptune turns direct again, you may be scrutinizing your motives and exploring the dark underside of your own psyche.

JUNE 2010

Tuesday, June 1 (Moon in Capricorn to Aquarius 2:08 a.m.)   If, as the song goes, living is easier now that summer is almost here, you may have some time in the next few days to simply enjoy life. If, on the other hand, your lifestyle or job gears up during the summer, then you should get your ducks in a row now to stay ahead of the competition. Complete projects; tie up loose ends. The moon enters your sign on Thursday.

Wednesday, June 2 (Moon in Aquarius)   Karma day. You may meet someone from a past life, and the recognition will be instantaneous. Even if you don't know which life or what your relationship was, you grasp the dynamics. And right now that may be all that you need.

Thursday, June 3 (Moon in Aquarius to Pisces 2:34 p.m.)
You're on top of things by this afternoon and prepared to go to bat for an idea, project, or venue. The stars are definitely on your side. With the moon, Uranus, and lucky Jupiter in your sign, Venus in a fellow water sign, and Pluto in a compatible earth sign, you're in the power seat.

Friday, June 4 (Moon in Pisces)   Whatever you can imagine, you can manifest. And because of your deep intuitive talents and your expansive imagination, the manifestation part is easier for you than for most signs. But be sure that when you're manifesting that you're in a positive frame of mind!

Saturday, June 5 (Moon in Pisces)   Ignore the naysayers who may be saying that you're unrealistic about a relationship or that you've got your head in the clouds and don't understand what's really going on. All you have to know right now is what *you* feel. Once you're certain of that, everything else falls into place.

Sunday, June 6 (Moon in Pisces to Aries 2:51 a.m.)   Jupiter enters Aries today, where it will be until September 8. By then, it will have retrograded back into your sign for one final pass. This transit should increase your earnings, but could also increase your expenses. So if you get a raise or land a terrific contract, be sure to pay yourself ten or fifteen percent first.

Monday, June 7 (Moon in Aries)   Mars enters Virgo, your opposite sign, where it will be until July 29. This transit ignites fireworks within a partnership—business or romantic. But the fireworks don't have to be negative. You and the other person can use this energy to increase sales in your business, to find new meaning in a romantic relationship, or to delve into respective needs and expectations.

Tuesday, June 8 (Moon in Aries to Taurus 12:42 p.m.)   Today's moon forms a beneficial angle to Venus in Cancer. It should bring a nice smoothness to romance, friendships, finances, creative projects, and anything you do for pleasure. A raise is possible or some advancement in your earnings, perhaps through royalties or an unexpected bonus.

Wednesday, June 9 (Moon in Taurus)   Ignore the ones who may call you stubborn today. You usually are quite easygoing and flexible, but a situation or relationship requires that you dig in your heels and hold your ground. If you can do this without seeming to threaten anyone else, you'll succeed and win over the opposition. You feel very strongly about whatever this issue is.

Thursday, June 10 (Moon in Taurus to Gemini 7:12 p.m.)
Mercury enters Gemini and will be there until June 25. During this period, expect discussion and lively debates at home. You may start a novel or book. And now, with expansive Jupiter in the financial sector of your chart, that novel or book could bring in a nice chunk of change.

Friday, June 11 (Moon in Gemini) Today's moon and Jupiter in Aries form a harmonious angle to each other, augmenting your optimism about your financial affairs. You may decide to expand or refurbish your home in some way, or you may consider buying property on which to build a home. Just be sure that you actually can afford to do this.

Saturday, June 12 (Moon in Gemini to Cancer 10:51 p.m.)
Today's new moon in Gemini attracts opportunities in communication and with your home and family. Neptune forms a wide and beneficial angle to this moon, so it's likely that your ideals play a part in these opportunities that surface. Saturn forms a challenging angle to this moon, indicating that you may have to first fulfill your obligations and responsibilities.

Sunday, June 13 (Moon in Cancer) Nurturing issues surface today: how you are nurtured by the people in your life, how you nurture others, or how you were nurtured as a child. You are urged to nurture your creative side, to give yourself permission and time to dive into your creative projects daily. In fact, you may want to set aside a particular time each day when you do exactly that.

Monday, June 14 (Moon in Cancer) Venus enters Leo and your sixth house, where it will be until July 10. This transit should bring ease and smoothness to your daily work life. But because Venus is in Leo, there could some drama playing out with coworkers and employees. An office flirtation may heat up as well.

Tuesday, June 15 (Moon in Cancer to Leo 12:55 p.m.) If you're searching for a new job, if you have submitted résumés and been pounding the pavement, then Venus's transit through Leo could bring the right job at the right time. You may be looking for work that excites you, that's emotionally or creatively satisfying. And with Mars in your house of partnership until July 29, it's likely you'll find what you're seeking.

Wednesday, June 16 (Moon in Leo)   The moon hooks up with Venus and the two planets form a harmonious angle to Mercury. So it's a great day for discussion and debate both at work and at home. If you're self-employed, you may be searching for a new location for your business and could be talking to Realtors and trying to negotiate a good rental deal. Or you may decide to work out of your home.

Thursday, June 17 (Moon in Leo to Virgo 2:41 a.m.)   The moon joins Mars and Saturn in Virgo, in your seventh house. The combination of planets brings a seriousness to bear on any business or romantic partnership. You're pouring a lot of energy into a relationship right now. Just be sure it's worth the time and energy!

Friday, June 18 (Moon in Virgo)   Delving more deeply into the details and nuances of a relationship, you may discover it's time for some fine-tuning. If you and your partner have been headed in opposite directions, it's time to regroup and reshuffle your priorities. It could be that your lives are simply so busy that you have to consciously make time for each other.

Saturday, June 19 (Moon in Virgo to Libra 5:13 a.m.)   Jupiter's largesse is beginning to work its magic with your finances. Suddenly, it's easier to make money, and the more money you make, the more prosperous you feel. The more prosperous you feel, the greater your sense of well-being. You realize that prosperity isn't just about money; it's about inner abundance and well-being.

Sunday, June 20 (Moon in Libra)   Balance can be challenging to achieve, particularly if you're absorbing the moods of the people around you. Time to detach from other people's issues and get back into the rhythm and flow of your own life. Only then will you achieve the balance you need and crave.

Monday, June 21 (Moon in Libra to Scorpio 9:14 a.m.) With the moon in fellow water sign Scorpio, your intuition deepens and so does your resolve. Decisions that seemed daunting yesterday are suddenly much easier to make. You're no longer torn in two or three different directions, but see the solution clearly.

Tuesday, June 22 (Moon in Scorpio)   Your dreams are especially vivid now. Before you fall asleep, give yourself a suggestion that you'll remember your dreams tonight and wake up to record the dreams and the insights you receive. Intuitively, you're plugged in to a source greater than yourself.

Wednesday, June 23 (Moon in Scorpio to Sagittarius 3:11 p.m.)   It's undoubtedly a relief that Pluto is no longer transiting the career sector of your chart. The jarring energy of Pluto's transit through Sagittarius created a lot of permanent change in your professional life. Today, the Sagittarius moon reminds you how far you've come professionally.

Thursday, June 24 (Moon in Sagittarius)   You grasp the larger implications of a project or issue in which you're involved. You may have to travel to implement the solutions or to expand your own vision, but that's fine with you. It's all about perception, and when you travel, your perceptions explode wide-open.

Friday, June 25 (Moon in Sagittarius to Capricorn 11:22 p.m.)   Mercury enters Cancer, where it will be until July 9. This transit makes it much easier to tap in to your creativity in a way that brings you joy and may make you money as well. It also favors conversations with a romantic partner, with your children, and with your muse, who is ready and willing to help!

Saturday, June 26 (Moon in Capricorn)   Today's lunar eclipse in Capricorn occurs in your eleventh house and may bring up emotional issues involving friends. Pluto is exactly conjunct to the eclipse degree, suggesting that the emotions that surface are powerful and transformative. Today, you're an agent of change.

Sunday, June 27 (Moon in Capricorn)   You get together with friends and family. The group may be strategizing or planning something and would like your psychic input. You may not like being put on the spot like this, but go within, and find the answers.

Monday, June 28 (Moon in Capricorn to Aquarius 9:53 a.m.)   The clarity of your vision surprises you nearly as much as it surprises the people around you. Sometimes, you say stuff that seems to come out of nowhere and its truth resonates. That's how it could be today with a relationship.

Tuesday, June 29 (Moon in Aquarius)   Tomorrow, the moon enters your sign, signaling a power period. So today complete projects, wrap up travel plans, figure out what you're doing over the long July Fourth weekend. You're preparing yourself for the new moon in your sign that ushers in each month.

Wednesday, June 30 (Moon in Aquarius to Pisces 10:11 p.m.) Tonight the moon enters your sign, and neither Jupiter nor Uranus accompanies it. That alone should make tonight and the next two days somewhat calmer, although maybe not as exciting. Tonight, set up your agenda for the next two days so you can maximize the lunar energy.

JULY 2010

Thursday, July 1 (Moon in Pisces)   Whether you're traveling or sticking close to home for the July Fourth weekend, you'll have your choice of things to do. Select activities today and tomorrow that please *you* rather than doing things just to please someone else. It's not selfish; it's self-preservation!

Friday, July 2 (Moon in Pisces)   Everything seems to go
your way today with very little effort on your part. Employees
and coworkers are helpful, you gain the support you need at
work and at home, and your mood is optimistic, even buoyant.
Whether you're leaving town or hosting the weekend holiday
at your place, you may want to knock off work early to get a
jump on things.

Saturday, July 3 (Moon in Pisces to Aries 10:45 a.m.)   The
tone of everything switches gears this morning. Excitement and
high passions enter the picture, and you're not sure whether
you're coming or going. Time to take a few deep breaths and
get back on track. The best way to do it is to pay attention to
your breathing. When you do that, you're firmly rooted in the
moment.

Sunday, July 4 (Moon in Aries)   Happy July Fourth! And
how appropriate that on a day celebrated with fireworks, the
moon is in fire sign Aries, and Venus is in fire sign Leo. Lots
of high drama and theatrics are floating around in your environment. Best to channel it somehow into something physical.
Get everyone together for touch football, swimming, softball,
or just a long, fast walk.

Monday, July 5 (Moon in Aries to Taurus 9:30 p.m.)   Uranus turns retrograde in Aries, in your second house. You may
experience a sudden reversal in your mood. If so, try to get
back into your optimistic groove by understanding that this
too shall pass. There's no sense in fretting about what hasn't
happened or what may happen. The only certainty lies in this
moment. So as Uranus begins its movement back toward your
sign, which it will reach on August 13, keep in mind that worrying has never solved anything.

Tuesday, July 6 (Moon in Taurus)   The stabilizing influence of the Taurus moon can't be overestimated. You feel it
today in the way you communicate—clearly, in a grounded,
resolute fashion. This moon enjoys its creature comforts, so
treat yourself to something you enjoy.

Wednesday, July 7 (Moon in Taurus)   This moon forms
a beneficial angle to your sun and to Mercury's current position in Cancer. The combination brings a steady flow of intuitive information that you're able to translate into something
practical and efficient that other people understand. If you're
asked where your ideas come from, just smile.

Thursday, July 8 (Moon in Taurus to Gemini 4:51 a.m.)
You're all charm and able to talk to nearly anyone about anything. You understand that the secret to connecting to others
is to give people your full attention, to actually listen to what
they're saying, and to encourage them to talk about themselves and their beliefs and opinions. This diplomacy goes a
long way toward settling issues.

Friday, July 9 (Moon in Gemini)   For today and only
today, Mercury and Venus travel together in Leo. This duo
brings about animated discussions between you and a romantic or creative partner. You're able to communicate easily and
clearly.

Saturday, July 10 (Moon in Gemini to Cancer 8:38 a.m.)
Venus enters Virgo, your opposite sign, where it will be until
August 6. During this transit, your focus shifts to a partner—
business or romantic—or to your spouse, if you're married.
This would be a good time to get married, to renew your vows,
to move in together, or to get engaged. Pay close attention to
details during this transit, and try not to be critical of yourself
or of others.

Sunday, July 11 (Moon in Cancer)   Today's solar eclipse
in Cancer, in your fifth house, brings double the pleasure in
new romantic and creative opportunities. In fact, if you've
wanted to start a family, sell a novel or screenplay, or land
a perfect role, this new moon can make it all happen. Mars
forms a beneficial angle to the eclipse degree, indicating a lot
of movement and activity around the time of the eclipse.

Monday, July 12 (Moon in Cancer to Leo 9:54 a.m.)   The
moon joins Mercury in Leo, in your sixth house. Today you

put your money where your mouth is. You join a gym or sign up for yoga or Pilates classes to take positive, definite steps toward redefining your health and body. These steps could include a new diet or nutritional program as well.

Tuesday, July 13 (Moon in Leo)   Uranus and Jupiter form beneficial angles to this moon, adding excitement and luck to events that unfold today. Be sure to stick to the speed limit while driving, and if you're angry about something, cool down before you get behind the wheel of your car.

Wednesday, July 14 (Moon in Leo to Virgo 10:15 a.m.) Whenever the moon is in Virgo, it means it is opposite your sun sign, so there can be tension in a relationship. It's the kind of tension that can be mitigated by ignoring obvious attempts to push your buttons. Rather than reacting, do nothing.

Thursday, July 15 (Moon in Virgo)   The moon and Saturn travel together today, but this will be the last time this year, because on July 21, Saturn enters Libra again. So for today, you have several choices. You can laugh at whatever the universe hurls your way, you can sit around feeling sorry for yourself, or you can keep moving forward.

Friday, July 16 (Moon in Virgo to Libra 11:25 a.m.)   It's a take-stock day. Where do your joint finances stand right now? If you don't share money with anyone—a parent, spouse, or child—then take stock of your own finances. Check over bank statements. Do your banking online, if possible, where you can keep easy tabs on what you spend and what you earn.

Saturday, July 17 (Moon in Libra)   Whether you're balancing your checkbook or the various responsibilities in your life, the bottom line is the same. You feel pressed for time. So to create more time and less pressure for yourself, take a few moments to sit quietly, emptying your mind. It's that inner dialogue that could drive you nuts. Best to quiet it.

Sunday, July 18 (Moon in Libra to Scorpio 2:43 p.m.)   If you're gearing up for a vacation, remember that Mercury will

277

be retrograde between August 20 and September 12. Try to travel on either side of those dates. For today, go virtual traveling. Spin the virtual globe on your favorite travel Web site, pick a spot, and then plan a trip and break down the cost. Can you afford it?

Monday, July 19 (Moon in Scorpio)   With Venus still in Virgo, traveling with Saturn in your seventh house of partnerships, there are residues of tension between you and a partner. However, today's Scorpio moon helps you to dig down to the bottom line about what's really wrong. So then you have to ask yourself if you can live with this, whatever it is. Chances are that you can, but don't make any hard and fast decisions until the moon enters your sign on July 28.

Tuesday, July 20 (Moon in Scorpio to Sagittarius 8:49 p.m.) Your professional sphere is your focus today. Whether you're working against a deadline or just doing what you normally do, you're acutely aware of the passage of time. Each minute brings you a little closer to the realization that your life is finite.

Wednesday, July 21 (Moon in Sagittarius)   Today your attitude has flipped completely. You see yourself as an infinite being with many lives, and you've got plenty of time to complete whatever it is you're doing. So what changed? Maybe you allowed the spacious present into your life. Feels good, doesn't it? And by the way, Saturn is now in Libra again, undoubtedly a relief for you.

Thursday, July 22 (Moon in Sagittarius)   Your flexibility and willingness to accommodate your schedule to fit someone else's is a major plus. Your boss and peers consider you to be an asset to the company and to the team. Just be sure that your flexibility is sincere. Otherwise, it may come back to haunt you down the road.

Friday, July 23 (Moon in Sagittarius to Capricorn 5:40 a.m.) The moon joins Pluto in your eleventh house. You experience powerful emotions about a relationship or about some issue in your daily life. You're determined to fix things, and you figure that if you really focus on the situation, if you really strive to find a solution, it'll be cleared up tomorrow. The solution is to release your concern.

Saturday, July 24 (Moon in Capricorn)   Today you're the one who lays out the strategy and the tactics, then steps back and lets other people implement your blueprint. There are times when you run with the ball, and other times, like today, when other people run for the ball you've thrown.

Sunday, July 25 (Moon in Capricorn to Aquarius 4:39 p.m.) Today's full moon in Aquarius illuminates something hidden in your life. You're able to use this issue to your advantage, thanks in part to Jupiter's beautiful angle to this moon. What you discover somehow broadens your horizons.

Monday, July 26 (Moon in Aquarius)   It's a powwow day at work. Big discussions ensue behind closed doors. If you're in the inner circle, then you know exactly what's going on. Otherwise, you hear it secondhand and probably should take the rumors with a grain of salt.

Tuesday, July 27 (Moon in Aquarius)   Mercury enters Virgo, and you and a partner are into honest conversations about what you feel for and about each other. You may be planning a trip some spot where neither of you has ever been. Emotional detachment is exactly what the day calls for.

Wednesday, July 28 (Moon in Aquarius to Pisces 5:00 a.m.) The moon enters your sign, and you're on a roll. There are many directions in which this roll can go—toward your profession, your personal life, your creativity, or your kids. And today you get to pick which area receives your undivided attention.

Thursday, July 29 (Moon in Pisces)   Mars enters Libra, joining Saturn in your eighth house. This strange combination could feel somewhat uncomfortable for you until September 14, when Mars enters Scorpio. Saturn restricts; Mars chafes to move ahead. It's like a dog straining on a leash. If you refuse to heel, your resistance hurts you. If you go with the flow, you're fine.

Friday, July 30 (Moon in Pisces to Aries 5:42 p.m.)   The moon joins Uranus and Jupiter in the financial sector of your chart. A surprise is headed your way. Initially, it may seem very uncomfortable. But when you grasp the larger implications, you count your blessings.

Saturday, July 31 (Moon in Aries)   As you head into the last month of summer, it's wise to take stock of your priorities. Are you on the track that feels right to you? Have you taken detours that seem to have dead ended? How can you correct your course?

AUGUST 2010

Sunday, August 1 (Moon in Aries)   You're on fire with ideas. Record them, write them down, and don't worry about trying to explain them to anyone just yet. You can do that when the moon is in Taurus or in your own sign. For now go with the flow, and trust that you'll be able to use these ideas.

Monday, August 2 (Moon in Aries to Taurus 5:13 a.m.) With the stabilizing quality of the Taurus moon, you can put these ideas into practical terms that other people can understand. Or not. It isn't really necessary that others understand them. Right now it's enough that you understand what you're doing.

Tuesday, August 3 (Moon in Taurus)   You're very centered and focused today. Your head and your heart are in strong agreement about a situation, relationship, or issue, so you are less apt to waffle and just sit on the fence. It's easy to charm the competition.

Wednesday, August 4 (Moon in Taurus to Gemini 1:54 p.m.) This moon forms a harmonious angle to Saturn, which is now

280

in Libra again. You're able to bring people together to discuss serious issues that could have far-reaching consequences. You and your group are able to find the proper structures for your ideas.

Thursday, August 5 (Moon in Gemini)   Mars and Saturn form beneficial angles to the Gemini moon, so you can expect a lot of frenetic activity that begs for a structured venue. You may not be the right person to find the structure, but you're definitely the right person for bringing everyone together.

Friday, August 6 (Moon in Gemini to Cancer 6:50 p.m.) Venus joins Mars and Saturn in your eighth house. Whenever Venus and Mars travel together, there's romantic and sexual chemistry. If you meet someone under this combination of planets, the relationship could be very intense and become serious quickly.

Saturday, August 7 (Moon in Cancer)   How do you nurture your own creativity? Do you spend enough time working on your creative projects? These are the kinds of questions you may be asking today. If you come to realize that you need more time for your creative projects, then carve out that time from your busy schedule.

Sunday, August 8 (Moon in Cancer to Leo 8:23 p.m.)   You may be trying out a new nutritional program or exercise routine. In your zeal, you may push your body to do things it isn't accustomed to, so work into your new routine slowly. Pace yourself. With the nutritional program, pace yourself as well.

Monday, August 9 (Moon in Leo)   Today's new moon in Leo ushers in opportunities to show off your abilities and talents. If you've been hunting for a job, this moon could attract exactly the right job at the right time. You could get a promotion, move to a different office, or have your job description redefined so that it suits you better.

Tuesday, August 10 (Moon in Leo to Virgo 8:02 p.m.)   By the time the moon enters your opposite sign this evening, you're ready for a vacation! You may be feeling irritable, critical of the people around you, and even self-critical. Stop these feelings before they overpower you. Focus on your breathing for a few moments to center yourself. Understand that this moment is all that matters.

Wednesday, August 11 (Moon in Virgo)   A partnership requires your attention today. If this is a business partnership, you may have to redefine the fine print. It could be that you and your partner are on the same track when it comes to your overall vision, but that you differ on the day-to-day stuff.

Thursday, August 12 (Moon in Virgo to Libra 7:44 p.m.) Other people's resources come into play today, perhaps through some sort of teamwork in which you're involved. You're quite the charmer, and you can win the support of even the most ardent skeptics.

Friday, August 13 (Moon in Libra)   If you don't have an external hard drive yet, you might consider buying one today. Mercury turns retrograde in a week, and you'll need to back up your computer files before that date. Get something large enough so that you can store digital photos as well.

Saturday, August 14 (Moon in Libra to Scorpio 9:27 p.m.) Tonight, there's a palpable change in your mood. You're more firm and certain about what you should do and when you should do it. Reach within. Your answers lie there.

Sunday, August 15 (Moon in Scorpio)   If you're traveling now, particularly if you're overseas, it's not strictly for pleasure. You're on a quest of some kind—searching for something ineffable that you can feel and sense, but can't describe. Even if you're not traveling, the searching continues.

Monday, August 16 (Moon in Scorpio)   The Scorpio moon forms a beneficial angle to Mercury right now, so it's easier for you to verbalize your hunches and intuitive insights and to talk about what you feel. And what you feel today is a certainty that things are turning in your favor.

Tuesday, August 17 (Moon in Scorpio to Sagittarius 2:35 a.m.)   With Mercury turning retrograde in three days, it's wise to firm up travel plans, finish negotiating contracts, and complete projects that are in the works. If you're in the market for a new computer or some other appliance, buy before August 20 and after September 12, when Mercury turns direct again.

Wednesday, August 18 (Moon in Sagittarius)   Professional matters take center stage. You're pursuing the big picture today, trying to figure out how your daily work adds up to the finished product or the service that you and your company provide. You'll figure it all out.

Thursday, August 19 (Moon in Sagittarius to Capricorn 11:18 a.m.)   Your social calendar starts filling up for the weekend ahead. Firm up plans today, because tomorrow Mercury turns retrograde—a certain invitation to swift, unexpected change in plans. Be prepared to review, revise, and rewrite between August 20 and September 12.

Friday, August 20 (Moon in Capricorn)   Mercury turns retrograde in Virgo. Reread the posts of the last several days and the content in the big-picture section about Mercury retrogrades to find out what this could mean for you. On other fronts, it's time to dust off that manuscript you stuck away in a drawer, that portfolio that you hid in your closet, or some other creative endeavor that you started but didn't finish.

Saturday, August 21 (Moon in Capricorn to Aquarius 10:38 p.m.)   You delve into your own unconscious—through dream recall, meditation, or a mind-body technique of some kind. What you uncover can be used as creative fodder for one of your many projects. By stirring up what's usually hidden from your conscious mind, you may initiate a whole new slew of synchronicities.

Sunday, August 22 (Moon in Aquarius)   Every month when the moon enters Aquarius, it's joining Neptune in your twelfth house. This house symbolizes your personal unconscious, what is unresolved, and any issues you brought in from past lives. Neptune and the moon together enhances your idealism, your visionary qualities, and your psychic ability.

Monday, August 23 (Moon in Aquarius)   This moon forms beneficial angles to Mars, Venus, and Saturn in Libra. It sounds like it's time to get together with friends who share your passion and interests and talk the night away. Make sure you include only upbeat, positive people on your list!

Tuesday, August 24 (Moon in Aquarius to Pisces 11:11 a.m.) The full moon in your sign illuminates some personal issue or concern that you have. Thanks to a powerful and beneficial embrace from Pluto, the news is positive, and it's time to celebrate. The next couple of days are power days for you. Use them wisely!

Wednesday, August 25 (Moon in Pisces)   Intuitively, you're connected to the holographic world today. You can see and feel these connections and you have a deeper appreciation for how these connections also extend to people—not just the people you love, but strangers as well.

Thursday, August 26 (Moon in Pisces to Aries 11:49 p.m.) By tonight, you're feeling like a trailblazer, an entrepreneur, an intrepid explorer. So for the next few days, act as you feel. Don't hesitate to think outside the box. Explore areas that you know nothing about. Learn. Keep an open mind.

Friday, August 27 (Moon in Aries)   You're on a singular path today. In a sense, you're like a horse wearing blinders moving ahead at lightning pace. This can work to your benefit if you remain clear about your destination and goal. But if you waver in your resolve, you could misstep.

Saturday, August 28 (Moon in Aries)   No matter how you look at it, you see only abundance and prosperity. This is a good thing. It means you'll attract more abundance and prosperity. And once you get into that groove, you'll understand completely how the laws of attraction work.

Sunday, August 29 (Moon in Aries to Taurus 11:36 a.m.)
Your relatives figure into the day's events. It could be that you all get together for a summer barbecue, the last before Labor Day weekend, or that you're planning for the Thanksgiving holidays already. Enjoy. The Taurus moon usually stabilizes your emotions.

Monday, August 30 (Moon in Taurus)   You're especially stubborn and resistant to something—a suggestion, an idea, a change. The only question you have to ask yourself is if you're resisting just to resist and rebel or if you're resisting because you know you're right.

Tuesday, August 31 (Moon in Taurus to Gemini 9:20 p.m.)
You're quite the homebody today, puttering around your place to complete projects you have put on hold. As long as you're not launching anything new, you'll finish in record time. Leave the new projects for after September 12.

SEPTEMBER 2010

Wednesday, September 1 (Moon in Gemini)   As you head into the final quarter of the year, you may want to take stock of where you are and where you're headed during these last four months. Have you achieved everything you set out to do? What is lacking? What are your triumphs?

Thursday, September 2 (Moon in Gemini)   Network and communicate. Even though Mercury is still retrograde, you can mitigate the risks of miscommunication by touching base through e-mail. It gives you a chance to think about what you want to say. Keep your contact to information only—no criticisms or rumors.

Friday, September 3 (Moon in Gemini to Cancer 3:51 a.m.)
You attract the attention of someone who interests you. Perhaps there's already an ongoing flirtation with this individual, and today things are taken to a whole different level. The other way the Cancer moon can work for you is through

285

your creative endeavors. Your muse is ready and available to help.

Saturday, September 4 (Moon in Cancer)   Mars and Libra are still traveling together in Libra, but won't be for much longer. Take advantage of this combination by getting together with friends or with a group to which you belong, and figure out how you're going to change the world. Change begins with just one person.

Sunday, September 5 (Moon in Cancer to Leo 6:46 a.m.) Stand up for yourself, and don't hesitate to say what's on your mind. Of course, if you do that, do it with the understanding that Mercury's retrograde could mean that the people around you don't understand what you're really saying. Maybe you should put it all in writing.

Monday, September 6 (Moon in Leo)   Something in your daily work routine changes soon. It may be something as small as when you eat lunch or take a break. But you realize that perhaps you're stuck in this particular routine. After all, as a mutable sign you welcome change.

Tuesday, September 7 (Moon in Leo to Virgo 6:54 a.m.) The moon enters your opposite sign. You know how to navigate this energy by now. Move ahead a step at a time, doing your best at every instant to perfect yourself. If you feel picky or critical, keep those things to yourself.

Wednesday, September 8 (Moon in Virgo)   Today's new moon in Virgo, combined with Venus's transit into Scorpio, creates fertile ground for opportunities for business and romantic partnerships, for engagement and marriage, and for your creative endeavors. Venus's transit through Scorpio lasts through the end of the year. You'll have plenty of time to enjoy this one, where romance with a foreign-born individual is a distinct possibility.

Thursday, September 9 (Moon in Virgo to Libra 6:02 a.m.) Another note on Venus. It will be retrograde between October 8 and November 18, which is why it will be in Scorpio for so long. But when it's moving direct, your love life should be humming along quite to your satisfaction. You may get a chance for some overseas travel too.

Friday, September 10 (Moon in Libra)   If you're thinking about refinancing your existing mortgage or applying for a new mortgage, wait until September 12, when Mercury will be moving direct. However, in the meantime you can gather your facts and figures, and do your homework about rates on the Internet.

Saturday, September 11 (Moon in Libra to Scorpio 6:22 a.m.)   The moon joins Venus in Scorpio, in your ninth house. Your thoughts and feelings seem to be turning to distant shores today. If you're planning a trip overseas, remember not to travel until after Mercury turns direct on September 12.

Sunday, September 12 (Moon in Scorpio)   Mercury turns direct in Virgo. Your love life is about to pick up big-time. Venus and the moon in Scorpio combine to trigger intense emotions and passions. The only risk here is that passions can run into the negative too—jealousy, envy, anger.

Monday, September 13 (Moon in Scorpio to Sagittarius 9:52 a.m.)   Pluto turns direct in Capricorn, in your eleventh house. The impact is subtle, but you should have a clearer idea now about how to implement the changes you desire in your career and in your goals and dreams. You'll be reminded of both when professional issues surface today.

Tuesday, September 14 (Moon in Sagittarius)   Mars and Venus are traveling together in Scorpio, a sign that Mars co-rules. This duo, in this sign, makes for a lot of intensity and deeply felt emotions. Flow with whatever you're feeling, but try not to let sarcasm or barbed speech enter the equation.

Wednesday, September 15 (Moon in Sagittarius to Capricorn 5:30 p.m.)   Now that Pluto is moving direct in Capricorn, its travel with the moon should be somewhat easier on you emotionally. Not as introspective, perhaps. Or as doubting. You can tap in to Pluto's enormous power—the sort of power that moves mountains, that makes things happen.

Thursday, September 16 (Moon in Capricorn)   Today's moon provides a solid, grounded foundation for your ideas. And now that Mercury is in direct motion again, it's a good time to launch new projects, pitch ideas, and generally consolidate your efforts. This moon also gives you a focus so that you don't have to weigh a dozen different options.

Friday, September 17 (Moon in Capricorn)   You could feel nostalgic for the good old days, whenever those days were. In fact, it's tempting to revisit the past, to look for former classmates, lovers, and friends. Just don't get stuck in the past. You've got too many things to do, places to go, and people to meet.

Saturday, September 18 (Moon in Capricorn to Aquarius 4:35 a.m.)   Once again, the moon joins Neptune in your twelfth house. By now, you should know the drill for this moon. Clear off your desk and fulfill obligations. You're making way for new experiences, people, thoughts, ideas, and situations.

Sunday, September 19 (Moon in Aquarius)   Saturn forms a harmonious angle to this moon, offering form and substance to whatever you do and feel. Your creativity is poured into a stronger, more viable venue. You may get help from supportive friends and family members.

Monday, September 20 (Moon in Aquarius to Pisces 5:15 p.m.)   By this afternoon, your mood has lifted; your attitude is more expansive and buoyant. The moon is in your sign, and you're ready to go! So hopefully you're prepared and have some idea of what you're going to tackle today.

Tuesday, September 21 (Moon in Pisces)   You're working up to the full moon in Aries in two days, and you could be feeling the chaotic excitement a little early. It concerns finances. Perhaps you've heard back from one of the places where you sent your résumé. If so, decide what you'll do when the moon enters Taurus on Saturday.

Wednesday, September 22 (Moon in Pisces)   You and someone in your personal life enjoy one of those glorious days when everything seems to unfold effortlessly, every moment clicking into place like pieces of some huge puzzle. So give thanks and express your appreciation.

Thursday, September 23 (Moon in Pisces to Aries 5:47 a.m.) Today's full moon in Aries is a humdinger of a moon, which will stimulate the other three cardinal points—Cancer, Libra, and Capricorn. News and insights surround your finances. You could get a raise, and it may be substantial.

Friday, September 24 (Moon in Aries)   The moon is now opposed to Saturn in Libra. This can feel pretty weird. The moon wants you to feel comfortable and cared for, but Saturn is over there on the other side, cracking that whip and demanding that you work harder and longer hours, and that you forget about sleep and fun. Best advice? Sleep in today!

Saturday, September 25 (Moon in Aries to Taurus 5:17 p.m.) The perfect Taurus moon day moves in later this afternoon, and because you're attuned to your inner world, you feel the impact immediately. So today is great for grounding whatever you're involved in. If a relationship has been experiencing bumps and bruises lately, then this moon makes it easier to discuss your mutual expectations.

Sunday, September 26 (Moon in Taurus)   How long should you stick with an idea, project, agenda? Well, with the moon in Taurus, you won't be quitting today or tomorrow—that's for sure. This moon urges you to stay in the race for the long haul. It also bolsters your self-confidence.

Monday, September 27 (Moon in Taurus)   Jupiter and Uranus are back in your sign, expanding and surprising you with twists and turns in the plot called your life. They form a beneficial angle to this moon that helps support your communications with others and that encourages you to keep moving forward with what you're doing. There's plenty of excitement and unpredictability to events now, but your life is expanded in some way by the final resolution to these events.

Tuesday, September 28 (Moon in Taurus to Gemini 3:12 a.m.) A situation on the home front could require your attention today. It puts some stress on you because you've got responsibilities at work too. So what's more important? Is there a way to balance these two obligations? Of course there is. Use your imagination!

Wednesday, September 29 (Moon in Gemini) With Mercury now moving in direct motion, it's a good time to apply for a mortgage or loan. Saturn is in Libra and your eighth house too, so you've got the proper venue for obtaining what you need. Just be sure that you can afford the mortgage or loan.

Thursday, September 30 (Moon in Gemini to Cancer 10:47 a.m.) Whenever the moon enters Cancer and your fifth house, it's time to play! To enjoy yourself. To have fun. What a concept, right? So get out there and discover what it means to enjoy yourself.

OCTOBER 2010

Friday, October 1 (Moon in Cancer) Here it is again, one of these wonderful days when the universe says it's your time to have fun. Of course, we should approach every day like that, but sometimes we don't know how to give ourselves permission. So the universe gives us permission.

Saturday, October 2 (Moon in Cancer to Leo 3:22 p.m.) Mars and Venus are still traveling together in Scorpio. You might want to keep notes on this duo transiting together. Has your love life improved? Your creative life? Have you become a better researcher? Do you understand other people's motives more clearly?

Sunday, October 3 (Moon in Leo) Mercury enters Libra and your eighth house. At some point between now and October 20, apply for a mortgage or loan (if you're in the market). Also, pay closer attention to things like taxes and insurance. If you don't have a will yet, have one drawn up.

Monday, October 4 (Moon in Leo to Virgo 5:00 p.m.) The moon enters your opposite sign. If this is usually a nutty time of month for you, there are ways to improve that. First, pay close attention to details. Whatever you're working on is like a diamond in the rough, and you're polishing it. Don't judge or criticize whatever this is. Just appreciate it. The Virgo moon loves it when you do that.

Tuesday, October 5 (Moon in Virgo) Now that Jupiter is back in your sign, you should be enjoying some of its good luck, expansion, and serendipity again. Today, in fact, there could be a sudden and unexpected turn of events that catches you by complete surprise. And you are in the mood to celebrate!

Wednesday, October 6 (Moon in Virgo to Libra 4:52 p.m.) The moon joins Saturn in Libra. Can you find the proper venue for expressing all that bottled-up creativity you have inside of you? This combination of planets says that you can. You may want to brainstorm a bit with a friend or family member, someone who appreciates the kinds of ideas you have, the way your imagination works.

Thursday, October 7 (Moon in Libra) Today's new moon in Libra ushers in opportunities in shared resources, teamwork, romance, art, and even in mundane stuff like taxes and insurance. If you've been wanting to apply for a loan or mortgage, do it under this new moon. In fact, get the process rolling today. Tomorrow, Venus turns retrograde until November 18, and the process might not unfold as smoothly.

Friday, October 8 (Moon in Libra to Scorpio 4:52 p.m.) Venus turns retrograde today in Scorpio. During this period, which lasts until November 18, personal and romantic relationships could suffer some bruises, and you and a partner may be rehashing old issues. It's smart not to buy big-ticket items under this retrograde; you may have to return them, or you'll discover something wrong with them. Former lovers or spouses may surface during this time.

Saturday, October 9 (Moon in Scorpio)   Intense emotions and passions rule the day. These feelings may involve a personal relationship, but could also involve change that you're seeking in your life. You have an enormous amount of emotional energy that can be brought to bear against a situation you would like to change for the better. Visualize, imagine, and then step aside and let the universe do its work.

Sunday, October 10 (Moon in Scorpio to Sagittarius 7:09 p.m.)   If you're feeling blocked in some area of your life, or have a problem that you can't seem to solve no matter what you do, then it's time to step back and regroup. Read books, talk to other people, and ask your dreams for insights.

Monday, October 11 (Moon in Sagittarius)   Professional stuff takes center stage. A boss or someone with whom you work may need your input on something. Your schedule is probably pretty busy right now, so before you commit to something long-term, make sure you have the time to devote to it.

Tuesday, October 12 (Moon in Sagittarius)   You're on a metaphorical mountaintop, looking out over the past year. Can you see how far you've come? Are you satisfied with the way things in your life have worked out? What remains to be done, understood, or achieved?

Wednesday, October 13 (Moon in Sagittarius to Capricorn 1:17 a.m.)   Strategy and planning are not usually your strongest attributes, but today you excel at both. A friend or a group to which you belong may approach you about putting together some sort of program that will need a strategy. It could be anything from a political campaign to a charity drive to a community project.

Thursday, October 14 (Moon in Capricorn)   Your social life picks up steam, maybe a bit more steam than you're ready for. Just go with the flow, and don't throw up any resistance. See where this flow leads you. You may be pleasantly surprised! A Taurus or a Virgo individual is helpful.

Friday, October 15 (Moon in Capricorn to Aquarius 11:24 a.m.)   You're going it alone today, which suits you fine. Whether you're working out of your house or your partner has gone away for the weekend, you welcome the solitude. This free time is all about completing what you've started. The moon enters your sign late on Sunday, and you intend to be ready to embrace the new.

Saturday, October 16 (Moon in Aquarius)   You have the emotional detachment now to tackle what could be a volatile project, relationship, or situation. Intuitively, you've read the pulse, you know the score, and you may even have a good grasp on the players and the rules. Now you just have to deal with it in a left-brain, rational way.

Sunday, October 17 (Moon in Aquarius to Pisces 11:52 p.m.)   Later tonight, the moon enters your sign. For the next two days, you're on the top of the world and off and running. Just watch events unfold with little or no effort on your part. And later, when the moon is in a less agreeable sign, and you're feeling a bit down in the dumps, remember how the happiness feels.

Monday, October 18 (Moon in Pisces)   With the moon in your sign, you may feel as if there are four of you, and all of them want to go in different directions. So you may have to let Pluto in Capricorn ground your ideas, feelings, dreams, and energy. Consider performing some small ritual that uses earth.

Tuesday, October 19 (Moon in Pisces)   Ask for answers and insights from your dreams tonight, and keep a pen, a notebook, and a night-light handy. You live with one foot in another world anyway, so moving fully into your dreams shouldn't be a stretch. You may even be one of those individuals who can wake up within a dream and then control the dream in this state.

Wednesday, October 20 (Moon in Pisces to Aries 12:24 p.m.)   Mercury joins Venus and Mars in Scorpio. It will be there until November 8, and during this transit, you'll be so tuned in to your intuition that you could be doing psychic readings for friends! These three planets combine to deepen the way you communicate with the people around you. You may also feel like you need to travel to a foreign culture, if only to open your perceptions in a new and different way.

Thursday, October 21 (Moon in Aries)   The moon in your second house can make you feel totally crazy, or it can bolster your self-confidence, or you may feel more vulnerable when it comes to your money. Or all the above and then some. So you'll be arranging your priorities.

Friday, October 22 (Moon in Aries to Taurus 11:31 p.m.) Today's full moon in Aries illuminates the financial sector of your chart. Perhaps a check arrives in your mailbox! Neptune forms a harmonious angle to this moon, indicating that your ideals come into play or that you don't have the full information and should hold off before making any financial decisions.

Saturday, October 23 (Moon in Taurus)   Your in-box is filling up with mail today. It could have to do with that Aries full moon yesterday. Since it's Saturday and you probably aren't at work, you catch up on your e-mail correspondence, post to your blog, and poke around on the Internet, catching up on what's going on in cyberspace.

Sunday, October 24 (Moon in Taurus)   Firm, stubborn, unbending—these are some of the adjectives that apply to you today. Quite a shock for the people around you, who know just how flexible you usually are. Or who know that sometimes you're a sucker for a sob story. Not today.

Monday, October 25 (Moon in Taurus to Gemini 8:48 a.m.)   This moon forms a harmonious angle to Saturn and Neptune, but it's still going to be a strange day. Saturn helps you to find the proper venue for saying what you think and feel, and Neptune helps to dissolve the barrier between you and others, so you communicate a lot with hugs. On a more serious note, get your e-mail addresses straightened out. If you're still using an old-fashioned Rolodex, transfer the addresses to an e-mail program and toss the Rolodex!

Tuesday, October 26 (Moon in Gemini)   A little tension at home today could escalate into something much larger than it is if you dwell on it. Solve the issue, and move on. Everyone will be glad you did, because once you do, they can. Some honest communication goes a long way toward mitigating the situation.

Wednesday, October 27 (Moon in Gemini to Cancer 4:15 p.m.)   Mars and Venus in Scorpio have one last fling today. Your love life or creativity may be about to go through some changes because tomorrow Mars enters Sagittarius and the career sector of your chart, so your career is going to take up a lot more of your time.

Thursday, October 28 (Moon in Cancer)   Mars enters Sagittarius and your tenth house, where it will be until December 7. This transit should activate career matters. Things start happening. You may be working longer hours and twice as hard, but you can feel the momentum building. Make this transit count. Don't get distracted!

Friday, October 29 (Moon in Cancer to Leo 9:39 p.m.)   The Leo moon forms a beneficial angle to Mars in Sagittarius, giving you just the kick you need. You're able to garner support among coworkers and employees and work tirelessly to make sure everyone understands what you're doing and why they should join your team.

Saturday, October 30 (Moon in Leo)   The last Mercury retrograde of the year falls between December 10 and December 30. So it's not too soon to start planning your holiday celebrations. If you have to travel, try to do so on either side of those dates. But if you find yourself in an airport during the retrograde, make the best of it. Think of it as research or as an adventure. So today, your assignment is to virtual travel. Pick a spot on the globe, and plan your trip.

Sunday, October 31 (Moon in Leo)   It's a good day to plan the week ahead. You're detail-oriented now; you have a pretty clear idea what you have to do and what the time frame is. Just be sure you schedule time for yourself next week too.

NOVEMBER 2010

Monday, November 1 (Moon in Leo to Virgo 12:51 a.m.) If you can, turn to close friends today to discuss something important to you. It's quite possible that you need another point of view. You might consider joining an Internet group that supports your interests or concerns. Sometimes the advice of strangers is better than the advice you get from people who know you.

Tuesday, November 2 (Moon in Virgo)   You and your partner could be involved in intense conversations where everything is laid bare, right down to the bottom line, whatever that may be. Think of it as clearing the air. It isn't the end of anything. It's the next step in your evolution as a couple.

Wednesday, November 3 (Moon in Virgo to Libra 2:19 a.m.) You may be looking for end-of-the-year tax write-offs. Look all you want, but if it's a big-ticket item, wait until after November 18, when Venus will be moving direct again. If the economy where you live is in decline, start looking for innovative ways to earn additional money.

Thursday, November 4 (Moon in Libra)   Teamwork and cooperation are the day's hallmarks. You may not be in the mood for either, but give it a whirl. As a member of a team, you may find that you enjoy working with people who have a common goal.

Friday, November 5 (Moon in Libra to Scorpio 3:16 a.m.)
The moon joins Venus in Scorpio, in your ninth house. This combination lends itself to some intense emotions in a romantic relationship, concerning a creative project or a child. You're locked in to your intuitive flow, so don't allow the emotional stuff to overwhelm you. Follow your intuition.

Saturday, November 6 (Moon in Scorpio) Today's new moon in Scorpio ushers in opportunities in higher education, publishing, and overseas travel. You may have the opportunity to take a seminar or workshop in some sort of spiritual discipline or about an esoteric topic that interests you. Neptune turns direct in Aquarius, so now you should have a clearer idea how to integrate your idealism more readily into your own psyche.

Sunday, November 7—Daylight Saving Time Ends (Moon in Scorpio to Sagittarius 4:28 a.m.) The moon joins Mars in the career area of your chart. This combination fires you up emotionally, and that emotion allows you to break through a barrier that has been impeding your progress. Sounds like an epiphany of some kind.

Monday, November 8 (Moon in Sagittarius) Mercury now joins the moon and Mars in your tenth house. This powerful combination puts you up on center stage, so be prepared to pitch your ideas, submit manuscripts, and send out job résumés. Whatever you're doing, you're a powerhouse of energy and determination.

Tuesday, November 9 (Moon in Sagittarius to Capricorn 9:37 a.m.) The moon joins Pluto in Capricorn, and suddenly, you're in the driver's seat again. Even if you're surrounded by naysayers who tell you that something can't be done, that you'll never achieve your dream because it's impossible, you just smile and go on your merry way. It's exactly what the situation calls for.

Wednesday, November 10 (Moon in Capricorn)   You may feel as if you're all over the place today. So it might be a good idea to pause in what you're doing, take a couple of deep breaths, and ground yourself in the present. Then run to your nearest bookstore and buy a book that will make you more deeply aware of being totally present in each moment.

Thursday, November 11 (Moon in Capricorn to Aquarius 6:33 p.m.)   Clear off your desk. Clean your closets, your attic, and your garage. By now, you know the drill for the Aquarius moon. It's the time to set your house in order and make room for the new. A Libra and a Gemini play into the day's events and activities.

Friday, November 12 (Moon in Aquarius)   You have the emotional detachment to tackle an old issue. It could be related to a past life or to something that occurred in your early childhood. You don't have to resolve it today or tomorrow. Just the fact that you're aware of this issue, whatever it is, means the healing process has started.

Saturday, November 13 (Moon in Aquarius)   November 18, every planet except Uranus will be functioning the way it should—moving direct. Until then, you'll have to make slight adjustments in your thinking, attitudes, and internal world. Your love life and creativity could be experiencing a few bumps still, but hang in there. In five days, that's done. History.

Sunday, November 14 (Moon in Aquarius to Pisces 6:25 a.m.)   The moon enters your sign early this morning. You may be touching base with relatives, friends, and neighbors about the Thanksgiving holiday coming up shortly. Whose house will host everyone else? How far will you need to travel? Do you feel like traveling over one of the busiest travel times all year? It all depends on how adventurous you're feeling.

Monday, November 15 (Moon in Pisces)   The moon links up with Jupiter and Uranus in your first house. It's likely that whatever you do today will be colored by some surprising and positive event that will lead to an expansion in your world-view or your spiritual beliefs. You're completely in the flow today and intuitively you know exactly which steps to take to get you where you want to go.

Tuesday, November 16 (Moon in Pisces to Aries 7:00 p.m.) Try not to spend your day fretting about money. If you concentrate on lack, you simply attract more of it. Better to make some symbolic gesture that arises out of an inner sense of abundance.

Wednesday, November 17 (Moon in Aries)   This moon forms a beneficial angle to Mars and Mercury in Sagittarius, in your tenth house. That means that today favors all professional matters. You may want to meet with a boss or peers to discuss an idea or project you have in mind. Or meet with the sales people. Regardless of your profession, you've got the energy—physical, mental, spiritual, and emotional—to nudge things your way.

Thursday, November 18 (Moon in Aries)   Both Venus and Jupiter turn direct today—Venus in fellow water sign Scorpio and Jupiter in your sign. The release of all this positive energy is a bonus for your love life and your creativity. But it also benefits plans you may have related to education, publishing, and overseas travel.

Friday, November 19 (Moon in Aries to Taurus 6:05 a.m.) Solidify the Thanksgiving holiday plans with relatives. In fact, while you're at it, you may want to discuss the Christmas holiday plans, too. This year, the last Mercury retrograde falls between December 10 and December 30, in Capricorn, which will impact December's holiday travel.

Saturday, November 20 (Moon in Taurus)   Surround yourself with beauty. Whether it's music that soothes your soul, or a vase of freshly cut flowers, a beautifully written book, or art that speaks to you, beauty is what you need today. You probably need a touch of it every day, in some form, but the Taurus moon loves to be coddled in this way.

Sunday, November 21 (Moon in Taurus to Gemini 2:46 p.m.)
Today's full moon in Taurus should be quite nice for you, Pisces. Jupiter and Uranus form close and harmonious angles to it, suggesting that the news and insights you gain come about suddenly and broaden your horizons and your options in some way. You may have to make an adjustment in a creative project or in your love life. No big deal. You're flexible.

Monday, November 22 (Moon in Gemini) You may sometimes feel a bit off with the Gemini moon. It's due partially to the fact that it's an air sign, and air and water don't mix. But it's also because it's the only other sign besides yours that is represented by two of something—the twins. So if you feel off today, find a way to relish the many facets of yourself. Indulge those facets.

Tuesday, November 23 (Moon in Gemini to Cancer 9:14 p.m.) Creature comforts are center stage. And it may have to do with guests who are arriving for Thanksgiving—or your travel plans for the holiday. Once you figure out your comfort zone, make the necessary adjustments.

Wednesday, November 24 (Moon in Cancer) If you take the day off from work or school, plan something special, something *you* genuinely enjoy. Also, delve into your psychic ability. You've got plenty of it, and when the moon is in a fellow water sign, that ability is enhanced. If your hunches lead you in a direction you've never explored before, follow them.

Thursday, November 25 (Moon in Cancer) Happy Thanksgiving! You're in a nurturing, upbeat mood today, surrounded with family and friends. But the holiday is about more than turkey and sweet potatoes and pumpkin pie. It's about gratitude. Express yours toward the people you care about.

Friday, November 26 (Moon in Cancer to Leo 2:01 a.m.)
Your inner dialogue may get louder today. If so, sit quietly for a few moments, and try to empty your mind of thoughts. Focus on feelings that wash through you—don't examine them. Ground yourself. Find your center.

Saturday, November 27 (Moon in Leo)   If you're continuing what you did yesterday with the inner dialogue, you may want to see how often negative thoughts flit through your head. Then watch how often positive thoughts go through your head. Are the negatives more numerous? If so, how can you change this?

Sunday, November 28 (Moon in Leo to Virgo 5:34 a.m.) The only planet left to turn direct is Uranus, in your sign. That happens on December 5. Sometimes, the end of a retrograde has as much of a punch as the beginning. If that's the case with you today, if sudden, unexpected events surface, just go with the flow. Don't resist what happens. Accept it.

Monday, November 29 (Moon in Virgo)   Pay close attention to details in everything that occurs. Are the dots connecting? You may be experiencing some odd synchronicities today. If so, figure out what the message is.

Tuesday, November 30 (Moon in Virgo to Libra 8:16 a.m.) Mercury joins Pluto in Capricorn—a transit that lasts through the end of the year. This transit should strengthen your conscious mind, give it more focus and direction. Remember that Mercury will be retrograde between December 10 and December 30. So make your New Year's plans soon, or suffer the consequences!

DECEMBER 2010

Wednesday, December 1 (Moon in Libra)   As you enter the last month of the year, pay close attention to the thoughts that run through your head. Are they predominately positive and upbeat? Critical? Complaining? If our beliefs create our reality, then take a look around at your life. All of it is a reflection of beliefs that you hold. The internal made manifest. So the thoughts running through your head provide valuable insights into what you may be creating for tomorrow.

Thursday, December 2 (Moon in Libra to Scorpio 10:44 a.m.) The moon joins Venus in Scorpio, in your ninth house. This duo defends itself if attacked—take a look at the barb on the Scorpio glyph—and the defense can be biting sarcasm. So if you're irritated today by someone close to you, try not to lash out. Bite your tongue!

Friday, December 3 (Moon in Scorpio) Romance and love are uppermost in your heart today. If you're getting a jump on holiday shopping, you may want to look for just the right gift for that special person in your life. In fact, you may want to wind up your holiday shopping before December 10, when Mercury turns retrograde—unless, of course, you don't mind standing in the long return lines at the mall on December 26!

Saturday, December 4 (Moon in Scorpio to Sagittarius 2:00 p.m.) The moon joins Mars in your tenth house. Think of Mars as the booster rocket firing up the moon to take risks, to leap forward with daring maneuvers and twists and turns. This could mean anything from requesting a raise or promotion, to pitching some outrageous cutting-edge idea.

Sunday, December 5 (Moon in Sagittarius) Today's new moon in Sagittarius ushers in professional opportunities. Any offers that come your way will be serious ones, thanks to the beneficial angle that Saturn forms to this moon. You could get a raise, find a new, better-paying, and more satisfying job, or be recognized in some way by peers.

Monday, December 6 (Moon in Sagittarius to Capricorn 7:17 p.m.) The moon, Mercury, and Pluto travel together. This combination snaps your focus onto power issues: your own power, the power of people who hold authority over you, how you use your personal power, how power is used against you. Today, you define what personal power is and take stock of your strengths and weaknesses. You may be discussing it with people in your circle.

Tuesday, December 7 (Moon in Capricorn) Mars joins Mercury and Pluto in your eleventh house. If ever there was a combination for long-term planning and strategizing, this is it. Mars helps you to build long-range goals, Pluto helps to make them powerful and profound, and Mercury enables you to discuss these plans in a practical way. Just remember that Mercury turns retrograde on December 10, so if you're going to be signing contracts, do it before then.

Wednesday, December 8 (Moon in Capricorn)   You and a group you belong to may be discussing the group's long-term purpose. You may be discussing ways to build your membership, to expand the services and benefits your group provides, and to reach out to the larger community in which you live. If this group is an Internet community, then come up with innovative ways to direct more traffic to your site.

Thursday, December 9 (Moon in Capricorn to Aquarius 3:32 a.m.)   Mercury turns retrograde in Capricorn tomorrow, for the last time this year. So back up all your computer files today, firm up your New Year's Eve plans, your holiday travel plans, and, if possible, wind up your holiday shopping! If you're still looking for end-of-the-year tax write-offs, purchase today.

Friday, December 10 (Moon in Aquarius)   Mercury turns retrograde. But this shouldn't prevent you from tying up your loose ends, revising and reviewing your agenda for the next week, and preparing yourself for the moon entering your sign tomorrow. During this retrograde period, old friends may resurface.

Saturday, December 11 (Moon in Aquarius to Pisces 2:41 p.m.)   Your mood lifts this afternoon, when the moon enters your sign. And with good reason. Jupiter and Uranus are in your sign, moving direct, so there's plenty of positive excitement and an element of luck to whatever unfolds. In addition, Venus is in fellow water sign Scorpio, adding a touch of mystery and seduction to your love life.

Sunday, December 12 (Moon in Pisces)   Creatively, you're on a roll. With Mercury retrograde, the roll seems to work in reverse, as you review and revise something you've been working on. You have to go back before you can move forward again. By doing so, you find ways to improve and polish your project.

Monday, December 13 (Moon in Pisces)   It's a warm and fuzzy day. You become nostalgic for something in the past, and the memory of that time stirs up a deep longing. The proximity of the holidays can be at fault. If you're in this frame of mind, best to focus on right this second. The steps you take from this moment to the next are important. Don't look back.

Tuesday, December 14 (Moon in Pisces to Aries 3:15 a.m.)   Holiday shopping got you down? Are you wondering how you're going to pay for these gifts? Time to switch to cash. Buy only what you can afford. Come January, you'll be glad you went this route.

Wednesday, December 15 (Moon in Aries)   The moon in the financial sector of your chart can help bring about innovative ways to earn extra money or to earn more money at what you already do. Even though it's not the time to launch something new, brainstorm all you want and keep track of your ideas. Write them down.

Thursday, December 16 (Moon in Aries to Taurus 2:49 p.m.) Your social calendar is getting crowded quickly. Today's events could involve your community or neighborhood. The event could be for charity or for an organization that is recruiting volunteers. You're in a giving mood and able to donate your time and energy.

Friday, December 17 (Moon in Taurus)   A week from today is Christmas Eve. If you're a last-minute shopper, it's time to finish up. Hopefully, you have bought the more expensive items before Mercury turned retrograde. But if not, then be sure to hold on to your receipts, because you may need them for returns.

Saturday, December 18 (Moon in Taurus to Gemini 11:38 p.m.)   You're in full frantic gear now, even if the frantic part doesn't show. Whether you're packing to leave town or making preparations for the arrival of guests, your home and family are the central issues today. Lots of communication is needed. Be clear and concise to mitigate the possibility of others not understanding you.

Sunday, December 19 (Moon in Gemini)   You may be rearranging things at home today to make your place more comfortable for gatherings. Whether it's rearranging furniture, buying new dinnerware, or putting up a Christmas tree, you're psyched for the holidays. You're in full command mode!

Monday, December 20 (Moon in Gemini)   Connections. That's what today consists of. Someone you met socially gives you the name of someone else and that person puts you in touch with yet another person. You know how it goes: the domino effect. And suddenly, you have the contacts you need to get the job done.

Tuesday, December 21 (Moon in Gemini to Cancer 5:22 a.m.)   Today's full moon in Gemini is also a lunar eclipse. News and insights connect to your home and family life. Something culminates. Emotions may run the gamut from euphoria to triumph.

Wednesday, December 22 (Moon in Cancer)   Nowhere is your ability to nurture more apparent than with your own family and friends. Among these people, you also discover who nurtures you and your abilities and talents. If possible, steal a few hours for yourself to jot down some ideas or to work on a creative project that has been front and center.

Thursday, December 23 (Moon in Cancer to Leo 8:51 a.m.) You have plenty of opportunities to show what you're really capable of doing. The only danger lies in how you do this. If you do it in a boastful, arrogant manner, it turns people off. In fact, your best bet would be to applaud and appreciate others.

Friday, December 24 (Moon in Leo)   Mercury will be retrograde for another six days. If there have been miscommunications, don't try to fix them yet. Wait until New Year's Eve, when everyone will be in a jubilant mood and Mercury will be moving direct. You may want to take a few moments to start your list of New Year's resolutions!

Saturday, December 25 (Moon in Leo to Virgo 11:15 a.m.)
Merry Christmas! However you celebrate, be sure to include everyone in the gift-opening festivities. Emotions can be fragile at this time of year for some people. You don't want anyone to feel like an outsider.

Sunday, December 26 (Moon in Virgo) Skip the return tradition at the mall today. The mall will still be there tomorrow. Complete your New Year's resolution list. You should consider drawing up goals for 2011 too. You're in a detailed place today, and some of the goals and resolutions you come up with may surprise you.

Monday, December 27 (Moon in Virgo to Libra 1:39 p.m.)
Your partner's income or resources come under your scrutiny. Or you're dealing with tax issues—gather all your receipts and pay stubs so you can tackle the tax stuff in an organized fashion next year. If you use a computer program to track your finances, be sure to back up any entries you make today.

Tuesday, December 28 (Moon in Libra) This moon forms a challenging angle to Mars, Pluto, and Mercury, which are all in Capricorn. This angle urges you to complete something and may cause you to feel irritable and unsettled. Try not to obsess about it. By tomorrow afternoon, you'll be feeling a whole lot better.

Wednesday, December 29 (Moon in Libra to Scorpio 4:50 p.m.) Are your New Year's plans in place yet? If not, then wait until tomorrow or even right up to December 31 to commit. By then, Mercury will be direct, and you'll have a clearer idea what you really want to do.

Thursday, December 30 (Moon in Scorpio) Mercury turns direct. You're after the bottom line, so start with a retrospective of where you have been this year and where you would like to be next year. Do this for both your internal life and for your external life. Then figure out how to bring the two into a seamless whole.

Friday, December 31 (Moon in Scorpio)   It's terrific that the year ends with most of the planets in signs that are compatible with your own. It means that today should unfold with amazing smoothness.

HAPPY NEW YEAR!

SYDNEY OMARR

Born on August 5, 1926, in Philadelphia, Pennsylvania, Sydney Omarr was the only person ever given full-time duty in the U.S. Army as an astrologer. He is regarded as the most erudite astrologer of our time and the best known, through his syndicated column and his radio and television programs (he was Merv Griffin's "resident astrologer"). Omarr has been called the most "knowledgeable astrologer since Evangeline Adams." His forecasts of Nixon's downfall, the end of World War II in mid-August of 1945, the assassination of John F. Kennedy, Roosevelt's election to a fourth term and his death in office . . . these and many others are on the record and quoted enough to be considered "legendary."

ABOUT THE SERIES

This is one of a series of twelve *Sydney Omarr® Day-by-Day Astrological Guides* for the signs of 2010. For questions and comments about the book, go to www.tjmacgregor.com.

Penguin Group (USA) Online

What will you be reading tomorrow?

Tom Clancy, Patricia Cornwell, W.E.B. Griffin,
Nora Roberts, William Gibson, Robin Cook,
Brian Jacques, Catherine Coulter, Stephen King,
Dean Koontz, Ken Follett, Clive Cussler,
Eric Jerome Dickey, John Sandford,
Terry McMillan, Sue Monk Kidd, Amy Tan,
John Berendt…

You'll find them all at
penguin.com

Read excerpts and newsletters,
find tour schedules and reading group guides,
and enter contests.

Subscribe to Penguin Group (USA) newsletters
and get an exclusive inside look
at exciting new titles and the authors you love
long before everyone else does.

PENGUIN GROUP (USA)
us.penguingroup.com